NEWSPAPER BOYS
ALWAYS DELIVER

FEB/2/16.

DEAR MADAME
NAKHOUL.

I Hope you
Enjoy this Story

NEWSPAPER BOYS
ALWAYS DELIVER

of all the GREAT

Events that Brought

us to our Times

Best of HEALTH

Joseph Gulesserian

ISBN: 1507898622
ISBN 13: 9781507898628
Library of Congress Control Number: 2015902253
CreateSpace Independent Publishing Platform
North Charleston, South Carolina

Dedication and Acknowledgments

To all the people I shook hands with and knew in days gone by who have since walked different paths.

To those endless nights we spent in after-hours eateries, celebrating and passionately wasting our youth away.

To the dreams we dreamed and all the dreams we should have dreamed.

This book takes us to a place in our minds where life was forever, and death was unfathomable.

And finally, to all those people who dreamed but did not have the courage to reach out and grasp their dreams.

This story takes us back to a special time and place when everything was possible.

This book is in memory of my father, whose infinite wisdom and courage guide me to this day.

To my wife, who not only encourages me but also somehow has the patience to come to terms with my indifferences.

I thank all the wonderful people who were kind enough to help me, including John McAulay, an old friend with a highly refined mind who gave me feedback and donated the most precious thing we have, which is time. I also have to make special note of the feedback and contributions of my friend, Loyd Miller, with whom I went to business school, and another friend, Professor Mike Wade, whom I know from teaching days. And, of course, Steve Boyle, for the lovely cover page design.

Contents

Foreword

Few will argue that it is difficult to question the notion that the last half of the twentieth century, as well as the first years of the current one, have seen the greatest technological, economic, social, and environmental changes that the world has ever experienced, and indeed that in these early years of the twenty-first century, these dramatic changes appear to be continuing at an exponential rate.

Those of us who compose the Baby-Boom Generation have not only borne witness to these changes but also have been largely responsible for bringing them about. As a result, perhaps Baby Boomers have a unique view of the world that previous, current, and future generations may not share. And as time marches on and we eventually leave behind our legacy, this period of history may very well be remembered as being particularly formative and memorable.

Joseph Gulesserian immigrated to Canada with his Armenian parents at a very young age in the early 1960s and spent his early years growing up in the Toronto suburb of Thorncliffe Park. Each of us is affected in our development by our environment in different ways. Childhood and adolescent influences vary greatly, and as a Baby Boomer, his were perhaps highlighted by some very specific social, historical, and pop culture events and phenomena that shaped his very personal and perhaps unique view and understanding of his environment and of the broader world in which he later found himself in adult life.

Newspaper Boys Always Deliver is a chronicle of this very personal journey of a member of the Baby-Boom Generation through the early stages of his life. It is a diarized and autobiographical account of his encounters with the major influences of his adolescence and early adulthood, as well as his current assessment of modern-day technological and cultural influences on subsequent generations. These are presented as what may initially appear to be a slightly disjointed and incongruous series of individual essays, but eventually they lead to a cohesive and comprehensive conclusion portraying an arguably somewhat unique understanding of those events. It is a viewpoint that is very much his own and one that may, in fact, challenge some of the more popular and conventional approaches to an analysis of both past and present cultural and technological developments.

Joseph survived adolescence and early adulthood, eventually earning an MBA, teaching business at two Toronto colleges, and subsequently establishing and operating a Toronto-based company that has created a variety of very successful brands that it markets both domestically and internationally. He currently lives with his wife in Toronto.
John McAulay
Lake Scugog, Ontario, Canada
January 2015

Preface

I had the great experience of delivering newspapers in the late 1960s to the early 1970s, in Thorncliffe Park, which is a Toronto neighbour-hood of high-rise rentals. Few who live there today know that once upon a time it was a racetrack, evidenced by the street named Milepost Place. It was through newspapers that I viewed the tumultuous age I grew up in and experienced so much.

One day, as I was pondering, or more accurately daydreaming, do-ing my latest rendition of Walter Mitty, I realized much had happened in my lifetime in this playground we call the world, some of it with little fanfare and some of it that awed us. It dawned upon me that in a span of fifty years, we went from the slide rule to the calculator, saw the space race—which culminated with landing a man on the moon (my father actually made parts for that mission)—the magical music of the 1960s, the appearance of the Beatles, the Motown sound, the Vietnam War, and the assassinations of Martin Luther King and Bobby Kennedy, all as we went from typewriters to desktop computers. I grew up in the world of the Cold War of East versus West; that is such a distant memory today, but we had thousands of nuclear missiles pointed at each other and in a moment, or so we thought, we could be faced with total human annihilation.

I had front-row seats to so many things that happened, including when the Soviets first visited Maple Leaf Gardens in 1972 to play our

Canadian professionals in that game we call hockey. My fascination with the inextricable relationship between villains and the virtuous glued me to the original *Batman* series of the 1960s, and when that series ended, it then led me to study the history of wrestling's finest villains. I met so many of my childhood heroes, from Bobby Orr to Neil Armstrong, and happened to deliver the newspaper to the mayor of Toronto. When I came of age, I lived through the rise and fall of disco.

I saw the introduction of the graphical user interface (GUI) and the diffusion of the Internet from a unique perspective, since, once upon a time, I worked as an office equipment salesman and sold some of the bridging technologies that took us from typewriters to word processors. This technology sounds so rudimentary today; as in so many aspects of life, there is a natural progression in the quest for evolution and enlightenment in both technology as well as pop culture. I first fiddled around with the Internet in 1993 when we were on arcane dial-ups: 7,200 bps versus today's 30 Mbps downloads.

Time passed by so quickly because perhaps we were all occupying the passing lane. Eventually the Berlin Wall came down, with much fanfare, for the cheering crowds to feel good about, thinking it was a turning point in human history as the end of the Cold War, only to realize that 9/11 pitted the West against a new boogieman who wants to draw us back into the Stone Ages, with a supporting cast of naïve accomplices in the West.

As much as I still find commerce and running a business quite interesting, I always thought there was a bigger purpose in life than having the nicest toys in the sandbox.

The question then becomes, how did we get here in the West, both technologically and in terms of pop culture? So, then, can I write and deliver a book that informs, titillates, offends, and entertains while discussing the events that touched so many of our lives to this day?

Newspaper Boys Always Deliver takes us to the nostalgia of yesterday, its epic moments that impacted the world, and how much of what happened before that eventually delivered us to the times we currently live in—namely, the techno-culture. It's more than that, though; we explore the journey of time while taking a sometimes-serious and controversial and sometimes-humorous look at much that has touched our times.

Newspaper Boys Always Deliver appeals across generational and cultural lines. On the surface, this book perhaps appeals mostly to the Baby Boomers, who will more than likely gravitate to the nostalgia and romanticism of reliving some of the epic moments that have slipped into the passages of time.

Then there is today's generation, which might be curious as to how we went from the first industrial revolution to the techno-culture, and while the book asks the question, "Did electricity and its inventors impact the world more than Google?" Perhaps this generation might be exploring the roots of its current pop culture and how we went from the Beatles to Motown to hip-hop music, and where all this techno-dance music came from.

Finally, we now have so many newcomers to the West, and many of these newcomers perhaps do not have a deep understanding of our culture in Canada and United States. But this much is certain: the West invented so much, from its technology, to its thinking, to its music that has impacted and catapulted the world like no other civilization in recorded history. So, then, how did all this come about? It did not come from thin air. So perhaps this book can help newcomers understand our pop and technological history in an entertaining way and have a richer experience in their newly adopted homeland.

This book in many aspects is an eclectic newspaper journal of major and indelible events that impacted my life and many others' lives, from inventions in pop culture and tied together through this writer's lenses. These events touched us all and helped shape today's world. Hence, this book allows us to create a better framework to understand the path that brought us to the times we currently live in. This is important, since before we draw the map of the future, we need to understand the map that brought us here.

I hope you enjoy this book and come away with a wealth of perspective, while asking the questions I ask myself each and every day: How did we get here? Where are we? Where are we going, and how do we plan to get there? So then, if one does not understand the past, how can one understand the present, and how can one have the depth to draw the road map of the future? I cordially invite you to sit back, relax, and take a front-row seat!

Front-Page News

WHY NEWSPAPERS MATTER

Our lives and times are neatly organized like sections of a newspaper, and each section we leaf through tells indelible stories of all we shared, and some we dared not, as we unfold this journey we call life. Newspapers are the social conscience of a community; they allow us to place our set of values as individuals against the collective norm, while through words and pictures we are serenaded into a different place.

Newspapers teach, inform, provoke thought, and manipulate how we think. Newspapers report the world around us as we compare the glee and agony that define our times.

Before the Internet age, the unmistakable crackling sound of turning pages and ink-stained fingers was the *modus operandi* of how we journalized our daily lives against the world at large and attained knowledge, while often falling victim to an agenda that had not yet made itself known.

Newspapers give us time to nurture critical thinking and ideas and foster robust debates to rival a Greek café on Danforth Avenue in Toronto, all the while adopting a civil code that helps us mask the savage in us all.

Newspapers help us imagine and allow the reader to indulge in digesting the artistic assembly of words crafted by high-calibre journalists or frown upon those journalists who write about things they faintly understand.

Newspapers exercise the imagination and educate and help us dream, imagine, cry, and smile. They allow us to compare the miracle of our individual lives with all that we simply cannot affect.

Newspapers help reconcile our emotions to truth when presented with critical evidence, no matter how unsettling it is to our core values.

Once upon a time, newspapers galvanized and polarized a community, a nation, and sometimes the world, as was the case in the Cuban Missile Crisis.

Newspapers tell a story of a childhood that was filled with delivering information that included the *Globe and Mail*, *Toronto Star*, and the now defunct *Toronto Telegram*, the ashes of which created the *Toronto Sun*.

It is those days I remember many years ago, as I waited for the newspaper truck to arrive with my bundles of papers, keenly waiting not only to deliver this assemblage of information but to read about the world as it was unfolding while daydreaming of so much future ahead.

Having the newspaper before the general public, and reading before the world woke up, was like having a monopoly on the Internet for two hours a day until the rest of the world caught up with you. And in many respects it was not much different than the Riddler taking over Gotham City, even if it was only for a couple of hours.

After all, learning to read and write in a classroom was somewhat less of an exhilarating exercise and too structured for those of us who were daydreaming our youth away as we tried to make sense of what was, what is, and the road that lay ahead. In any case, we were in an ambitious yet naïve dream of how we were going to change the world. It is this mindset that is the right of passage, concomitant with youth and the innocence that afflicted us all.

More important, the delivery of newspapers provided income for the finer things in life, such as candies, Becker's pop, paying off tough guys to protect one from other toughs, buying model rocket ships, reading about the solar system, and, of course, hockey magazines.

Yes, printed newspapers are static compared to the dynamic real time of the digital media, but they were indelible, and they captured and gave so much in a time when we had so little.

I delivered newspapers from 1968 to 1973 and had the privilege of reading just about each and every edition of the *Globe and Mail*, *Toronto Star*, and, of course, the *Toronto Telegram*. It was during that time when I started to interpret my environment while unknowingly reinforcing my elementary school education, which did not always show up on my report cards. After all, school was the time for daydreaming about what we were about to become and conjuring up acts of heroism. Was it not?

As I reflected, waiting for the newspaper truck to come by to deliver my bundles of papers, I looked into the sky and pondered what the future might look like. What lay ahead in the map of life was still unknown. Many years went by since those dreamy days of my childhood in the late 1960s, and the future of tomorrow finally unveiled itself against the romanticism of our ideals, alongside the events that defined our times.

Like some sleepy dream woven into a future that had not yet revealed itself, I fall into a beautiful and soft sleep and try come to terms of how nearly a half-century went by at a blink of an eye and took away the gift we can never bring back; that is the gift of time!

Little did we know that the future of tomorrow lay in wonder and tragedy wrapped in a misty enigma, beckoning for a truth that perhaps we did not have the courage to accept or explore.

Time eventually opened its hand and revealed what it once concealed in its mystic unknown, as the pages of our lives are by now mostly written. The reunion that we hoped for eventually came as all the people we once walked with took different paths and became strangers against a backdrop of a cold wind. Time had moved and changed us all, since we could only talk about the past and no longer the future. In its sadness, we somehow realized that perhaps the perfect moment had passed.

It is this story I present to you!

People Section

SWINGING SIXTIES

Thorncliffe Park: 1966

The place where our story begins is Thorncliffe Park. In 1966, from the quiet and predicable working-class neighbourhood of Avenue Road in Toronto, we arrived at the doorsteps of this community. Thorncliffe Park, which was a dusty old racetrack converted into a planned semi-premium rental neighbourhood, was probably the first multicultural community in Canada. I'm not sure if we noticed, since today's self-ordained social engineers had not had their day in the control rooms yet to make us aware of such things.

In Thorncliffe Park, one could occasionally run into pro athletes who lived there, or Toronto Mayor Dennison, to whom I delivered newspapers. Many of the parents were still young enough to groove, while teenagers were wearing a very hip look, since they were about to grow their hair long for the rehearsal for the summer of '67.

I remember my father surveying the people he considered the carnage of civilization namely the hippies, who he considered "the walking dead." I was on the receiving end of many lectures to the effect of, "When you grow up, don't you dare grow your hair long." In contrast, we are entertained today by the latest generation doing their version of *Rebel without a Cause* in the way of the hip-hop culture. Many of today's youths make a fashion statement as though they just got lost at a disorganized pajama party while taking the last train to a clown reunion. Their only real fear is that their smartphones will be taken away and their pop music heroes will run out of words that rhyme with *bitch*!

It was a different time where we had different experiences and learned a set of social skill sets that were well...different than today. We learned to play, learned to fight, learned to sue for peace if the other guy was bigger and/or when the outcome of the fight seemed predetermined. We learned to trade baseball cards and to play hockey without helmets on natural ice or supervising parents in our every moment. We learned to make money from discarded beer and pop bottles and to be alone to discover our own psyches. There was more, though. We learned to consolidate power. We learned to negotiate, and we learned cool-speak. Most of all, we learned to survive in preparation for life.

We knew that most of our parents could not afford to buy us everything we wanted, and this wanting is what perhaps created the fuel for dreams. This, in short, in a very peculiar way is a most privileged of upbringings.

It was such a special time, when the world was still creative enough to manufacture real heroes and leaders that you would respect and aspire to be like. It was a time when everything didn't seem so uptight and contrived.

We couldn't wait to grow up so we could experience the type of future where everything was possible.

Around us there was much social upheaval, war, and incomparable pop music from the Motown sound to the British invasion. It was against this special backdrop that my friends and I dreamt together in this world that was ours to shape.

It was not a perfect time, but it was *our* time!

Thorncliffe Park, my old neighbourhood, circa 1960s.

The last publication of the Toronto Telegram that
I delivered, of which I still have a copy.

New York's a Go-Go and London Swings

The epicentre of Western culture is London, and indeed London was swinging in 1966, as Carnaby Street was the backdrop for so much inventiveness that defines pop culture. From the hip fashion of bell-bottoms, handkerchief neckties for guys, and miniskirts for young ladies, a voguish look defined a cool yet narcissistic type of hip. Oh! Did I mention the music of the British Isles that had captured the imagination of youth culture? If the French gifted America with the Statue of Liberty, the British Invasion gifted them and the world with a musical sound that was perhaps the Empire's swan song.

Not to be outdone, Greenwich Village in New York had gone into hip mode, and San Francisco was rehearsing for the summer of love as beautifully clad lovelies were wearing go-go boots and doing what they did best: well...go-go dancing. Some claim it originated in the early sixties in New York's Peppermint Lounge, or were its roots enveloped at LA's Whiskey A Go Go?

It was stylish, voguish, and full of vitality, a pristine stage on which to exhibit the eccentric formats of energy and pop culture while simultaneously devising the art of the current generation deeply questioning the moral fibre of the previous one.

Star Trek first proposed in a visually sophisticated way the idea that other worlds were possible, and science and morality had to find a way to reconcile as we peeked into the future of all that was possible. But in 1966, it was a great time to be alive and an even greater time to be young!

What lay in the future of tomorrow was unimaginable at the time: Vietnam, the drug culture, soulful instruments, *Sgt. Pepper*, dispersion of colour TV, the assassinations of Bobby Kennedy and Martin Luther King, the moon landing, and Woodstock. What is telling is that all this happened in a span of four years.

A view of Expo 67 with a peak into the future.

London's Carnaby Street, 1969.

EXPO 67

In the summer of 1967, my parents and I shared the excitement of Canada's centennial birthday. I remember falling asleep in the back of their 1967 candy-apple-red Ford Meteor Rideau 500 on our way to Montreal to see that special event called Expo 67. That summer, Canada exuded confidence.

In the background were the smooth, jazzy sounds and the pop music of the sixties to serenade the young into a dreamy place.

The moment that we entered Expo 67, which was a World's Fair, I realized that I had walked into a place where the future was now. Mankind's quest to play God gave us a romantic peek into the future of tomorrow that was dreamt up by the most imaginative.

That summer, Expo 67 was the place to be if one couldn't make it to San Francisco.

The monorail took people around the grounds, and with over sixty countries exhibiting, it was a thrilling place to be, from the US pavilion, a stunning round biosphere that exhibited the Gemini rocket, to the Russian pavilion, which was an architectural joy to behold. All this transpired with the backdrop of the Cold War as each side was involved in a mud-slinging fest of propaganda, one side with not enough freedom and the other one with too much and not enough discipline to better harness it.

Many of the buildings conjured the future that was promised, and this link—http://www.westland.net/expo67/map-docs/architecture.htm—gives a more detailed look at the pavilions and architectural thinking of the day as the world came to peek into the future that was promised.

Expo 67 had it all: technology, art, and the energy of a youthful nation that was celebrating its one hundredth birthday. On May 7 and 21, 1967, *The Ed Sullivan Show* was broadcast from the grounds, where the Supremes and Petula Clark performed.

Many of the well-heeled and influential attended Expo 67, including Bobby Kennedy, Queen Elizabeth, Ethiopia's Emperor Haile Selassie,

Charles de Gaulle, Harry Belafonte, President Lyndon Johnson, and of course the very refined Jacqueline Bouvier Kennedy.

The world was ours to hold in our hands and shape it into a place where everything was possible and no barriers existed to human thought. Change was in the air, and the urgency of our own microcosm made us forget that, in the end, we are irrelevant specks in the universe, for it was our destiny to explore and dream; it made us feel that we had purpose by challenging the parameters of possibilities.

It was a beautiful backdrop for planting the seeds of lifelong optimism against the warmth of the Montreal sun in that summer of 1967.

The road ahead was to take us to that storied July night in 1969 when we greeted the stars with the famous words, "The Eagle has landed." From the way-ahead-of-its-time *Star Trek* TV series, which has influenced industrial design forty years later—including today's smartphones, to the sweet sound of the Fifth Dimension, one couldn't help but notice that we were promised "The Age of Aquarius." There were a host of events that shaped this period, interlaced with painful nostalgia and gasping hope. The decade saw America lose three absolutely great men who have touched and shaped us all today. Within a span of six years, our heroes were carried out of this world: John F. Kennedy, who headed America's Camelot; Martin Luther King Jr., who encouraged us to look at ourselves for what we had become; and Bobby Kennedy, who gave us an opportunity to flirt with hope again. These and other heroes allowed us the courage to dream, made us feel significant and made us believe that we did matter.

There was so much going on around us with clandestine speed and inertia of its own, but perhaps we were too young and innocent to realize that we were on a remarkable journey.

Often this journey takes us to a place that asks us to consider the delicate roles of both the virtuous and the villain. How history treats the villain is written by the victors, either in war or prevalent ideology. For it is the victors who write the epitaph of what was, and ensure that the villain has no voice in the plethora of current thinking. But when the equation of morality is considered in a balanced light, the virtuous and the villainous each have blood stained hands, their only difference is that one has washed it away with time and the other has left behind an ink that is conveniently imprinted in historicity. Together the villain and the virtuous unite in a peculiar way as to write each other's unrehearsed script and by doing this, they unknowingly create the greater story that eclipses their individual efforts. It is this story that naturally needs to be told and this takes us to the boulevards of Gotham City.

Arts and Entertainment Section

BATMAN AND 1960S HIP!

Our fascination with the villain and the virtuous is as infinite as time itself; each nurtures the other, since being by themselves would create a loneliness they are not prepared to consider. There has always been this great, unanswered question of civilization—namely, what was *Batman* really all about?

In retrospect, we sometimes ask questions about things that put them in a better light, yet with all the value of hindsight, there are still some enigmas that beg even more questions as time goes by. A place that needs to be better aligned in proper light might be Gotham City, where the vigilante in a caped outfit was aligned with an idle police chief and an unemployable commissioner who forever could not deal with the consortium of so-called villains that frequented their town. They had to rely on Batman for that while they collected full salaries, regardless of their gross incompetence.

Who Is Going to Save Gotham City?

The never-ending quest to be the hero continues as Batman fights for human justice and finds something worth protecting and fighting for while promoting his position and demonizing opposing forces. Meanwhile, he is discovering the demon in himself so that he can have the set of requisites to better understand the psyche of his foe. Together, heroes and villains walk into a psychodrama of enigmatic inebriation in order to find purpose in each other while they discover themselves. Unknowingly, or perhaps not, they are crafting a morality of virtue for the audience, so the audience can now have a righteous yet tenuous blueprint for their lives. The hero has a seemingly moral code of equitable justice, but when peeled to the core, it reveals itself to be a sanctuary of extreme thinking and collective virtue that hides within the savage in us all while inoculating the reality of human tragedy. Deep in their psyches, heroes admire the creativity in the villain, and the villain might long for the perceived societal stability of the hero, but in the end, neither can stand to be anything but themselves.

The original *Batman* TV series, which debuted in 1965 in Technicolor, took its roots from the original comic strip of the 1940s. The hip ultra-surrealism has roots perhaps in the Playboy Club in Chicago, where ABC executive Yale Udoff attended a party to watch the very popular serials of *Batman* from the 1940s (see http://www.youtube.com/watch?v=fRgfipzWmo0).

It is here that Mr. Udoff and company got the idea of putting together a very hip Batman television series in the style of *The Man from U.N.C.L.E*, making it a pop culture icon with a dual-target marketing strategy to audiences that included children and hip adults alike.

Slowing down for a moment, we have to remember that this was a very inventive time in television that saw Ed Sullivan first introduce the Beatles to North America, *Laugh-In*, *The Man from U.N.C.L.E.*, the *Star Trek* series, and the *Smothers Brothers Comedy Hour*, which nearly every big pop star of the day performed on. However, none captivated my childhood friends, or at least me, like the *Batman* series.

Some of the greatest celebrities of the day would make appearances on *Batman* as villains. To name a few, there were Milton Berle as Louis the Lilac, Frank Gorshin as the Riddler, Cesar Romero as the original Joker, and the list went on.

But wait, don't touch that dial, there was more! Each week, Batman and Robin would have a "Bat Climb Cameo," and as they were climbing up a building, a new celebrity would open the window and start talking to them. Some of these included Dick Clark, Sammy Davis

Jr., Jerry Lewis, and even Bruce Lee, who played Kato on *The Green Hornet.*

Batman had it all: the Bat Cape (Eaton's department stores actually sold these in Canada); the Batmobile, with its advanced computer systems and radar-detection systems (quite a chick-magnet ride); the Batman Utility Belt gadgets; the Bat Taser; and even the Batcopter, which even today the Toronto Police Force does not have. But Bruce Wayne somehow found the funds (by the way, not many budgetary meetings at Wayne Manor) to have the most high-tech arsenal of his day, and together with the Boy Wonder, they faced foe and friend alike with a new bag of gadgets in the never-ending saga of good versus evil.

Each week the villains were rounded up by the caped crusaders, but a few weeks later they were back in commission, something like the current justice system.

The Problem with Batman

When midlife has sobered up one's childhood quests and perceptions, or so I hope, it might be a good time to revisit the 1965 series to get a more balanced view of Batman and his supporting cast.

So let me see if I understand this correctly. We have this masked man obsessively fighting crime, running around in a leotard, hanging out with a seventeen-year-old Boy Wonder as his protégé (who also wore leotards), and hiding out in a reclusive cave that sat below a mansion. Hmmmm!

All this with substantial money for his excessive list of expensive crime-fighting tools like the Batmobile (remember, it takes money to fight crime) and other high-end gadgets. With unlimited finances that could rival the credit line of Wile E. Coyote, Batman, just like Wile E., had no real job, but had boundless funds due to a hereditary predisposition, hence, he had means to purchase high-tech equipment to bring so-called villains to justice in his quest to deal with the alleged underbelly of society.

Each week, Batman rounded up a host of criminals (who, incidentally, never received fair trials) that all seemed like undesirables but curiously enough looked like they were having a great time. Today, even gangbangers get a fair trial so they can turn their miserable lives around and be budding calculus professors at MIT.

With time, we have the luxury of perspective, so why not fast-forward to 2015 and deal with the fact that if Batman showed up for a trial with his notes and fact dockets, while considering today's judiciary process, he would spend more time in court and less time rounding up some of those exquisitely dressed characters such as the Joker.

Consider that the Joker arrived in pressed suits, while gangbangers, who seem to be poorly imitating him, look like they could take some cues from a Milan fashion show. Many look like they stayed too long at a pajama party or attained part-time jobs at the circus as part of their society reintroduction course after they did their time in the big house. Whereas the Joker had an Oxford-inspired oratorical grasp of the English language to titillate the audience, in contrast, today's gangbangers are in peril with their lower double-digit IQs as they abominate the English language with their Philistine treatment of communications. Gangbangers show their true resourcefulness, though, once they exhaust their twenty-word vocabulary, their repertoire often degenerates into an orgy of proletarian hand gestures that usually point toward coordinates in the groin area.

Moving back to the analysis of the *Batman* series, it included a very straight-looking Commissioner Gordon (another bureaucrat who wouldn't last twenty minutes in the private sector) and an Irish cop, Chief O'Hara (no police force is complete without one), who was thrown in for good measure. Both were in a state somewhere in the twilight zone, that place between incompetent and comatose, but they still managed to collect their salaries.

Therefore, it would seem logical that there was a requirement for the caped crusader to bring some law and order to Gotham City. It seemed like Batman and Robin were the good guys, and the host of villains were the bad guys, however, things are never really that clear-cut, and in retrospect, one wonders if this was the case; perhaps Batman was intolerant of these so-called criminals who were likely marginalized as children, leading to their adulthood eccentricities.

So, then, what was the problem with *Batman*? Had the original show writers really created a credible case for why he did what he did? Or perhaps we should fast-forward Batman into the current politically correct era, where rational thinking and accountability are thrown under the bus as we all learn to walk on eggshells. Thus, I thought we might want to take a closer look at these unconvicted and downtrodden so-called villains in the series within the context of our so-called modern value systems. Perhaps this would provide a different perspective on everyone's motives while creating a case that Batman was, well…"intolerant"!

Batman and Robin, played by Adam West and Bert Ward, 1966.

Chief O'Hara, played by Stafford Repp, 1966.

The Penguin, the Riddler, and the Joker, 1967.

Catwoman, played by the unforgettable Julie Newmar, circa 1966.

The Villains

We always seem to honour heroes, when in fact villains are not given the accolades they sometimes deserve, and we forget to pay homage to their genius within. Because, after all, without villains to point at and to reinforce our own sense of righteousness, we would be in the uncomfortable position of discovering the beast within, while our heroes would lose purpose and face a future of irrelevant idleness. This alone could easily metamorphose the hero into the villain while allowing the villain to come out and declare that his actions are heroic; put differently, the equation between these two polarized forces is more balanced than one might think! In terms of the villains, each one was dressed in suave attire custom-made by a bespoke tailor, and in the case of Catwoman, her fashion statement seemed to be sensuously painted onto her curvaceous assets.

There were a host of villains that seemed to frequent Gotham City and create havoc; whereas when one would be caught, another one would appear, just like today's casts of boogiemen passing off as virtuous political leaders—the same ones that through collective virtue finance thugs dressed as freedom fighters to beat up their latest prearranged boogieman. This is, of course, until these hired thugs break their leashes and turn on their Western masters and mutate into our latest made-in-the-West Frankenstein. Then, as we turn our attention to our latest Frankenstein, it naïvely never occurs to us to consider the genesis of our ill-fated collective misguidance. Since, by destabilizing foreign regions, we end up destabilizing ourselves. Eventually, our political leaders (who only occupy positions of leadership), with ill-equipped intellectual road maps, come to realize that their original appointed boogieman was a figment of their imagination when compared with the real Frankenstein they created. Naturally, after a dietary supplement of CNN and its all-star cast of talking heads, (whose mouths move, but nothing of note is said) the mostly naïve public passionately calls on our leaders to gather the services of the cavalry to beat back the "made in America" Frankenstein into his shoebox.

Getting back to Gotham City, it seems that virtue and truth can be separate things, and perhaps it might be good to start our story by celebrating flamboyancy. And who better depicts this than the Joker?

The Joker

Here is a gentlemen who had a getup that might look like an ostentatious pimp—or maybe he just needed to go to Macy's to get a straight man's outfit—but at the same time, he seemed joyful and always smiling despite the fact that he never received a fair trial, and unlike Batman, he was not uptight. In fact, the Joker was quite an entertaining guy to be around, with great humour, despite the constraints put on him by society. The Joker, for the most part, was always happy, positive, and energetic, to the point where he looked like he just completed an Anthony Robbins seminar on positive thinking. The Joker seemed like a level-headed guy, and he did not drive around town in a chick-magnet car, yet he could still attract women. Deep inside, perhaps he probably wanted to be, and could have been, a flamboyant wrestling manager, or in today's world he could have had a better place to rant, such as a hashtag (#) on Twitter, so he could have joined the many who actually think they are going to change the world by tweeting.

Unlike Batman, the Joker was not born with a silver spoon in his mouth, and all he could do to carve out a living was drop by Gotham City and redistribute the wealth, like some modern-day Robin Hood, since he read in the *Wall Street Journal* that five percent of the people control ninety percent of the wealth. After all, is this not what modern socialists do by punishing employers and the wealthy, by acquiring what isn't theirs through draconian taxation, societal kleptocracy, and the creation of a sanctuary for human mediocrity, while addicting and bribing the electorate with societal welfare, gift-wrapped in benevolence? Eventually, most realize that businesses create jobs not governments, hence; the best role for governments is to create rules of engagement for commerce, and take more of a laissez-faire approach.

In retrospect, the Joker was not raiding the national treasury; all he was doing was redistributing wealth. He was not selling drugs and certainly was not employing firearms in the commission of a crime. Perhaps all he wanted was a few lovelies on his arms and to purchase a set of wheels that could rival the Batmobile and a closet full of fashion grandeur. Really, was this so bad?

Did anybody think that all the Joker needed was maybe a job-training program or perhaps "hope and change"? It is quite possible that his problems started as a kid when his mother wouldn't rent a clown for his fifth birthday party, and he was sure that if Dr. Phil was around back in 1966, the Joker would have found his inner self and stopped dressing like a surrogate New York City pimp.

Did anyone realize that with this getup he was discriminated against and profiled, while constantly being arrested and incarcerated without trial or legal counsel? For all we know, he could be held, as we speak, in Guantanamo Bay without due process. Is this any way to treat someone who is reaching out for help?

Furthermore, the Joker had great fashion sense, with an exquisite wardrobe, and it is quite possible that with some outreach programs, he could have been retrained as a fashion critic for the *New York Times*, at which I am sure he would have flourished with his keen eye for colour coordination. Alternatively, with very little training he could have carved out a flourishing career as a stand-up comedian at Yuk Yuk's.

Then this begs the question: if we had more social safety nets in place, would he have been reformed and perhaps worked as a social counsellor for clowns with anger-management issues? We may never know!

When one studies the original 1966 *Batman* series, it becomes evident that the Joker was quite articulate, and he even pointed out that the Batman utility belt was unconstitutional—and he was right! It was overlooked that Batman did not have a license for his utility belt. The Joker, being a good sport, did not take the issue to the Supreme Court, even though Batman carried a host of other weapons, including chemical weapons, contrary to the UN charter on war tactics. Then again, one should ask where Batman got these chemical weapons. Where was his stockpile, and after they needed replacing, were they falling into the hands of al-Qaeda, or, even worse, ISIS? Is it possible that these theologically intoxicated psychotics obtained discarded weapons from Batman? Did any US Secretary of State warn Batman of the consequences of using chemical weapons? Did the FBI pay him a visit? Where were the authorities? Where was the equal treatment under the law, which is, after all, the kernel of democracy? So, then, it seems the hero, in this case Batman, has a different set of laws to abide by than mere paupers of society, and this would defy the tenets of equal treatment under the law. Perhaps Batman was an elitist.

Regardless of the Joker's perceived conniving ways, he had a stroke of imprinted genius as he found ways to foil Batman, and at one point, he even sat on the board of directors of a bank, even though he was quickly ousted. Today, we have all types of jokers as heads of the US Federal Reserve and the Bank of Canada, who seem to print money, inflate assets through monetary policy, and manipulate inflation numbers, while creating structural distortions in the economy, and hardly anyone notices or seems to mind. This, of course, would not be stood for, if as children, we all watched more *Sesame Street* and especially paid more attention to the episodes featuring Count, since he taught us how to well…. count with numbers.

It becomes evident that the Joker had a destiny and a résumé of superlative accomplishments that were suffocated by societal norms, amounting to a double standard.

In summary, the Joker had an incredible knack for fashion and very inventive schemes that at times had Batman overwhelmed. The Joker could also have turned out differently if there were some outreach programs that would have transformed him into a more conforming and productive member of society. Perhaps if the state had provided him a toy circus set as child, he would have turned out differently, but being denied this was more than likely the root cause of his issues. So again, when looking for the root cause, we conclude that it was not his fault; it was the state's fault, since self-reliance and accountability are phobic words in our new culture of victimization.

What Batman did with the Joker was actually quite callous, arresting this flamboyantly dressed individual with excessive force, using closed fists. How do you think this would stand up in court today? And the sad reality is that after a marginalized youth, he did not even get a fair trial, with no right to counsel, in accordance with US law. Gotham

City, it seems, was like frontier justice, and one has to ask if this was in accordance with the tenets of fair play and legal due course.

But I guess that the only card handed the Joker was, well…the joker card!

The Riddler

At first, we dismiss the Riddler (who was played by Frank Gorshin in the 1966 series) as some twisted villain whose only purpose was to disrupt the congenial ways of life in Gotham City. A man without a cause, according to some, but when we delve deeper into his existence, we see that this individual really gave people a free game of Scrabble and challenged adults' and children's minds alike with his ingenious riddles. Just because that self-righteous man in the cape did not dig his riddles does not minimize this complex man and his societal contributions. Here are a couple of titillating examples that give away his genius trait; "why is a quarrel like a bargain?" "Because it takes two to make one"; or better still, "why is a welder like a woman in love?" "Because they both carry a torch!"

It is only when we examine him in a more thoughtful way that we see this man for his great contributions to education, and, furthermore, without the use of modern algorithm vehicles such as today's Google, he asked complex questions that stimulated yet perplexed the self-proclaimed authorities of Gotham City.

The Riddler, in retrospect, should be commended for being the walking, talking predecessor of Google who came up with a host of enigmatic riddles that stimulated the minds of the youth of the day, and of course Batman's. Debatable as it might be, this is how he unselfishly benefited Gotham City. Yet not even the Riddler could stimulate the mind of the comatose Commissioner Gordon and the lackey police Chief O'Hara. As opposed to vilifying the Riddler, educators should have had him published in all high-school curriculum under new courses for having original and dexterous thought patterns. Because, much like in life, we must solve riddles, since we do not have the good fortune to pass just for showing up, unlike the K-12 education system which is a noble lesson for both students and educators today, who are often detached from life outside of school.

Going back to the Riddler, he could have had his own game show that would make *Jeopardy* look lame. In many ways, he was artistically painting the minds of youths and challenging the perimeters of current thinking of the day. Put simply, the Riddler was a great educator who made people think, and just because of his funky getup and intellectually challenging repertoire of riddles hardly qualify him as a villain.

Today's "easy information age" world, with all its marvels, does not exercise the mind when exploring the truth or solving an enigmatic question, since Google and Wiki sites seem to have all the answers. In fact, much of this technology has left the mind lacking intellectual energy and drowning in an orgy of information overload. Obtaining information is so easy that we could rent out our minds, assuming anyone would want them. Instead of answering the questions within, we go to the internet to soothe our insecurities through the sanctuary of collective thought that inoculates us from inventiveness and the painful challenge of stretching our minds to find the original within. This is evidenced by the fact that we pay money to download Lumosity to exercise our underworked minds.

The Riddler, armed with his obsessive-compulsive neurosis condition, promoted inventiveness with his array of seemingly unsolvable riddles. He sent all the so-called authority blockheads of Gotham City on twists and turns and made Police Chief O'Hara think for a change and earn his keep. Put another way, through his psychosis, he inadvertently created an array of riddles that made the more intellectually challenged Gotham City police department and the straight-laced caped crusader challenge their minds by tampering with their imaginations. After all, isn't imagination the starting point of all creativity?

The Riddler is another fine example of a man who was incarcerated without trial, which makes one think that Gotham City invoked frontier justice and order, and acted like a state within a state, something like multiculturalism. The Riddler was a perplexing individual who painted questions and wrapped them in mystery, like the timeless work of Michelangelo; both were geniuses, yet one was renowned and the other vilified.

But when one tries to make sense of the enigmatic nature of the Riddler, it seems we have to delve into his childhood and find out what caused him this pain. Perhaps in public school he asked questions that were unanswerable, and this evolved into a scar that never healed; or perhaps one Christmas someone stole his *Jeopardy* game set from under the Christmas tree. Much like the Joker's childhood predicament, there were not enough social safety nets to rescue him from himself.

This much is for sure: the Riddler had a great mind, and when we put aside his differences with Batman, we see someone with an incredibly high IQ who should not have been put in jail but instead had a library or a wing at Harvard University named after him. With his mathematical skills and problem-solving abilities, he could have worked at Goldman Sachs as a derivative analyst. All he needed was a chance. Nevertheless, society dismissed him as an outcast rather than recognize a great educator. Because even Batman knew that, unlike the US public and Canadian K–12 educational systems, you had to pass the Riddler's test to move to the next grade.

So, in some inexplicable way, the Riddler was a benevolent so-called criminal who could not help but leave clues to his dubious deeds to tip off his detractors to catch him so they could help him discover the enigmatic creature within, to share and soothe his pain through comforting arms.

Clearly, Batman had a twisted admiration for the Riddler because evil and virtue in a strange way are each other's mentors, since they owe much to each other.

A Feline and Villainous Entrapment

The femme fatale slithered into Gotham City with a sensuous strut that bore a resemblance to the feminine walk of a lady refined at Madame Claude's Swiss Finishing School. Debonair and innately bourgeois, she exuded femininity and weaved it into a dreamy magnetism to intoxicate the unsuspecting heart.

Many young ladies today could take cues from her and willfully lift themselves from their lowbrow, substandard character deficiencies and their associated desperate attire that screams for help day after day on the social media and beyond!

Julie Newmar originally played Catwoman in 1965. Adam West called her every boy's wet dream—and with good reason, since she was perhaps the Creator's finest example of femininity. Catwoman used the sometimes-self-serving vulnerabilities of a lady and enticed Batman into a hopeless web of lust and intoxication of the heart. As much as he wanted to reform her, Batman had a deep admiration for her villainous ways as he displayed his vulnerability to her sensuous irresistibility.

Catwoman understood haute couture, with an exquisite eye for detail, complemented by a deep understanding of discriminating attire, and carried herself like the upper bourgeois refined lady that she really was. With her *perrrfectly* manicured nails that were elegantly prepared to claw into a man's heart, stunningly high cheekbones, and hourglass figure to complement this superb arrangement, she was, well...the cat's meow!

Batman had it all, if we really think about it: a mansion, an alter ego that made him the go-to guy for crime fighting in Gotham City, and a hot ride in the way of the Batmobile. However, there was one missing element in the otherwise perfect repertoire of his obsessive-compulsive fascination with fighting crime, and that was a woman in his life.

A woman whom he could come home to after a tough day of crime-fighting against the illustrious parade of villains of Gotham City.

He needed the comfort and loving arms that only a woman could provide. He needed someone to tell him that everything would be okay, and that his cause was righteous.

He should not have taken her rehabilitation to such a logical level but appealed to her emotions instead, while perhaps it was time for Batman himself to let his hair down and tune into the plethora of hip musical activity that was all around in 1966.

Catwoman, after all, was ahead of her time in demonstrating her own brand of modern femininity by not depending on a man, but instead fending for herself. Did she depend on marriage or divorce for economic furtherance? Did anyone think that she turned to her depraved ways because she had put herself in a mountain of debt with her prodigious spending habits? Society in the 1960s did not have the social safety nets and other derivatives of welfare addiction programs that we have today, and all Catwoman needed was perhaps some credit counselling to help her reconcile her debits and credits into positive cash flows. In fact, debt-ridden Western governments that issue bonds based on fiat currencies could have joined her and seen if they could get a group rate on debt relief. At the very least, Catwoman was a textbook case of the glass ceiling, and out of sheer survival and lack of equitable opportunity, she turned to a life of villainous virtue. When put in perspective, Catwoman was not a villain but instead a pioneer for female modernity.

Yes, Batman did have some teasingly romantic interludes with Catwoman (Julie Newmar), but he spent more time debating her like some idle Harvard debating club member. Perhaps in order to change her ways, he should have dropped the professorial lectures, and at least have the decency to take her out and get her nails done. Perhaps a "Bat Shag" was in order, as an attempt to change her villainous ways?

Catwoman had a very kind side to her and even extended an olive branch by offering to be partners with Batman, admitting that she needed what every woman needs, and that is a good man. In one episode, she even confided to Bruce Wayne that her heart belonged to Batman. Perhaps Batman should have had a more laissez faire attitude and taken more of a swinging London approach! Or perhaps he could have taken her to San Francisco in 1967 for the Summer of Love.

As Catwoman said, "If you just come off your high horse for a moment, Batman, we could make such beautiful music together." In retrospect, this is what Batman should have done and filled a void in both their lives.

With all the money Batman had, he was chintzy, and he did not even have the gentlemanly class to take her shopping, instead he would go on one of his professorial lectures that would put most people into a coma. What would have changed her felonious and conniving ways would be a whirlwind shopping folly on New York's Fifth Avenue, as well as Milan for shoes, Gucci bags, and Versace couture, which could then be followed by a lovely dinner in Rome and a gondola tour of Venice, wonderfully ending in a prolonged horizontal leap.

But the issue with Batman was that he simply did not know how to seal the deal with the ladies and let his hair down a bit. Simply put, Batman didn't quite understand women. So, Batman, I say, what do girls really want? Not always this intellectual, rational stuff, that's for sure. Why didn't Batman just buy Catwoman shoes, Italian-made clothing, hairspray, a trip to the spa, take her to get her nails done, lend her his platinum America Express card for shopping in Paris, give her quality time with her friends for gossip, and, well…just buy her lots of bling-bling? Oh, and of course, don't forget to give her quality time to be alone and cry.

Yes, Catwoman, with her inventive schemes and ability to organize her crew, including managing men (which can be quite challenging at the best of times), with a common corporate vision, was a true female entrepreneur and championed women's rights, while maintaining her female charms. She was not one of those hardline unbalanced feminists who forgot to shave her legs and wore construction boots. On the contrary, she was a refined lady in the Jacqueline Bouvier Kennedy tradition. Catwoman pioneered independence and opportunities for women but still understood that yin needs yang for a proper fit.

If Batman let go of his tight utility belt and took her cruising in his Batmobile, he could have sealed the deal. Because after all, as Batman himself once said, "What good is a dream if it is not a blueprint for a courageous act?"

Just as the Joker and the Riddler, Catwoman also needed to be heard, and perhaps she had something that affected her in childhood, like her doll was stolen in fifth grade or she was bullied, or her mother kept her training wheels on until she was ten or something. When all was said and done, her intellectual wiring, her curvaceous assets, and her perfect charms were too much for Batman to handle.

If Batman had been strategic or had vision and believed that every woman is a charming diamond (although some in the rough), he could have reformed her into a *perrrrfectly* unrivalled asset for Gotham City and turned her loose on the Joker, Riddler, and the likes with her incomparable attributes of feline enticement and insidious scheming. But she was put in jail without trial or due process and not given a fair chance to claw back into the norms of society, while incompetent bureaucrats like Commissioner Gordon were drawing exorbitant salaries at the expense of taxpayers. Furthermore, if it were up to Chief O'Hara, she would have ended up in a women's shelter.

It is this paradox that Batman did not see, and his inability to reform the Catwoman and his callously having her incarcerated shows his failure as a healer.

Batman had his moment to be the "cat's meow" but did not know how to capture that *perrrfect* moment!

The Penguin
The Penguin, born as Oswald Chesterfield Cobblepot, was a fascinating character who got past his disability of walking with a double-sided

limp. Yet with his disability he did not get special treatment nor asked for a handicapped parking permit. He did not ask for pity, social assistance, or any other form of societal handout and didn't have associated addictions of dependency. He was quite entrepreneurial, self-sufficient, and evoked the tenets of the Protestant work ethic, which has been largely responsible for the rise of the West and everything it has created, affecting the world at large.

The Penguin was teased very much in his childhood due to his short stature, obesity, and bird-like nose but somehow had the courage to overcome a difficult hand of cards that he was dealt.

The police have some outstanding officers they call a "cop's cop," but, drawing a parallel, Penguin was a "bird's bird", not a birdbrain, as some would make him out to be. Quite on the contrary, he was an intellectual giant with keen, refined, and cultured tastes, and furthermore, he had a well-grounded education in scientific knowledge that allowed him to create weapons to ward off bullies like Batman who incidentally picked on a disabled person.

He was also obviously schooled in the economic philosophy of Adam Smith, with his refined sense of intellectual energy and enterprise. He understood capitalism and all the fine things it could provide, which is supported by the fact that he even frequented the Millionaires' Club in Gotham City.

The Penguin could have been a professor had he chosen to, instead of being hassled by the cast of the self-righteous Gotham City police, their do-gooder caped crusaders, and idle administrative cronies at City Hall. Or, quite possibly, he would have been an asset in the police colleges as a credible lecturer on criminology.

Despite all that the Penguin brought to the table, Batman was a verbal abuser by calling him a "bush-league bird," and this further tainted the Penguin's sense of self. Certainly, Batman's actions were not becoming of a self-proclaimed pillar of society. Furthermore, just because he dressed in a well-pressed Penguin outfit, he was unjustly profiled as a criminal by both the Gotham City police department and the caped crusader, who obviously did not tolerate diversity.

In fact, the Gotham City police department and the caped crusader should have been mandated to take a course on diversity training to better understand the concept of societal inclusion of our feathery friends, especially ones with pre-existing hip disabilities. Too bad Gotham City did not have such training, since it could have then employed what it learned as police forces do today.

With all this progress today, look how we all live happily ever after as we embrace cultures that advocate honour killings by reaching out to them and allowing them to sponsor more psychotic relatives into the country. Better still, had they received more diversity training in Gotham City, authorities could have learned how to send a social worker out in a middle of a gangbanger shootout to help keep the neighbourhood safe by reciting messages of hope and peace. Or perhaps Batman, with his new diversity training, could have lectured at universities on the root causes of suicide bombers, which of course is no fault of their own or their supporting culture. Hmmm!

Now, getting back to the Penguin, he desperately wanted to join society and at one point even ran for office as Gotham City mayor, and his eloquence was at a level that could be adopted by a certain infamous former Toronto mayor. Unlike Mayor Ford and President Obama, he did not have a razor-thin curriculum vitae, with no real experience or qualifications for the position. On the contrary, the Penguin was certainly more qualified with his business and administrative background, and at least he had hands-on experience creating jobs in the private sector, even though some of it was a bit on the seedy side. In furthering the case for the Penguin, he was a master orator who knew how to assemble the finite complexity of the English language, and he displayed his articulate verbiage when he put together a grand campaign for mayor on a bird's budget:

(See http://www.youtube.com/watch?v=I63SRpGXBHE).

Masterfully, he debated Batman on numerous points, which included the reason why Batman concealed his identity, while the bumbling Chief O'Hara was outraged at the idea of the Penguin becoming mayor of Gotham City. Again, this was a deliberate attempt by the police department to interfere in a free and fair election and to throw the electoral process under the bus. This is something like Americans, who encourage democracy abroad in the name of freedom, and when their preferred candidate turns the place into a theocracy or ends up being our friend's enemy, they cry foul against the wishes of the majority.

If we had left the election process to the Gotham City police department, Commissioner Gordon, and its entrenched plutocracy of cronyism, Gotham City would be a junta. The Penguin stood up against these oppressors of the truth and so-called guardians of a civilized society, and for doing that he was unjustifiably tarred and feathered!

So there you have it. Penguin had it all, when we look at things through the clarifying lens of retrospect: great attire, a vibrant and articulate persona, a strong following (including his lovely armpiece, Chickadee), strategic vision, and the ability to overcome disabilities. At the same time, he ran in a city that was shamefully intolerant of birds (more specifically, penguins) and the potential flight to rescue they could provide.

So, when all is said and done, the Penguin might have been feathery, but he was definitely not for the birds!

Police Chief O'Hara
What is the point of his shenanigans, Batman?

Dating back from the 1850s, the Irish have a fine tradition in North America, of doing dangerous jobs, which led to them dominating many of the police departments. Back then, the risks were high and the pay was low, but things eventually changed. No police department is complete without the presence of an Irishman; having a police force without one would be like a book with no ending. Simply put, it is unfathomable, and Gotham City was no exception.

Police Chief O'Hara came from a fine tradition of Irish police officers, but he laid shame against all the police traditions of gallantry by simply being unable to do his job. With his fat salary, he was relegated to an idle role as a bureaucratic lackey of Commissioner Gordon, as opposed to leading his police force by example. Did he not study how many of the generals in history led their troops to battle, as opposed to those who cowered behind the safety of an administrative sanctuary?

Instead of meeting with his detectives when a crime was committed, he would call in the caped crusaders to do the job for him. This must have demoralized the detectives and special investigation units of the Gotham City police force. This is like a grown man calling his mama every time he's in a pinch. Yes, the Irish one-liners were good, but the chief had no organizational skills, and he had none of the following departments in place:

- guns and gang squad
- homicide squad
- drug squad
- hold-up squad

Police Chief O'Hara was a pseudo-law enforcement officer, always in the office, never in the field doing real police work. This is not an unusual line of thinking, since Winston Churchill, the Prime Minister of the United Kingdom in the Second World War, insisted that he gallantly join his troops for the Normandy invasion and was eventually talked out of it by King George. The only thing O'Hara was competent at was remembering the Dunkin' Donuts menu. I never saw him walk the beat with his police constables and do real police work. Every time Batman was in a compromised position—for example, being immersed into boiling acid by the Penguin or being pummelled—O'Hara and his coppers were nowhere to be found. Having one's command post at Dunkin' Donuts does have its disadvantages.

O'Hara did not have logical intelligence and intellectual curiosity. Did it not occur to him to find out whom the Bat Line phone was registered to? This would give him a better understanding of where the calls were coming from. Unlike Batman, he didn't even have a computer on his desk; how can one have a computer-illiterate police chief? Could he not at least check the billing address of the Bat Line with the local phone company? All we are asking for here is some basic police investigative work.

It seemed that a new villain would pop into Gotham City every week or so, and did it occur to the police chief that his detectives should have put a tail on Mr. Freeze? They could have monitored him and harassed him for parking too close to the curb, going two miles per hour over the speed limit, put the heat on his associates, and all the other regular tactics that police departments employ to stall the unsuspecting while they muster a rap that will stick.

Chief O'Hara's lack of police investigation and administrative skills made him incompetent for such a position, but Commissioner Gordon probably reappointed him out of cronyism. This bumbling master of blarney was dressed as a man of societal accomplishment with his uniform of justice, but outside of state dinners, he was in a state of semi-consciousness; true, he had some good one-liners, but when we peel back his layers, the suit was empty!

Batman, Then and Now!

So there you have it, Batman and Robin keep Gotham City safe by putting the more entertaining members of society behind bars, but there are a host questions still cannot be answered and many that were not pondered; for example, did Batman do a budgetary review on the Batcycle, Batcopter, Batmobile, and utility belts, and was the Gotham City taxpayer willing to help him foot the bill for all these toys?

Even the greatest philanthropists have limits to what they can give. In terms of being fair and equitable, Gotham City could have at least reimbursed him for all these out-of-pocket expenses, since catching villains often requires money. Then again, where did he go to get the oil changed on the Batmobile? Perhaps he just drove through a Jiffy Lube, hoping to find a standard filter. Where did the Batmobile go for servicing? Assuming he built the vehicle, there was a host of GM parts he more than likely used during the assembly of his car. Even the non-sceptic would have to admit that there were some holes in the story.

There are additional questions for the discerning minds, for example, did Bruce Wayne have shareholders to answer to, if so, what would the effect be on his stock valuations? How did he repair all these contraptions; did he consider applying for tax breaks from the IRS for all this wear and tear on his crime-fighting assets? Why was Robin not in school and living the dreams of President Johnson's *Great Society* that included higher education, considering the fact that only nine percent of Americans over twenty-five had four years of college or more in 1964? Instead, the Boy Wonder was living off the avails of the Bruce Wayne manor and trust fund, with no real job and an academic record that was obscured by Hollywood. Was Robin hiding the fact that he was a lethargic hippie-in-the-making but kept himself clean-cut until his true agenda came to light? Was Robin, in some obscure way, at a dress rehearsal for Woodstock? Was Batman furthering his agenda at the expense of throwing Robin's education under the bus?

Still, more questions go unanswered; was Batman part of the five percent wealthy, and the Joker, Riddler, and their cohorts in favour of more equitable wealth distribution in a socioeconomic sense?

But wait, even more perplexing is when we consider that the IRS never did a wealth attainment audit on Batman's cave, or have we considered that crime-fighters have a right to disability, critical illness insurance, and pensions? Would Bruce Wayne's insurance company cancel his various personal life policies if they knew what he really did for a living? So then, this would mean that Batman, aka Bruce Wayne, lied on his insurance policy, and this begs the question of what else he lied about.

Fast-forwarding to today, how would Batman feel about dealing with gangbangers and sitting in city courts these days, while bleeding heart judges let them off easy? Would the Riddler be tweeting, and would Batman be retweeting? What if someone texted the location of the Batcave or put it up on Facebook, or worse, how about if Google Maps blew the whistle as to the location of the Batcave? I am sure that given the chance, the Riddler would have audited the source of Batman's wealth. Perplexing as it may be, there are some things we may never know about Batman and will perhaps leave it beside other seemingly unanswered questions such as, "Are we alone?"

The enigmatic Batman leaves us wanting to know more, and we gasp in sadness as the evasion of clarity eases into the annals of time, where memories fade, folklore pervades, and truth is perhaps permanently obscured, leaving us all in a conundrum.

But then possibly we forgot about all this when the sixties came to a close in the year 1969, which brought an event to change our psyches forever. Because staring at the evening sky without ever touching it was no longer enough. What happened next was simply out of this world!

News Section

OUT OF THIS WORLD

On July 22, 1969, there was one great event that stirred the imagination of anyone who was alive to see it, an event that created an unrivalled phenomenon while collecting the intellectual imagination, prowess, and energy of mankind. It was the calling card for those who believed in the endless creativity of humans and more specifically encouraged us beings to embrace the future with vigour, energy, and purpose. For those of us who saw it, as I did, on a black-and-white Admiral television, early morning Toronto time, it left us in awe. For those who did not experience this most magical moment, I encourage you to read on.

We might take for granted that in 1969, when America sent a man to the moon, it helped define all that was possible, attesting to what human ingenuity could accomplish. What made it especially touching for me was that my father, who worked in the 1960s at General Electric on Eglinton Avenue in Scarborough, helped make some rocket thrust components of the Saturn 5. Additionally, his closest and lifelong friend, engineer Levon Babluzian, an orphan of the Armenian Genocide, designed the reflectors that brought back the first live pictures from the moon.

Recently, after hearing one of my boyhood heroes, Neil Armstrong, speak in Toronto in 2008, it brought me to such a nostalgic moment of the passage of childhood dreams that the moment Armstrong walked on stage, I could feel that I was in the presence of greatness and humbleness, all wrapped into a storybook that brought me back to July 22, 1969. As I listened to him speak, my mind wandered back to being nine years old, sitting in front of our television with the world in awe as mankind introduced itself to the universe. As I watched his hands tremble, since time and age had caught up to him, I wanted to reach out and touch him, my heart sinking, and wished that he could defy mortality because, like many of his generation, he gave to us so unselfishly. Once again, I was transported back to the morning after, sitting in the park in Thorncliffe, passionately discussing the slingshot that propelled our dreams and defined our tomorrows.

It was during that unforgettable moment Neil Armstrong delivered to us in 1969 that I learned how greatness was within us all, if we only had the courage to pursue it. We just could not wait to grow up and touch the world as we lay in a childhood bastion of quasi-poverty and dreamy-eyed intoxication.

Once again, I felt the same type of energy I had flirted with on that storied night in July 22, 1969; I listened as he explained how close the Soviets had come to landing a man on the moon first. He mentioned that little did we truly understand the gap that existed between President Kennedy's inspiring moon speech and the technology of the times in 1962. This gap was closed by the people who had the courage to pursue the dream of an assassinated president who helped energize and define perhaps our greatest moment to date.

What makes it even more remarkable is that it was all done with computer memory chips that, at best, could not rival today's modern calculator.

East versus West

The moon landing did not happen by chance; it involved a series of initiatives, events, and competition for scientific and philosophical supremacy between East and West. But to really get an appreciation of this marvellous human accomplishment that was known as the moon race, we should consider the backdrop of the times and take a quick look at the post World War II period.

The end of the Second World War carved a new map for Europe that included Western Europe being under the protective umbrella of the United States and Eastern Europe under the influence of the Soviet Union. Winston Churchill first coined the term Iron Curtain in his "Sinews of Peace" address of March 5, 1946, at Westminster College in Fulton, Missouri. *Wikipedia* offers the following excerpt:

> *"From Stettin in the Baltic to Trieste in the Adriatic, an 'Iron Curtain' has descended across the continent. Behind that line lie all the capitals of the ancient states of Central and Eastern Europe. Warsaw, Berlin, Prague, Vienna, Budapest, Belgrade, Bucharest, and Sofia; all these famous cities and the populations around them lie in what I must call the Soviet sphere, and all are subject, in one form or another, not only to Soviet influence but to a very high and in some cases increasing measure of control from Moscow."*

—WINSTON CHURCHILL, *1946*

Winston Churchill, Harry S. Truman and Joseph Stalin at the Potsdam Conference, 1945.

A United States Navy P-2 of VP-18 flying over a Soviet freighter during the Cuban Missile Crisis, October 1962.

President John F. Kennedy at Rice University, delivers *"The Moon Speech"*, September 12, 1962.

A 1963 conceptual model of the Apollo Lunar Excursion Module.

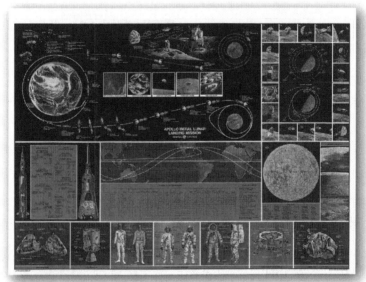

Apollo 11 mission poster my father received from General
Electric when he made parts for the moon landing.

Buzz Aldrin, walking on the moon, 1969.

Leonid Brezhnev and Richard Nixon speak, 1973.
Regardless of one's political leanings, Nixon was quite possibly the most qualified U.S. President in the last 100 years, with a vibrant intellect.

Sir Winston Churchill was a visionary, a genius who read over five thousand books and wrote over thirty, while he had perhaps the finest grasp of the English language and wrote all his own speeches, including the masterpiece that he delivered in Fulton that was well ahead of its time. Churchill understood the savagery of Joseph Stalin on the numerous occasions they met, while President Roosevelt was indifferent to the Soviet dictator. Churchill had, after all, gallantly fought wars on four continents (he was truly fearless) and insisted that he be on Royal Navy boats to lead his troops into the Normandy invasion in 1944 at the age of sixty-nine; it was only at the desperate urging of his wife, Clementine, and King George that he was persuaded not to join the invasion. King George felt that if Churchill was lost at sea, neither he nor the British people had counsel that could replace him in wartime. After all, many in the British inner circles were ready to capitulate in the darkest days of the war, but Churchill would have none of it. He was politically incorrect, even in his own time, and he did truly lead as opposed to worrying about the next election.

It is no secret that America did not want to be dragged into a European conflict as it had been in the First World War. American isolationism, as political doctrine at the time, had deep roots. What is interesting, though, is Churchill's ability to see the Soviet agenda. Truman, as well as a host of British Parliament members, dismissed Churchill as an alarmist after his famous Fulton speech and felt it was inimical to the cause of world peace. President Truman disowned him after the Fulton speech and denied he had seen the speech in advance, which he of course did see, during the train trip to Fulton, while the *Wall Street Journal,* in the spirit of isolationism, felt America should not align itself with Britain. *Pravda,* the Soviet newspaper, and Stalin pounced on the former prime minister when he stated in the Iron Curtain speech that "the principles of freedoms and the rights of man...were the joint inheritance of the English speaking world," and perhaps he was right.

Two years later, after the blockade of Berlin split Europe in half, Communism and its tyrannical agenda became apparent, and Truman later realized that Churchill was right during that afternoon in Missouri. This is the difference between politicians and leaders, since one of two are not the same! Boris Johnson, the mayor of London, stated in his book, *The Churchill Factor*, that "it was Churchill's moral and strategic framework that set the stage for the world he was born into".

The Soviet nuclear program did not emanate out of thin air. In the early 1930s, the Soviets were instrumental to the advancement of nuclear physics during the age when protons and neutrons were first discovered. Much to the dismay of the West, the Soviets detonated their first atomic bomb in 1949. True, they employed some espionage including recruiting the American couple, the Rosenbergs, as Soviet spies, in attaining blueprints to accelerate their knowledge, and much like the West, they recruited German scientists and/or German know-how after the war. But the fact of the matter is that the Soviets had brilliant scientists of their own, including Igor Kurchatov and Andrei Sakharov, as well as educational institutes in support of this endeavour.

Then the plot of East versus West thickened in 1950 during the Korean War, when the United States and its allies fought in Korea against the Soviet Union, which was providing proxy support for North Korean Communists and the Chinese. The Japanese, many of whom are descendants of the Koreans—there was a mass migration into Japan proper from Korea in about 300 BC—were ousted from the Korean Peninsula in 1945, an obvious vacuum formed. At the end of the Second World War, as part of the Potsdam agreements, US administrators carved Korea, with its five-thousand-year history, along the thirty-eighth parallel, where they oversaw the South, while the Soviets as their part of the deal, brought the North into their hemisphere. Thus, all the actors were in place for the 1950 Korean War, which lasted until 1953 and cost the greatly decorated General MacArthur his career, since President Truman would not let him finish the job. The powers of the day created an enigma that still has not been resolved today, and it is this politics of tragedy that our modern world still lives with.

So, the conflict between communism and capitalism manifested itself in the Cold War, and its derivative, the Red Scare. Entering the ring from stage right was none other than Senator Joe McCarthy. Without supporting his position with cold, hard facts, he claimed that Communists had infiltrated the State Department, Voice of America, and other key American institutions. He even accused certain Hollywood types of being Communists, or sympathizers, and had a host of actors blacklisted without trial. Perhaps it was true that some of these Hollywood types were indeed Communists; however, we may never know, since victors of history bury the facts in emotional obscurity. The events of the time made anti-Communist crusades an easy sell, especially when we consider the fall of China into Communist hands, the Korean War, and the Soviet Union detonating an atomic bomb in 1949; this all happened in a span of three years.

Hence the term "McCarthyism," which is part of the dartboard repertoire for professors in academia. To better explain McCarthyism, it was something similar to the intolerant witch-hunt orchestrated by the political correctness we see today. Both are built on a foundation of twigs, whereas logic and self-expression are thrown under the bus. In other words, if one does not toe the line of the current culturally deprived and intellectually suffocating value system, one will be blacklisted as intolerant, without a trial or a litmus test. But this is the price to pay for proposing fair and logical arguments against the defective groupthink of the politically correct.

So, going back to the moon mission and what led up to it, perhaps the first silo that was launched of the moon mission was when the Soviets shocked the West by sending the first artificial satellite into orbit, *Sputnik* in 1957. This, of course, caught America flat-footed and was a blow to its prestige and confidence—confidence can sometimes evolve into arrogance, which in turn can melt into fear—this was perhaps true in America at the time. *Sputnik* showed how advanced the Soviet rocket technology was and how it could be adapted to pointing intercontinental ballistic missiles (ICBMs) at the United States and its allies. This was perhaps the largest fear factor generated in the West by the *Sputnik* success. Then, in September of 1959, the Soviet Union made *Luna 2*, which made an uncontrolled landing on the moon. The space race had started, and on April 12, 1961, aboard the spacecraft *Vostok 1*, Soviet cosmonaut Yuri Alekseyevich Gagarin orbited Earth in eighty-nine minutes and came home to a hero's welcome.

Needless to say, the national swelling was bad enough for the United States that it had to put an ice pack on its collectively bruised ego. Soon after, in February 1962, John Glenn became the first American in orbit with the Mercury capsule, *Friendship*, and circled the earth three times in four hours and fifty-six minutes.

Then, on September 12, 1962, Camelot's most prominent member in the United States entered the stage with what is known as the "Moon Speech" and eloquently energized the nation with these great words:

> There is no strife, no prejudice, and no national con-
> flict in outer space as yet. Its hazards are hostile to us
> all. Its conquest deserves the best of all mankind, and
> its opportunity for peaceful cooperation many never
> come again. But why, some say, the moon? Why choose
> this as our goal? And they may well ask, why climb the
> highest mountain? Why, thirty-five years ago, fly the
> Atlantic? Why does Rice play Texas?
>
> We choose to go to the moon. We choose to go
> to the moon in this decade and do the other things,
> not because they are easy, but because they are hard,
> because that goal will serve to organize and measure
> the best of our energies and skills, because that chal-
> lenge is one that we are willing to accept, one we are

*unwilling to postpone, and one which we intend to win,
and the others, too.*

—JOHN FITZGERALD KENNEDY

President Kennedy would not see the moon landing because of the horror of November 22, 1963, but the world would. The space race was in full flight and thus, the contest was to find out who could best challenge the parameters of human exploration.

This was not just some ordinary friendly competition; this was a contest between two archrivals that happened to have thousands of nuclear missiles aimed at each other. This was the era of the Cold War, and the destruction of civilization was a press of a button away, or so we thought. This was a time when the two ideologies of communism and individualistic democracies were on a daily collision course; it was us against them; it was good guys versus bad guys; it was East meets West, and in many ways a clash of civilizations and ideologies—much like the modernity of the West today versus the backwardness of religious zealotry. One camp feels guilty about its unparalleled accomplishments in the last five hundred years and the other intoxicated by backwardness and mythologies.

Perhaps this contest was the part of an unconscious effort to debunk the teachings of Karl Marx and his consortium of societal and economic illiterates, who did not understand our quest as human beings for individualism, self-gain, exploration, and selected compassion. This was perhaps a contest between egalitarianism and human idiosyncratic freedom—our way of life versus their way of life, democracy versus totalitarianism. Each side, through its respective propaganda apparatus, vilified the other; each side had its respective flaws, and each side believed its own stories, but the West, as a way of life, had so much more to offer.

Former Soviet premier Alexei Kosygin visited Toronto in 1971, and I remember crystal-clear the events of that day against the backdrop of this confrontation between the Soviet and American political systems. I particularly remember the protests by Jewish groups at the Ontario Science Centre against the Soviet premier, who was accompanied by the then-Prime Minister Trudeau, since these groups were less than pleased with the treatment of Jews in the Soviet Union.

As a side note, within Russia, Jews have had strained relations dating back even to the czars' time and before. However, what made this protest ironic was the fact that many of the key leaders of the Bolshevik Revolution, including Trotsky, were Jewish academics who had bought into the egalitarian philosophies of Karl Marx.

The police were brought in on horses for crowd control, but the most unforgettable moment was the procession of limousines and security detail. Now, let me turn back the clock, recreate this day and the way it touched me; I still lived in Thorncliffe Park, and was attending Valley Park Junior High School when this event was creating incredible buzz. I looked out the school window on the top floor, facing north onto the Don Mills neighbourhood, and I saw this endless convoy of limousines that included Prime Minister Trudeau and Premier Kosygin as they were making their way to the Science Centre. I remember all the commotion in the school of this visit, but what struck me the most was looking at the main towers of the Inn on the Park hotel (today a Lexus dealership) and seeing the RCMP (Royal Canadian Mounted Police) on the roof with modern machine guns dressed in camouflage. One must remember that we were living in a Canada before the mass importation of guns and gang violence, and to see this open display of arms was a first for me.

This was the leader of the Iron Curtain visiting us in Canada two years after the moon landing. But it was taking place against the backdrop of us versus them that made the moon landing so significant.

Why the Moon?

Arguments against the moon mission and The Space Race, as it was termed in those dreamy days, included a host of reasons. If I remember correctly, many said that we should eradicate our problems on Earth before expending our energies and money into space. This boulevard of reasoning was short-sighted and was considered wishful thinking, at best, since history has shown that this battle within ourselves may never be won.

We as humans have an exploratory spirit that thirsts for knowledge as well as wants to perhaps better understand God's engineering. The DNA of mankind's curiosity is not static, as its quest for progress is insatiable, and much of this is discussed later in this book under technology and disruptive changes. Then again, perhaps a better reason to explore space would be that there seems to be little evidence of intelligent life on Earth, hence we should seek and explore the universe for signs of intelligent life, and possibly we can mimic it to accelerate our own progress.

However, there might be an instinctual dark side in our collective psyche that does not readily surface, since it resides somewhere in the deepest areas of our souls. Being in denial of or possibly not perceptive enough to see the hidden, it may be possible that somewhere in our subliminal thinking, we know that it is our destiny to destroy ourselves here on Earth, and for this reason we need to leave this planet before we do. Hence, we must explore.

The question then of humanity's survivability is arguably based on a very fragile future, where we still have to use our imaginations and abilities and strive to reach for the stars in order to discover and colonize other planets, denying our passionate and strategic inertia to destroy our own species. In other words, will destiny give us the time to attain the technological know-how to colonize other planets before we destroy ourselves here on Earth? Ultimately, whichever camp is faster in its quest will determine mankind's future, or lack thereof. Quite possibly, here is where our manifest destiny lies.

The Deniers

Even today we have people who believe that the moon landing was a Hollywood production that fooled the world as they text away their lives with irrelevancies to their so-called virtual friends.

This line of thinking, along with people who believed the Earth was flat, suffers from backwardness and makes these types the "fools of time."

The moon landing stretched our minds, and for many it overloaded their personal sense of relativism.

There are a host of reasons for denial of the empirically obvious; for some, the only way they could suffocate modernity was through denial; in another camp, the moon is so seeded in ancient mythology, enveloped into religious thinking that they could not come to terms with this phenomenon; for others, the moon landing touched them on a primal level, deep in their psyche, since it unsettled five thousand years of human thinking, going back to Mesopotamia and even before.

My personal favourites are conspiracy theorists who narcissistically have a sense of supreme collective knowledge above the pauper masses, they wish to edify as they see it. Hence, with no real training in physics, engineering, mathematics, metallurgy, or hands-on assembly in complex equipment, they preach their poorly and selectively reasoned unscientific research, hoping that they can enlighten the intellectually oppressed masses, like some modern-day messiah. And of course, by doing this, they will become social media stars as they sip on some Starbucks java and figure out how to pay back their student loans for programs that have weak job prospect opportunities.

Their arguments usually start with the fact that the flag on the moon looked like it was waving, when in fact there is no gravity on the moon. This can be easily explained, since the US flag was supported by light steel mesh in the backdrop to make it appear as if it were waving (see: http://en.wikipedia.org/wiki/Lunar_Flag_Assembly).

The fact of the matter is that most of the flags placed on the moon are still standing, based on a review of photographs taken by the Lunar Reconnaissance Orbiter Camera in 2012.

Of course, we cannot forget about the Soviet scientists who tracked the *Apollo 11* and accepted the fact that the material brought back being from the moon landing, which could only come from the moon. Also, one should consider the fact that the reflectors placed there by Neil Armstrong and Buzz Aldrin are used today as a mathematical guiding point for Earth's telescopes, as any astronomer will confirm.

Certainly then, we should also entertain the absurd theory of how five thousand scientists, engineers, technicians, maintenance people, master tradesmen, mathematicians, astronauts, and filmmakers conspired to create the hoax, not only at NASA but at private and public companies that provided parts, know-how, and special services—which included advanced metallurgic components. And obviously, if one believes their school of thought, this would mean they all worked together in perfect harmony to coordinate such a hoax!

Anyone who has worked with scientists, mathematicians, and engineers knows the integrity of the scientific mind and how it must reconcile decisions based on empirical reasoning and follow litmus tests in order to further the parameters of knowledge. What makes it more absurd is that these people could conspire to keep this a secret all these years. As the CIA says, once two people know a secret, it no longer remains a secret!

Here is the fact: the Americans went to the moon four times, and there is not a credible scientist, including the Russians, who would deny the moon landing on July 22, 1969, or the subsequent three moon landings. In the end, the conspirators reek of envy and use their inebriated conspiracy theories as an attempt to sound intelligent about things they are ill-equipped to even discuss during their delusionary groupthink state of mind, as they dream their lives away, much like Walter Mitty.

Just because they are not accomplished in life, it does not mean that others are not more successful.

Some Final Words on the Moon

The story of the moon landing goes much deeper with political and philosophical ramifications; it helped to show the world that Western ingenuity could accomplish. As much as the rest of the world's peoples loathe the West, they deeply admire it as mankind's last great hope, even though it walks with a wounded knee today. As much as most cultures are worth preserving, they could never compete with the unbridled psyche of the West or have had the imagination required to send a man to the moon forty-five years ago. Many criticize the West, which is their right, but deep inside they know they need the West more than the West needs them.

The moon landing was a psychological blow to the Soviets, perhaps more so than *Sputnik* was to the Americans. But when the Americans put the first man on the moon, it perhaps showed that the Soviets no longer had the technological or political philosophy to compete with the West. Certainly, the moon landing was not the reason the Soviet Union fell in the 1991, but that episode had placed a deep bruise on Soviet confidence, which possibly cascaded in an immeasurable way in addition to its economic and philosophical setbacks toward its decline.

But when all is said about the moon landing, today we still play in this sandbox that we call Mother Earth, the same one that our ancestors played in and we grew up within, but once we landed on this faraway place called the moon, our playground was all put in relative perspective.

Somehow, my mind wanders back to 1969, as my father and I put together a complex model of the *Apollo 11* Saturn 5 Rocket, meticulously painting each component, including the red fire of the booster rockets, and with the finite precision of the highly accomplished artesian that my father was, we assembled the components of the lunar landing module. Each day, the rocket became closer to completion, until one day the model was finally complete. I stood before the three-foot model of the *Apollo 11* in complete awe as I cast one eye on my father's contagious smile and the other on the future of tomorrow, while considering all that was possible!

Sports Section

FROZEN ICE

Growing up in Toronto in the sixties, life without hockey was unimaginable; after all, the sport is woven into the Canadian fabric. It is our gift to the world, and hockey can best be described as a highly skilled game on a sheet of ice that integrates the finest in ballet, exquisite skill, and barbarianism, depending on the cast.

No building could inspire emotions for a child growing up in Toronto like the iconic Maple Leaf Gardens (the Gardens) did. As a group of eight- to twelve-year-olds, my friends and I would take the subway to watch a game at the Gardens. Many winter Sundays, we would go there to watch the Junior 'A' Toronto Marlies play in the OHA. I believe at the time that hockey tickets for this venue were in the $1.50 range. Some of the players would become big-name NHL stars, such as Mike Palmateer and Mark Howe. When these junior games became a bit boring, we would play tag for hours, running up and down the hundreds of stairs that were part of this iconic building.

On rare occasions, some of us had the good fortune of actually seeing an NHL game at the Gardens, if we were well-connected, assuming some of the suits gave up their tickets. The tickets we most often obtained were in the pauper areas of the green and grey seats of the building, but this was where the true fans were, and we were so thrilled to be watching our heroes.

Hockey is quintessentially Canadian and might be the common bond that binds this country. When some people who immigrated to this country first saw the game, they were so struck by the speed that they thought the television stations had the game running on fast-forward, which of course was not true. To the untrained eye, many people who see the game for the first time consider it violent, calling it barbaric, which at times it might be. However, to those who truly understand this breathtaking sport, it is art and skill at its highest levels on ice, and it is not a sport that can be played by just anyone without substantial training or self-learning.

In terms of the skill level required for even rudimentary and functional ability to play, it is quite involved. If someone wants to learn how to play hockey, one must first learn how to skate and then coordinate this with a stick and learn how to stickhandle and shoot a puck in perfect symbiotic motion, while moving in and out of human traffic at quite high speeds.

Most people who try this casually without instructions for the first time would risk injury, possibly severe, if they fell without knowing how. And if they tried it without a helmet, like my peers did, the possibility of head injury lurked against the hard coldness of a sheet of ice. Putting things in perspective, most people cannot even walk on ice without risking injury, never mind skating at thirty kilometres per hour. For many, they would never be able to master the most rudimentary levels of skill required even to play a basic pickup game at an outdoor rink.

In contrasting it with other sports, most people could kick a soccer ball after a minute or so, learn how to play basic hoops on a basketball court, and run with a football, since all these sports seem to more innately inclusive. This isn't to say one would be skilled at the initial stages, but one could throw a basketball or pass or run with a football without the risk of injury, since the mastery of a multitude of skills is simply not required at the rudimentary level. This is in no way a knock against these other fine sports, but just a relative comparison in terms of a physical barrier to entry due to the amount of coordination required. Some of hockey is innate, but much of it is quite alien because it is played on a sheet of ice, which is foreign to our natural human instincts.

When on those special hockey nights we take the proletariat behaviours of clutching and grabbing from the game, and then give back the game to its rightful owners, the true artistry emerges. In its glory, the rightful owners are the Lemieuxs, Gretzkys, Hulls, Perreaults, Yakushevs, Orrs, Pavel Bures, Lafleurs, Crosbys, Toewses, and the like. It is at that moment that we witness this symphony on ice of highly skilled magicians in a tango of a precise ballet that evolves into what we call "fire-wagon hockey." It is this magic moment that the game of hockey promises as it galvanizes the country and stirs the imagination like no other sport. Simply put, hockey is Canada's gift to the world.

It is on those naturally frozen rinks, like the one we had in Thorncliffe Park, that many Canadian boys learned how to play the game. It was where we learned to dream and expend the boundless energy of youth; the place where we hoped we would someday be wearing the blue Maple Leafs jersey and leading our hometown team to the Stanley Cup in front of more than sixteen thousand fans at the Gardens.

As we played, we emulated the broadcast of our game, pretending we were Foster Hewitt, imitating our heroes, skating around ice that was broken and cracked, unlike our dreams. Once we had picked teams on those cold Canadian winter nights, we must have played for hours at a time with no water or food, and the only sources of energy were adrenaline and perhaps a nutritious candy bar (well, not exactly nutritious), if we had bothered to bring one. It was a perfect venue on which to learn how to skate, deke, and pass through ten players, since many of these games had twenty kids on the ice at the same time. No real referee, something like professional wrestling, and in terms of keeping score, it was in our heads. After all, we had to put all that math we learned to good use, since the times tables were required learning in elementary school.

Our organized hockey was played in Leaside Memorial Gardens, where Frank Mahovlich's (a famous Leafs player and along with Dave Keon probably the main reason the Leafs won four Stanley Cups in the sixties) father ran the skate shop and prepared the ice before many of the games. He was a chubby, patient, and kind man. I remember standing by him after my game when he was watching his sons play on TV that afternoon, the notorious Broad Street Bullies (Philadelphia Flyers) against the Montreal Canadiens, which turned into a donnybrook. As he gestured, you could see he did not approve of his sons' involvement in a free-for-all with the Broad Street Bullies.

In the winter, each Wednesday and Saturday night, we would watch the Leafs on my family's black-and-white Admiral TV. In those days, TVs were still made by and large in North America, even though the Japanese were on the doorsteps of our market. It was perhaps a total of six-channel world, and stations would go off the air at about midnight. This was how winters were spent, at least in my neighbourhood, playing hockey, daydreaming in school, quivering when our parents received our report cards, and following the Maple Leafs. And since we had not yet quite discovered girls, hockey was the most important creation of the universe. Well, at least until we reached puberty!

On Saturday mornings we gathered our flimsy equipment, which in those days included styrofoam-type helmets, and dragged our hockey bags from Thorncliffe to Leaside Memorial Gardens for our games. This was about a two-and-a-half-kilometre walk, since we rarely took the bus, and no, parents did not hold our hands, stumbling over our every whim. It is no wonder that some kids grew up psychologically balanced and strong, while others were wanting.

Did parents come to our Saturday morning games? Some did, but I certainly do not remember them coming in to scream and act like overaged imbeciles. My father was too busy starting his business, and my mother was not exactly a hockey mom.

Each week we would play, imitating our heroes that were gifted to us by the hockey gods. Then one evening we all heard the villains were coming to Maple Leaf Gardens to challenge our heroes, and snatch away our dreams and our gift to the world in what turned out to be the greatest episode in international sport, of the virtuous versus the villainous, perhaps more calculating than the Riddler in the *Batman* series, and at times more insidious than the Joker. We thought we had chased their philosophy away when we landed a man on the moon, but evidently this was not the case, as a new chapter was about to reveal itself.

THE MAGIC OF SEPTEMBER 1972

That magical September in 1972, we were about to witness history in the making as we defended the Canadian version of the Holy Grail: hockey supremacy. Yes, our favourite and most mysterious villains landed on our shores, not with amphibious vehicles or with tanks and rifles, but with hockey sticks and skates. Eventually, we had to visit them behind the Iron Curtain in a Cold War world to settle the rivalry that was mixed in a mysterious brew of sports, politics, and economic philosophy.

I think it is difficult for this generation to get an emotional grasp of what went on that September, but the nation was galvanized like never before or since, unless of course you call Facebook galvanizing. For us seasoned souls, it is always worth reliving both the agony and glory of this magical moment of our youth.

Those who lived through it knew the raw emotions that this series evoked. With the background of the Cold War still in relative full swing, these foreigners with a different political and economic philosophy than the West first came to learn and then to challenge our supremacy of hockey, and perhaps in some way our way of life. We were not England and were certainly not prepared to give away hockey supremacy like the motherland did with soccer. The game of hockey was about to change as we once knew it.

Finally, after all the years of the Soviet national team beating our amateur teams, it was time for our professionals to administer redemption. In some way, it was like we were tired of our kid brothers getting beat up, and we were finally allowed to face this inevitable confrontation.

After all, it was our professionals against a Soviet team mostly drawn from their Red Army team.

The day before the summit series started, the three daily Toronto newspapers—the *Globe and Mail*, *Toronto Star*, and *Toronto Sun*—had special sections dedicated to the pre-series assessment; hockey writers stated in interviews with the Soviet coaches that they had come to Canada to learn, but we were in for a surprise. Writers of the day were also saying things like Canada skated better, but we could not play a physical game against the Soviets by hitting them, coupled with outlandish overconfidence. The summary of all the pre-series assessment by the sports journalists was that our NHL team of all-stars would win in a romp; after all, who could beat our bona fide heroes? It would be like Shakespeare teaching the finer points of literary *savoir faire* to Don Cherry. Even though we were warned by Billy Harris and the Team Canada coach Harry Sinden, who had previously played the Soviets as amateurs, that their team was quite capable, no one paid much attention to this advice. This, of course, was about to change, as arrogance was about to transform into fear.

On September 2, 1972, the first game was about to commence, and in attendance was Prime Minister Pierre Trudeau to witness the horror of Canada losing. The rest of us watched with dismay the unravelling of our national psyche in our own living rooms. In many respects, this loss was the worst realization of Canada's nightmare. It was worse than when Orson Wells broadcasted *War of the Worlds* on October 30, 1938, with the Martian invasion storyline that was thought to be real by many, but in the end, it was radio theatre and to this date has not manifested itself in reality, even though some people act like they are not from this world—especially during elections. Even when the Cuban Missile Crisis struck in October 1962 and the world spiralled into anxiety, in the end, our worst fears were never realized. To make an American analogy, it would be like the New York Yankees with Mickey Mantle in the lineup losing in front of the nation to a Soviet baseball team during the height of the Cold War in the 1950s, with President Eisenhower watching. Or "Broadway Joe" Namath and the New York Jets Super Bowl champions getting beaten at Shea Stadium by a visiting Soviet team while President Nixon watched. But unlike the fears of *The War of the Worlds* and the Cuban Missile Crisis, our worst fear of losing hockey's Holy Grail was manifesting.

The Russians handed the Canadian team a seven-to-three thrashing before a shocked television audience, and what made it more humiliating was that it happened at "the most storied building in hockey history," the Montreal Forum, the place that Maurice "Rocket" Richard and Jean "Le Gros Bill" Béliveau built, a building that was filled with ghosts of legendary hockey glory that were somehow intertwined with our national fabric. Even if French Canadian and Anglo Canadian teams despised each other, we needed this rivalry, much like Batman and the Riddler, to help sew the game of hockey into mythical proportions, because diametrically opposed forces are inextricably linked, and adversity is the seed that sows character. Much like brothers and sisters that might not get along but can put aside their differences when faced with a common foe, in the end we were family, and our infighting was a private matter when it came to protecting our national treasure.

I remember like yesterday the horrible, empty feeling all Canadians of a hockey persuasion felt after game one at the Montreal Forum. It was embarrassing, and the shock of the loss can be compared to a national wake. While the Soviets had studied our team deeply, including briefings on each of our players, our team had not done the same with theirs; little did we know how well they could skate, shoot, pass, and score, but this was further augmented by their playmaking abilities. Clearly, Team Canada was playing an able and disciplined team with a host of legitimate superstars. I remember a few of their players with their foreign sounding names: Yakushev, Kharlamov, Petrov, Mikhailov, and the list goes on. Though the Soviet team studied and respected Team Canada's abilities, we made the fatal mistake of being arrogant and marginalized their abilities. But perhaps it was our metamorphosis into fear that was the most unsettling.

It was a different time; back then the norm was for the professional players to come into training camp overweight from a summer of hearty living and liquid indulgences, and the NHL players would play themselves into shape during the playing season. Off-ice training and strict nutritional intake were not part of their training regimen, unless one calls alcohol part of a recommended and balanced meal plan. The Soviets, however, came into this Summit Series in top shape; they trained on and off the ice and made for, at least in the beginning, a more cohesive unit than the Team Canada players. In fact, when the series was over and the 1972 NHL season began, the players who were in the Summit Series were in top shape and were for the first few weeks flying past the other NHL players, which was quite obvious on TV broadcasts.

I remember my mother receiving a phone call on Sunday morning, September 3, from a family friend who ran a ticket outlet; to my excitement he had tickets for me, to hopefully witness redemption at Maple Leaf Gardens. Little did I know I was about to witness the making of history in game two. It was a dream come true and a really nice place to be for a Thorncliffe Park newspaper delivery boy, with one side of my mind on the thrill of being there and the other hoping the agony of the loss in Montreal would not repeat itself.

But we all wondered if redemption or pain would make its way onto the stage in the hockey mecca called Maple Leaf Gardens.

Bobby Orr scores to win his first Stanley Cup in 1969; his
skills were sorely missed in the 1972 Summit Series.

Frank Mahovlich's father was the skate sharpener and Zamboni driver when
I played minor hockey at Leaside Memorial Gardens in Toronto, 1967.

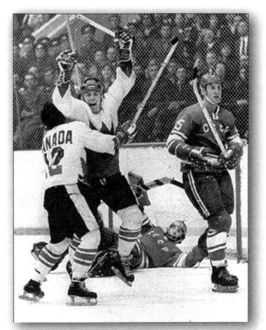

Paul Henderson scores with 34 seconds left in
game eight to save the Nation, 1972.

Game Two: Maple Leaf Gardens

Game two of the Summit Series was played before a shell-shocked
nation that was trying to come to terms with the loss of game one in
Montreal, a nation that was emotional, a nation in deep thought about
the game that is woven into our national fabric. Canada had switched
from confidence to insecurity about its favourite child. Much like stock-
market psychology, greed had turned to fear.

I believe it was a Monday, and I remember my mother's friend taking me to the game from Thorncliffe Park, where we all lived. I cannot remember the bus ride to Pape Avenue subway station, but I can
remember emerging from the College Street subway station. The
commotion, the emotion, and the electricity had ignited the air, the
heckling of scalpers and the smell of chestnuts sold on College Street,

as we all came to watch and find a way to mend the pride that consti-tuted our national framework. We came to discover whether we could find a way to heal together in Hockey's Mecca. This grey building called Maple Leaf Gardens was built during the despair of the Great Depression; it held eleven Stanley Cups and concerts by the Beatles, Elvis, and the Rolling Stones, a speech by Winston Churchill. This was the iconic place where Cassius Clay and George Chuvalo fought (Clay said Chuvalo was the toughest man he ever fought), and of course it was the place that Duke Ellington, and Ol' Blue Eyes himself, Frank Sinatra, performed. It was where our gym teacher, Mr. Thomas, who once played for the Harlem Globetrotters, took us to watch the team he once played with.

Maple Leaf Gardens is not only a storied building in Canada but also internationally, and it was this building, which we dreamed of so much as children growing up in Toronto, that would help us discover just who we were on September 4, 1972.

I vividly remember the ovation the Canadian team received for the pre-game warm-ups; it nearly brought the building down, and imme-diately we could tell that this was a more disciplined, respectful team. We could see during the warm-ups that they were skating much bet-ter, even though their conditioning was lacking, and at the same time, I remember how passionately we sang "O Canada!" To be this openly patriotic in Canada is, well, very un-Canadian.

From my family's black-and-white Admiral TV set to being in the presence of history at Maple Leaf Gardens, I was in awe, and I never felt more fortunate as I watched our heroes step onto the ice. They electrified the building. Since helmets were still not widely used, we could connect to the faces and personalities better, and there they were: Phil Esposito, the greatest goal-scorer the game had ever seen then without the incomparable Bobby Orr, Stan Mikita without Bobby Hull, the Mahovlich Brothers, Yvan "The Roadrunner" Cournoyer, Brad

Park. Names that are only historical to today's generation, but I saw them all when they were young, their pulses emanating with energy and the fate of our hearts within their grasp.

I sat in the north-end of the arena, which was always a beautiful vantage point to see the artistry of the plays. If one knows Maple Leaf Gardens as it once was, we all know the north-end and south-end seats of the building, and it is from these points that one could see blueprints of the plays turn into the high-speed game we love.

Breaking down game two, Canada came out very strong defensively and offensively. Incidentally, when assessing the Soviet team's style, their Achilles heel was that their defense was prone to breakdowns, and much of this has been lost in the overall assessment of their style of play.

The first goal in the second period was classic Esposito, parked on the doorstep. The second goal came from a beautiful pass from Brad Park to Yvan Cournoyer, and Canada had the momentum. The Soviets scored to narrow the lead to one goal. However, what I remember was the most beautiful goal I had ever seen; with Canada shorthanded, Peter Mahovlich took the puck from just outside his blue line, deked the Soviet defender literally out of his mind, and then put the shift on Tretiak, the goaltender. From the north-end of the Gardens, I saw this incredible moment forming like a choreographed ballet, and the energy it gave to Team Canada and the nation was too insurmountable for the Soviets to recover from that night. Canada won game two by the score of four to one. For the moment, my world was saved, but still it was not a good evening to grow fingernails.

As the story turns out, it was a night of redemption, but the story of the Summit Series was still in the making, and new heroes were about to make their way to the stage.

Eventually, the series shifted to the Soviet Union. Parents were starting to keep their children home and advising teachers that they felt watching the games was a moment that would live in historical folklore—and they were right! Subsequently, schools agreed to allow students to watch the game in school. At the time, I attended Valley Park Middle School in Toronto, and I remember the black-and-white TVs that were raised on portable support beams so we could watch the defense of our national game. Phil Esposito showed the incredible leadership that comes with Canadian grit; with some help from the hockey gods and Paul Henderson, Team Canada won that series with thirty-four seconds left in game eight.

That iconic Canadian moment of Yvan Cournoyer hugging Henderson in the Moscow Palace after the goal that shook the world with thirty-four seconds left in the game gave our nation redemption. This moment has now vanished into our collective memories. First captured on television, and then photographs, and then etched in paintings, it fades into the annals of history and turns into folklore. The following day, the *Toronto Sun* called its paper the *HenderSun* after the goal that was heard across the world.

Afterthoughts of the Summit Series

The Soviets always felt that the injured ankle of Kharlamov, compliments of a slash by Bobby Clark, is what caused the Soviet team to lose. But what people quickly forget is that the greatest player who ever laced up did not play in this series. For those who did not see the most gifted athlete of our time, it would be worth breaking down his skill set, outside of the fact that he revolutionized the game for defensemen and actually won a scoring title in 1974–75, which has still never been accomplished by any other defenseman. I speak about none other than Bobby Orr.

The statistics of this gifted athlete do not tell the complete tale when we remember that defensemen are supposed to defend, and that he did as well as anyone. But first thing's first: Bobby Orr was the most gifted skater, in terms of lateral dexterity, and at explosive speed, that has ever played the game. Spending much of his career on one leg, since the other knee was injured, he still dominated the sport of hockey like no other, and I would venture to say that he was more dominant relatively than Pele in soccer and Michael Jordan in basketball. Simply put, no other player ever dominated a sport like Bobby Orr did in hockey. He could control the complete ice surface and the tempo of the game, while he had passing abilities that were spot-on, like Gretzky, and explosive speed, like Pavel Bure. His playmaking abilities and inventiveness were outstanding, and he could electrify a building by just stepping on the ice. Simply put, he was incomparable as a complete hockey player.

And when we look at the total eight-game series, I can assure readers that Bobby Orr would not have come to training camp out of shape. Furthermore, Team Canada was lacking the dexterity and speed on defense that Orr would have provided. I am confident that a healthy Orr would have given the Soviet team fits with his explosive rushes, defense, ice presence, and playmaking abilities and would have brought down the Soviet scoring by at least eight goals over the series, while perhaps being responsible for an extra seven goals directly or by assist. In the worst-case scenario, this alone would have been good for at least two games, since Valeri Kharlamov would not have been able to skate around Orr, while at the same time he would have intercepted those blind Soviet passes. Team Canada badly missed the exhilarating Bobby Orr and his incomparable skills, and those who watched him play easily understand the thrill of what we were all deprived of.

Gordie Howe once said that the day Orr prematurely retired with bad knees was the worst thing that ever happened to the NHL. For those who have never seen him play, his ice presence can only be described as exhilarating. Injuries faded his skills, and yes, he finally played the Soviets in 1976, and even though he won the MVP, he was playing on one leg, and he was only a shadow of his former self. As Bobby Hull said about Orr in the 1976 series, "He was better on one leg than the rest of us on two."

But with time, we can become much better Monday-morning quarterbacks and armchair critics. For example, Team Canada was without Bobby Hull, and his scoring and skating skills were sorely missed. When one looks back at the series, the Canadian players that performed the best were the ones who could skate well: Cournoyer, Henderson, and Esposito, who did not appear fast but could cover a lot of ice quickly, and of course the dexterity of Brad Park. But what Team Canada missed sorely, and to this day I cannot understand why, was that Harry Sinden did not pick Dave Keon. His two-way play, coupled with his outstanding skating skills, would have been the exact remedy for the speedy Soviets, especially Kharlamov. Keon did not have a good prior season in the NHL, but still he was probably the best two-way player in the world. He was a master of the geometry of the rink, knew how to cut off angles, and made his opponent pay for mistakes by scoring. Even today, watching Keon on YouTube video, one can witness his speed and grasp of the game that is incredible in any era: (see: http://www.youtube.com/watch?v=_Q1OhaYNSkk).

So, when all was said and done, Canada won, the Soviets lost, the game of hockey changed forever as the fusion of two styles improved the game, and we saved our psyche as a nation. Somehow, the elation of winning masked the pain of almost losing, because in winning, we had to unmask the villain in us while saving what was left of our virtue.

THE MAIN EVENT

Man's fascination with evil versus good transcends history, folklore, and mythology. What can raise the human consciousness like the spectre of heroes versus villains? Would Batman have a purpose without the Riddler? Would Western thinking lack energy if it did not diametrically oppose the tenets of Soviet thought during the Cold War? Would Osama bin Laden have had purpose without the West? Perhaps without the West, Osama would not have been able to deflect the failure of himself and his disturbed followers.

If Snidely Whiplash (a classic cartoon villain) did not tie women to railroad tracks, what purpose would Dudley Do-Right of the Mounties have? Would Karl Marx be relevant without the tenets of Adam Smith? What would Hannibal be without Rome? And what would Irish cops do without bad guys, since one can only hang around a pub for so long? Bad guys and good guys are strange bedfellows, but nevertheless, they are inextricably bound by fate, since they mutually provide purpose.

Do we ostracize villains because we do not want to recognize the imperfections of our heroes? To despise something that does not agree with our morality and our principles is perhaps a way of coming to terms with our core beliefs and alleviating the wrongs of our own mindset. Do villains in an absurd way promote our sense of justice?

The villain is in all of us, and our denial of this flirtatious behaviour in the deepest parts of our minds creates the counter-culture of morality and collective justice of what we call, well, the "good guy." It is in this quagmire, which stirs in the deepest areas of our souls, that we do not have the courage to discover the demons within ourselves, but point in haste, as we wag our fingers at others, while cowardly hiding in the anonymity of the collective public forum.

So then, why speak about wrestling? What makes it so entertaining, and why do some of us gravitate towards such events? Is professional wrestling predetermined? Perhaps, but then again, so is theatre and film, and so is a losing sports team that diehard fans cannot help but waste their lives away on.

Wrestling has a combination of factors that fill the gaps other sports cannot provide. Many professional sports come up with a grandiose billing but fall short. For example, is every hockey game exciting and emotionally touching? What about some basketball games that are ho-hum or football games that are hyped, but cannot deliver? Consider some Super Bowls that sponsors have overpaid for advertising spots without considering the fact that the audience is suffocating on nachos and too intoxicated by liquid enhancements to comprehend the core message. Ever watched a boxing match that was too civilized?

If you carefully watch interviews with professional athletes, they are for the most part less than titillating. Who really cares about a ball or a puck that will not in any way change the outcome of civilization or one's personal life? The athletes are surrounded by otherwise intellectually stagnant commentators, interviewers, or writers, like a consortium of overaged groupies. So then, does the great sporting event change the course of things, or why does the thrill of victory mask the pain in us all?

Simply put, most of our sports heroes lack verbal creativity, charisma, or on-the-fly inventiveness. Have you heard hockey players interviewed, or the way football players answer prescripted questions? "Look, I saw you pass the puck or drop the hoop or catch the ball." Now exactly what is so titillating about redescribing their moment of glory?

Their oratorical skills are not exactly on par with Winston Churchill's, and these athletes did not steer Britain in the Second World War, so let's all keep things in perspective.

Watching paint dry is more entertaining than many professional sports interviews, perhaps with MMA and boxing excluded. Today's athletes have a script playbook that falls within the sports brand guidelines, with a rehearsed set of answers. Hence, the question begs itself:

what is more exciting, watching a pre-game interview with an athlete or being lullabied into a deep alpha level of sleep? With all the interview guidelines that are in their contracts, it is no wonder that when they do speak, they sound much like a politician, meaning much noise exudes from their lips, but nothing is really said!

The only people who would find this remotely interesting are fans who are in a state of animated inebriation. Perhaps fans who attend professional sporting events are looking for a way out of inner loneliness through television or the live event or perhaps a sense of escape. It goes then, that sports fans might not achieve fame on their own, they can live in grandeur through the athletes they worship by spending their hard-earned money to collectively celebrate the thrill of victory or the agony of defeat. Win or lose, both outcomes have little bearing on their personal lives, but the collective gathering inoculates them from the sad reality of what they have become, as well as the fatalistic nature of life. So, then, the question becomes, why the fascination with professional wrestling?

Professional wrestling has its television roots in the 1950s and came into its full splendour under Vince McMahon in the 1980s. Professional wrestling has it all: glory, scripts on the fly, and off-the-cuff articulation. It all starts with a creative dress code, if you will, that in many instances resembles a Philadelphia pimp, followed by the inventive pre-fight interviews and eloquent trash-talk to create an air of venomous hatred toward their adversaries. The good-guy wrestlers (baby faces) portray virtue that never seems to reconcile with justice that seems almost but never quite attainable, because somehow the bad guy keeps slipping away, like some immoral Teflon dream. No matter what happens, this melodrama continues until a new feud is established.

One has to admire someone who can stand in front of the microphone and eloquently trash-talk into our living-room TVs, tablets, smartphones, or any other electronic gadgets, and this is mostly done on a non-scripted basis. Professional wrestling is an enigmatic combination of athleticism, theatre, and movies, wrapped into an addictive soap opera that has endless layers of storylines, taking us on an expressway of the unknown without exits. And as one would expect, finality is eluding. It is the only place where good versus evil attempts to get settled week after week, first with eclectic trash-talking, followed by pugilistic misadventures. In a sense it mimics the story of humanity.

In many respects, it is even better than a soap opera, and often with a better supporting cast and more titillating scripts, especially in the eighties. The wrestling show has a never-ending chance of realistic closure, since it allows us to discover the inner psyche of the villains and heroes each week, peeling off a little more of the onion, with the promise of showing the core but never delivering it (something like a friend you thought you knew that vanished into time). It is a vehicle for allowing our alter egos to meet societal norms, a place where, in a twisted way, we enjoy the power of a villain walking into the building and being vehemently booed by twenty thousand people who pay money to voice their displeasure. These same people would not have bothered to attend if the scene was some type of collective love-in, but there's an unbarred opportunity to hiss at the villain wrestler who might very well be representing in effigy of sinister bosses they have to face the next day at work. Perhaps it may be the in-law or the neighbour they are fearful of confronting due to potential political fallout, but in the stadium, the audience gathers to let off collective steam, which is much cheaper and more effective than visiting Dr. Phil.

Watching wrestling and seeing the live event is far more exciting than reality TV or a Spanish soap opera (often populated by scorned women), since the good guy and villain can play out their feud in front of a live audience. This is what touches the skin! During its zenith in the eighties, professional wrestling was perhaps as exhilarating as gladiatorial contests would have been in Ancient Rome.

Some argue that professional wrestling is scripted, though in my view it seems more spontaneous and perhaps much less scripted than a TV series, a movie, or a sporting event between a good team and poor team, where the outcome is predetermined.

It is the great forum for the nefarious to explain their strange sense of fair play, selective reasoning, and equitable justice. It is where good meets evil and a place where we flirt with our alter egos without admitting it to the world; it is a place where our demons are hidden in the dark and unknown areas of our psyche. Only in wrestling can the so-called unscrupulous villain take a man's championship belt, steal his wife, move into his house, and have the opportunity to get on television the following week to brag about it; it is a place where good turns bad and bad turns good in the hope that the hero will arrive to distribute equitable justice. It is this and much more that quintessentially attracts the viewer, all wrapped up in a soap opera with no beginning and no end.

Wrestling at Maple Leaf Gardens, Johnny Valentine vs. Dory Funk Jr., 1973.

Wrestling at Maple Leaf Gardens, The Sheik and his manager Abdullah Farouk.

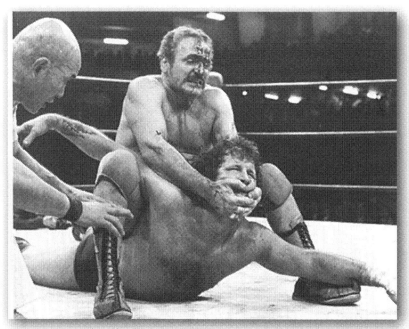

The Sheik destroying another opponent.

The Iron Sheik, not to be confused with the original Sheik, played
the villain from Iran with his partner Nikolai Volkoff who played
the sinister Russian, accompanied by their American manager
"Classy" Freddie Blassie, who billed himself as a fashion icon.

Wrestling at Maple Leaf Gardens and Oh My! Who Is Going to Beat the Sheik?

It must have been a Saturday afternoon in 1969; I was watching television that was tuned in to Channel 11, CHCH Hamilton. The promotions at that time were an arrangement with Channel 11 acting as a
vehicle for Frank Tunney Wrestling promotions at Maple Leaf Gardens.
Tunney was probably the greatest wrestling promoter of his time, until
Vince McMahon came along. Mr. Tunney brought all the great names
in wrestling to the Maple Leaf Gardens: Whipper Billy Watson, Bulldog
Brower, Lord Athol Layton (who was not really an aristocrat), Hulk
Hogan, Bruno Sammartino, and other greats.

This particular Saturday afternoon, I was eating my balanced and
nutritious lunch, which consisted of crumpled Wagon Wheels mixed

with ice cream and Hershey's chocolate, a splendid diet I might say (to bring up the concentration level to do math and science). Hmmm! After all, I had to be alert for my ritual of watching Saturday afternoon wrestling. As I watched the next wrestling match come on, the announcer stepped up to the microphone and introduced the greatest villain I had ever seen: "Ladies and gentlemen, now entering the ring, from Syria, at 250 pounds and accompanied by his manager, Abdullah Farouk: the Sheik."

He stepped into the ring in a Bedouin outfit, worked up in a frenzy of confusion, and ran around the ring like a madman, muttering what sounded like Arabic words but weren't, and his slick-talking manager in the Mustafa hat, Abdullah Farouk, would add to the mayhem. Even though the Sheik was not a Shakespearean orator, he had a message to the effect of: *"Abu alabu dubou yo yo adabu abu al-akhtu"*. Perhaps he was a pioneer of rap music!

That first time I saw the Sheik, I was fascinated with, startled by, and scared of this nefarious villain who displayed such disorderly performance. Canada, after all, is a country founded on the British principles of rule of law, order, and fair play, and when the Sheik, along with his even more sinister manager, Abdullah Farouk (who was actually a Jew named Ernie Roth), showed no respect for this tradition and value system and a shocking demonstration of the breakdown of law and order, I felt fearful and intimidated. Eventually I was taken aback to the point where I called my father into the room in a panicked state. He quickly observed the match on TV and could not hold a straight face, since he spoke fluent Arabic from the time when he lived in Syria, and he knew that what the Sheik was mumbling was nothing more than an attempt at Arabic.

Before he started his match, the Sheik would bring in his prayer rug and pray to Allah and then disrobe from his Arabic head garb and go through stretches of his strange blabbering while he ran around the ring, pointing at things in the sky as part of his repertoire of mayhem.

At one particular match, he bit his opponent's forehead and spat out what I thought was a piece of flesh, and since this usually led to bleeding, I had no doubt about the authenticity of his actions. But it did not stop there. He then added to the theatrics by continuing to bite his opponent as he rolled his eyes back, staring into the closest camera, followed by a never-ending stream of saliva drooling from the side of his mouth as the camera honed in on him. By now he had worked up the studio audience into a frenzy, (after all, this is the role of the bad guy) and then he would apply his signature submission hold, which was called the "camel clutch" (we later practiced the camel clutch on quite a few kids in the schoolyard—ouch!). Since my father was an Armenian from Syria, I role-played the villain, even though I could not speak any Arabic, and thus I came out on the receiving end of a few good make-believe pummellings. For those who do not know the submission hold, it involves lying your opponent on his stomach, sitting on his middle to lower back, and then pulling on his neck and arching the back. In retrospect, a rigorous immersion at Swiss finishing school would have been a good prescription for this wrestler's gratuitous behaviour. (More of the Sheik can be seen at: http://www.youtube.com/watch?v=E2GoQJip2lk).

I explicitly remember one kid in school, Nick Pablouzarou, who was skilled acrobatically, and he would play Flying Fred Curry, magically laying gentle drop-kicks into the chest of his opponent, and he would go flying back. Thus, when we were role-playing in the yard, I would do my flying backward, while a third kid would do the play-by-play announcement. Nick was Greek, but he did not play the role of a Greek wrestler, since they were all heels, and I am not sure he wanted to play the heel. Our theatrics in the playground, though, were our first attempt to emulate a professional sports entertainment spectacle, which included some excellent trash-talking, fully equipped with pre-fight interviews, stunning manoeuvres, a homemade 7.1 surround-sound of groans of pain, and emulating the sounds of Maple Leaf Gardens audiences in the background. I sometimes wish we'd had media technology at our fingertips the way we do today to have recorded these shenanigans, but I suppose the mental archives of our romantic recollection of our childhood is the only way we can reminisce.

Going back to that Saturday afternoon in 1969, the Sheik put his no-name opponent into this dreaded submission hold as he rolled back his eyes, complemented by another generous supply of drooling saliva, and the poor helpless opponent would submit. However, this was not good enough, since he would let forth another verbal tirade of "Abu Abu da boo" and would further maim his opponent. He would not immediately release the hold, even after his opponent's submission was official and the referee had called for the bell. This is the equivalent of mixed martial arts submission, with the pummelling continuing after the bell had been rung. Can we just imagine that even after a tap-out, the fighting continued in MMA? At the very least, the fans would salivate some more as they made Neanderthal chants, and the next day they would pay lip service and say it was barbaric and offensive, but deep inside they knew they got their money's worth.

Each Saturday afternoon, the wrestling show would put some flunky no-name wrestler out to take a beating from the Sheik, and his slick-talking manager, Abdullah Farouk, would equate his wrestler with nobility, quickly dismissing his wrestler's barbaric conduct and advising the television audience that he came from Bedouin royalty. The show was really a vehicle for the twice-a-month big event bouts at Maple Leaf Gardens, where, as promised, some big-name hero would be on the wrestling card to put an end to the Sheik's villainous ways as the last great hope for redemption.

Nobody could beat the Sheik. Oh, they all tried: Whipper Bill Watson, Bo Bo Brazil, Lord Athol Layton, Haystack Calhoun, Andre the Giant. From 1969 until 1974, the Sheik was undefeated in 125 matches at Maple Leaf Gardens (see: http://en.wikipedia.org/wiki/Ed_Farhat).

I remember when they finally had Bruno Sammartino (the Italian favourite) scheduled to fight the Sheik, and the prebout trash-talking that Abdullah Farouk (aka the Weasel) would get into; it went on something like this: "I want all you paisanos to come to Maple Leaf Gardens to watch that spaghetti-bender be beaten by my noble Sheik and watch his carcass carried out of the ring as the Sheik defeats that poor excuse for a real champion."

Needless to say, every self-loving red-blooded Italian would show up the following Sunday at MLG to see his or her hero take on the venomous Sheik and his even more evil manager, Abdullah Farouk, who would whip the crowd up into a rage as the nefarious two would use a host of tactics that would include flame-throwing and biting the forehead of the opponent. Abdullah Farouk had unsurpassed microphone skills (he was an ex-DJ after all), with a barrage of trash-talking that was in a league of its own, and he could work a television audience up into a lather. When he went to US towns, Farouk would insult Americans and was a master at inciting the audience, which in some cases resulted in near-riots. He carefully carved his wicked image. He perhaps pioneered outside-ring interference and would say and do things that would make today's politically correct cringe and crawl back in their shoeboxes. Here are just a few excerpts of his never-ending barrage of insults:

"After you fight the Sheik, here is what we are going to do for you. We are going to buy you a tin cup to stand on the corner of the street for the rest of your life."

"So my noble Sheik put you in the hospital last time, and you want a rematch? So it seems you have more guts than brains. But this time you are permanently going to be in the hospital."

It did not matter who fought the Sheik; he would somehow find ways not to lose. When Andre the Giant had him near a loss at Maple Leaf Gardens, he threw dust out of nowhere into Andre's eyes, and the giant was blinded, while the Sheik worked him over. It seemed that redemption was elusive to all the fans waiting to see justice served against the sinister Sheik.

Some of the Most Memorable Bouts

Depending on the age of the reader, perspective might be different, but a few great matches at Maple Leaf Gardens come to mind, at the expense of excluding some WrestleMania classics, so here we go!

The Sheik versus Bruno Sammartino, July 13, 1969

This was the first wrestling card I remember attending at Maple Leaf Gardens. My memory of this bout is a bit foggy after forty years, but I still remember it for the most part. Bruno Sammartino entered the ring with cheering fans (many of them Italian), as Abdullah Farouk, the Sheik's nefarious manager, egged them on to come see the demise of their paisano hero.

Sammartino, the world champion and Italian favourite, was met by a roar of cheers, and then shortly after, the Sheik, accompanied by Farouk, entered the ring. Needless to say, when Mr. Farouk entered the ring that night, he was met by the Italian fans with jeers, and he really worked them into a lather. As the match started, Bruno was working over the Sheik really good, but guess what? Abdullah Farouk handed the Sheik a brick with a string on it, and they worked Bruno over in the corner by knocking the brick over his head. Then again, this tactic should not entirely be dismissed, since it works for some people, in terms of knocking some sense into their heads! The final outcome was a disqualification—and some very disappointed Italians, who were out five dollars a head, with no justice in sight. Yes, their hero did not lose the championship belt, but he took an illustrious beating.

Flying Fred Curry versus the Sheik

Flying Fred Curry was an acrobatic wrestler who would send his body into the air horizontally and drop-kick his opponents in the chest, they would then go flying. Unlike his father, he was not a brawler but more of an acrobatic artisan in the air, and I am sure he had some type of gymnastics training.

It must have been around 1970, and he was billed to go up against the Sheik, who had an undefeated streak going at the time. But the results were always the same, either through cutting open the forehead or bringing out a fireball. The Sheik would always prevail. Still, no one could beat the Sheik, and all the big names of wrestling kept trying, but it seems none succeeded, with the outcome in the favour of the villain, while justice continued to be elusive. The Sheik would be taking a good pummelling to give some satisfaction to the paying fans, but lo and behold, he would find an illegal foreign object in his trunks and start stabbing his opponent with a screwdriver, nails, or even produce fire out of his hand and burn his opponent's eyes. The hero had been done wrong, and the fans went home distraught because there was no closure to this never-ending injustice. It was, in many ways, the first time young males were exposed to a soap opera where justice rarely prevailed, and better still, it was in a live theatre of sorts.

Every famed method known to mankind was tried to stop the Sheik—having two referees, a cage match—but in the end, the Sheik would either win or get disqualified, which meant that he would retain his US champion's belt. What's worse is he put more salt into the wounds, since a supposed madman from Syria had the US belt, and his character as well as demeanour were not even remotely American.

In real life, the Sheik's name was Ed Farhat, a second-generation Christian Lebanese who grew up in the Detroit area and enlisted in the US Army during the Second World War by using his brother's birth certificate, since he was too young to enlist. Prior to being a professional wrestler, he was an accomplished amateur athlete who attended Michigan State University. He was not only a professional wrestler but also became a wrestling promoter. Farhat, better known as the Sheik, pioneered hard-core styles of wrestling that included bringing sharp foreign objects into the ring, the use of fire, and profuse bleeding and biting of the forehead. But all this still had something missing…

Naturally, a fight, staged or otherwise, really requires an element of verbal tenacity to make it complete and full. This particular skill is needed to complete the theatre of entertainment; without the trash-talking, wrestling would compare to a stage without lights. So, I would cordially like to take this opportunity to introduce the "fine art of trash-talking."

Best Trash-Talkers of All Time, Well Kind of…

Not taught in any university curriculum, trash-talking is an art form from the old school; it is designed to psych out opponents while entertaining an audience. Even though George Foreman did not look rattled at all when Cassius Clay laid the sound bite on him, it is a way to rattle someone's cage, and as children, we all had to indulge in it to protect ourselves and mask our fears. It is articulate, obnoxious, and titillating, all encapsulated in one. My first exposure to this skill of verbal innovation certainly did not come from Shakespeare but from Cassius Clay, who knew how to hype an event and work everyone up into a lather, including himself!

I would, however, say that generally speaking, the best trash-talkers were wrestlers, who have the power as a heel (bad guy) to work the crowd into a frenzy. I think what enthralls me the most is how I used to watch a villain wrestler come up the ramp at the old Maple Leaf Gardens, stop halfway up the ramp, raise his arms to brag about how great he was, and then get ceremoniously jeered and booed by sixteen thousand fans who came to let out their frustrations on him. But I always wondered about this perverse power a man has when he can walk into a building and get jeered by the crowd yet consider it a good day's work. When one goes to work and defines success by how much venomous hatred is directed toward him, one must ponder how all this is reconciled when the lights go out and the stage is bare.

So, then, what does the heel tell his wife when he gets home, especially when she asks how his day was at work? He'd probably say something like, "Oh, well it was a great day, honey; the fans jeered me, the whole building threw garbage at me, old ladies pointed at me with their canes, and my boss said if I keep this up, I will be getting a promotion. And oh, by the way, dear, here is my paycheque!" Then we wonder when the wife goes to sleep beside her husband, is it the villain in him whom she loves or the hero? Which alter ego is he really? What was also remarkable in wrestling matches was the pure joy the heels demonstrated when the whole building hated them. The antihero takes such pride in the fact that he can protect the fans from the pain of being themselves by aiming their hatred at one individual who represents anarchy and evil, all woven into a murky nightmare, because the villain is the wall that holds back the utopia that we are all searching for, but elusively never find within ourselves. Since the utopia we seek disappoints when compared with our conjured imaginations, it is for this reason we keep on reaching for the branch that eludes us all.

Without any further ado, here goes to my personal list of best trash-talking personalities and their respective quotes.

Cassius Marcellus Clay

Cassius Marcellus Clay Jr. grew as a top-performing trash-talker. Although he honed his basic verbal skills on Sonny Liston, he did not become the established elite trash-talker until he laid the jazz on Smokin' Joe Frazier, who was a no-nonsense type. Here are some of his quotes:

"The man to beat me hasn't been born yet!"

"You beat nobody, ugly Joe Frazier, and this might shock and amaze you, but I am going to destroy Joe Frazier!"

When Howard Cosell suggested that Clay might be a shell of his former self, he turned around and said, "That's exactly what

Cosell's wife is saying about Cosell, that he isn't the man he was two years ago."

Abdullah Farouk (aka the Weasel, or Sometimes the Grand Wizard), the Manager of the Sheik

He was first introduced in 1969, and he played the nefarious manager of the Sheik who would travel back and forth to the Middle East to look after noble but sinister matters. His name in real life was Ernie Roth; he was of Jewish descent and originally started as a disc jockey before turning to wrestling in the sixties. He played the part of Farouk perfectly, especially in light of the fact that the Sheik did not speak English and made sounds that resembled a combination of Bedouin and Neanderthal chants. The Weasel really knew how to metamorphose a sinister act into upstanding and defensible morality with his sense of circular logic. One had to love his sense of objectivity, considering that his noble Sheik used to walk in the ring with illegal objects, including nails and even bricks. Here are some of his finest rants:

"Eddie Creatchman, I trusted you, but what did you turn out to be? A twentieth-century Judas."

"You have illusions of grandeur in that empty head of yours, Rocky Johnson, if you think you can beat Superstar Billy Graham."

Once, when the Wiesel was accused by Vince McMahon of being given an object to win a wrestling bout, he responded, "Vince McMahon, you need to get in touch with the AMA (American Medical Association) and get your eyes checked."

Rowdy Roddy Piper

Who recently passed away, may he RIP. Unlike his claims, Rowdy Roddy Piper did not grow up in the Parkdale district of Toronto, which is quite well known for pugilistic disputes. A lawyer I knew, Christopher Cox, told me he actually grew up in Don Mills, Ontario. As a wrestler, he knew how to work the crowd up into a rage and had a great reputation as a heel. Here are some of his dramatic quotes:

"I have come here to chew bubble gum and kick ass."

On Jim Duggan: "Does the tongue hanging out help his balance?"

"I'm the reason Hulk Hogan lost his hair!"

"When you were young, did your mommy and daddy place the swing too close to the wall?"

"I was pissin' Vince McMahon off when the red on the back of your neck was diaper rash!"

"Do you know you couldn't get a date with a twenty-dollar bill taped to your forehead?"

"I can't blame Muhammad Ali for changing his name; this way he won't be as embarrassed after every beating."

Ric Flair

Ric Flair really knew how to infuriate an audience and was one of the greatest narcissists of all time. With his dyed-blond hair and his "Glamour Boy" robe and reputation, he was quite a piece of work. Flair once noted that he was the reason women came out to watch professional wrestling, while boasting that he was thirteen-time world champion, while—not considering why he lost the belt twelve times! Many will remember him most when he left the NWA and came over to the WWF to challenge then-champion Hulk Hogan, and he said these famous words: "Ric Flair. Whooooo! The real world champion." And that was the calling card that started a run-in with the Hulkster. Not to say that he had the best one-liners, but with his attitude, delivery, and look, he had a strong visual presence. Ric Flair was born in 1949 and left college before completing his degree. He was a trained amateur state wrestling champion and also worked as a bouncer. Without further fuss or delay, let me quote some of his best verbiage:

"To be the man, you gotta' beat the man!"

"When I die, I hope it is on top of a wild woman."

"I'm Ric Flair! The stylin', profilin', limousine-riding, jet-flying, kiss-stealing, wheelin' and dealin' son of a gun!"

"All the women want to be with me; all the men want to be like me."

Bobby "The Brain" Heenan

Bobby Heenan has to be among the best trash-talking wrestling managers of all time, along with Abdullah Farouk. Born in Chicago in 1944, Heenan started out as a wrestling manager in 1965 and built a reputation as a tough-talking bigmouth who promoted bad guys and had a special gift for interpreting the nefarious nature of bad guys and depicting them as being done wrong by the hero. Put differently, he had a reputation for articulating selective reasoning.

He eventually joined the WWF in 1984, when Vince McMahon lured him into the wrestling company as a noted bad-guy manager. It is about this time that most remember his career as the noted manager of a stable of heels. One of the heels he managed was Big John Stud (whom he claimed was the only man who could not be slammed, even though he was slammed by Andre the Giant). Nevertheless, Heenan, who offered a prize of fifty thousand dollars to anyone who could slam Big John Stud, would run away with the prize money when anyone did. This act further cultivated the weasel image for him, being referred to as Bobby the Weasel by the fans. The feud that Big John Stud had with Andre the Giant, directed by Heenan, is considered to be one of the finest promotional pieces in the history of professional wrestling. He later created a complete stable of heels that included names like "Mr. Wonderful" Paul Orndorff, King Kong Bundy, and Ravishing Rick Rude (whom I saw at Venice Beach), to name a few.

One time I remember going to Maple Leaf Gardens with some friends to watch Andre the Giant fight Big John Stud. When things were not going well for Mr. Stud and he was taking a good pummelling, Bobby "The Brain" Heenan went to the dressing room and brought out King Kong Bundy (no slouch at over four hundred pounds), and they turned the tables on Andre the Giant by double-teaming him. While John kept Andre down, Bundy climbed the ropes and gave the giant ten big splashes, to the delight of both myself (I liked the heels) and Bobby Heenan. There lay Andre, at over five hundred pounds, out for the count in front of his adoring fans. I was not sure how they were going to carry out his carcass, perhaps with a forklift, but they eventually got him back to the dressing room.

As mentioned, Heenan assembled a stable of heels that would gang up on the good guys; it was often referred to as the "Bobby Heenan family." Later, he became an announcer in the WWF, along with his colleague, Gorilla Monsoon, and Heenan made a new career of rooting for the bad guys. "The Brain" left school early but was incredibly witty, while he was biased by rooting for the bad guys, which made for some fine entertainment. Here are some notable quips:

"By the time the Iron Sheik gets to the ring, it will be WrestleMania 37!"

In reference to Hillbilly Jim (a noted redneck): "For crying out loud, McMahon, you're talking to a guy who thinks the bathroom should be fifty feet away, outside in back of the house!"

"I'd rather have some money than a skirt."

"When we finish with Andre the Giant, you won't need ambulances; you will need a big trash truck to take him away."

"I know all about cheating. I've had six very successful marriages."

"I'm a legend in this sport. If you don't believe me, ask me."

On North Dakota State University: "What do you have to do there to graduate? Milk a cow with your left hand?"

"There's the downtown area of Tupelo. Did you see the skyscrapers? Two storeys."

"There's nothing better than a good, blind referee."

"The money's the same whether you earn it or scam it."

Jesse "The Body" Ventura

Born James George Janos, Jesse "The Body" Ventura was a US Navy Underwater Demolition Team member during the Vietnam War. He looked body-builder strong but could not wrestle, otherwise he would have risen further. But he was a skilled trash-talker, and that eventually served him well by elevating him into politics as the governor of Minnesota. He carved a nefarious reputation as a bad-guy wrestling commentator and then had his own segment on WWF titled the "Body Shop," where each week he would usher in and embrace a new heel on his show, but when baby-face wrestlers showed up, they were verbally ridiculed. I remember meeting him once outside Maple Leaf Gardens, and he came across as a regular and decent person, unlike his ring persona. But I always remember him as the heel colour commentator who always said that he called it the way he saw it, which often ignored the illegal antics of the heels. A type of circular logic, if you will! Here are some of his best one-liners and verbal exchanges:

"Mean Gene, everybody wants to know about Jesse the Body's private life, because I date and take out some of the most beautiful women in the world."

Referring to Tito Santana: "Chico or Tito, what's the difference? He's still a taco salesman from Tijuana."

"I'm not one of those three-dollar rock stars."

One time, when he was a heel announcer with Gorilla Monsoon and they were doing the colour commentating on a bout where Macho Man was being escorted into the ring by the lovely Miss Elizabeth, Gorilla Monsoon said, "That is despicable how he treats that woman, Jesse."

Jesse said, "She knows where her meal ticket is coming from."

In reference to Mr. T, he said, "I had earrings before Mr. T was away from his mama."

Before a bout started: "I had a guy give up during ring instructions."

The Iron Sheik

Not to be confused with the original noble Sheik, the Iron Sheik was originally promoted as being from Iran, which he actually is. His real name is Hossein Khosrow Ali Vaziri, and his early résumé includes being a bodyguard for the Shah of Iran. He participated in the 1968 Olympics on the Iranian wrestling team. After that, he moved to the United States and became the assistant coach of two US Olympic squads in the seventies. In 1971, he was the Amateur Athletic Union Greco-Roman Wrestling champion. He was also an assistant coach to the US team for the 1972 Olympic Games in Munich.

His professional wrestling career began in 1971, and he became world champion when he defeated Bob Backland in the WWF, and then had his title taken away by Hulk Hogan, which he still rants about thirty years later via YouTube shoots, many of them under the influence. Eventually he built up his Middle Eastern Persian background. His gimmick was quite good, and during the closing days of the Cold War, with his partner Nikolai Volkoff, allegedly from Russia, they would play the Iranian and Russian duo of heels that would go into US cities and spew the following lines that would work the crowd into a rage: "Iran, number one! Russia, number one! America pee-ew!" as he spat on the ring canvas. This would then be followed up with the announcer asking the fans to stand up as Nikolai Volkoff would sing the Soviet national anthem. This would work the fans up into a salivating frenzy, which was why they were there in the first place.

So, with these credentials, he and Volkoff would find ongoing feuds with American baby-face wrestlers. Oh, I almost forgot, to really make the audience venomously salivate, they would show up with the Soviet and Iranian flags, and for a while, they were world tag-team champions.

Watching his career as a trash-talker, it became evident that he evolved his craft, and I would have to perch him in the higher rankings of the all-time trash-talkers' list, not because he had the best lines but because of the way he sometimes delivered them in illiterate, intoxicated, and somewhat induced rages. Remember, one had to be funny without using profanity before the digital age.

Even today, with the advent of YouTube, his popularity is probably unmatched, and unlike television, profanity is quite allowed. So here we go with the Sheiky Baby's best lines:

On Rob Ford: "You eat da hamburger and take the crack cocaine."

On Brian Blair: "That jabroni, he says his background amateur high-school wrestling better than Iron Sheik. I say he's a no-good liar, piece of garbage. But Brian Blair sucks. He's no-good jabroni piece of garbage."

On Jay Leno: "Jay Leno, you are an ugly double jaw. You always want Terry Bradshaw, Hulk Hogan to your show. Why you don't invite the Iron Sheik, the legend, to your show? Jay Leno, you can go f*** yourself. But I want to tell that double ugly jaw piece of s***, you are not Jay Leno; you are Gay Leno."

On Tiger Woods: "Tiger Woods, he becomes the best golfer; he gets excited. After he becomes the best, he forgot about his background. He wanted more women, and he messed it all up. Tiger Woods, you deserve life in Islamic country, in a Muslim country. We suplex him; we put him in the camel clutch. We make him humble, and he never, ever again cheats his wife. He's a number-one gold digger. He cheat his wife. I hate that "bleepf***er.""

On Randy "Macho Man" Savage: "He is a cheap Jew! Why, you sons of da gun."

On Hulk Hogan: "I am the reeeeeeal world champion, not like that jabroni Hollywood Hulk Hogan. Dat Hulk Hogan, I should have suplexed him and put him in camel clutch old country way and make dat son of a gun humble. I make dat Hollywood Hulk Hogan famous; without Iron Sheik, Hulk Hogan, you would be still bouncer at gay bar. Without Iron Sheik, Hulk Hogan, you would be a janitor."

The whole topic of trash-talking and setting up a more inclusive study of the subject could fill a book on its own, since the list could be much longer. We could, of course, include the Tolos Brothers, the Rock, Hulk Hogan, the Macho Man, Dusty Rhodes, and the likes. But this much is for sure: working an audience into a lather with a barrage of articulated and impromptu verbiage, all without rehearsed lines or a teleprompter, is a commendable art form.

The Business of Selling Wrestling Dolls

Much of my knowledge and intrigue with professional wrestling came to me in the mid-eighties when I was buying and selling the latest fads. I remember one Christmas when there was a shortage of the WWF dolls on the market. I had a contact at Coleco Toys in Montreal through a friend of mine, Ivan Pallet. Together we used to work at flea markets, and this episode makes an interesting story.

The national wrestling TV specials on Friday nights drove up the demand for these wrestling action figures, and I ended up buying some wholesale, and once that stock was finished, I went to every Toys "R" Us and the now defunct BiWay locations I could get to and bought the rest at retail price. At this point, there was about an 8 percent difference between the retail and wholesale prices. I believe the wholesale was at $7.30 each, and the retail price was $7.99, which is often practiced in retail as a loss leader. Since the supply of these action figures on the shelves were spotty at best, and with my crew of spotters, I went to every retailer and bought everything on the shelf to corner the market; the Greater Toronto Area was literally sold out of these items. Thus, I had a monopoly of sorts, even if it only lasted about a couple of weeks.

The tenets of free-markets posit that all market participants have a right to a level playing field, unless of course one controls the field. "Monopoly" is one of the most sinister words in modern political speak, and naturally, we turn a blind eye toward labour unions that have a monopoly on labour at the expense of consumer welfare in the way of higher prices. Then again, our governments have a monopoly on tax collection, with no real competition, which is a form of desensitized thuggery. Our current medical system in Canada has a monopoly on health care choice. So, the underpinnings of fair play, at least in economics, comes with *caveat emptor* in law, as it is in one's self-interest to try to hang on to the monopoly as long as possible, which is exactly what I did, but only for about four weeks. In contrast, this is common in developing countries where people get corrupt government licenses that allow them to be the only player in the domestic industry. Nigeria is a good example, where there is only one soap bar maker in a protected market, and India is quite well known for industry protection, which is to protect a few at the expense of many. On the other hand, this is what consumers do to firms until they get an unfair advantage over them or literally drive the firms out of business by forcing razor-thin margins. At the expense of getting off course, in economics this is referred to as "perfect competition," meaning price is the only determinant of choice. Of course, consumers have no remorse and are clueless about the fact that they just drove themselves out of a job and are so delusional that they blame firms and scream "government job action plan," when in essence they are often the genesis of the problem. Then again, a government job action plan, in many respects, is delusional, since it amounts to the downtrodden asking the mediocre for assistance.

So now that we have veered off course with some market participant analysis, let's get back to the wrestling action figure toys.

I sold many of these action figure toys for $12 each at the flea market in Pickering, Ontario, and the balance went to various independent retailers that were in my Rolodex. So with my finite knowledge of what happened the week before on Friday night TV broadcasting of WWF events, I would recreate the pummelling of the good guys in detail (usually re-enacted in a displayed toy ring within the flea market). I made sure the dolls resembled certain outtakes from all the mayhem of the fight the week before, and this realism resonated quite well with the kids. The one I remember most is when Andre the Giant had both arms tied up in the ropes and could not free himself as Big John Stud and King Kong Bundy were laying a two-on-one pummelling on the Giant while the referee was out cold. It was a great moment for the heels and, in a sense, frontier justice for the underappreciated.

I also had friends with younger brothers or kids of their own. I would employ these little kids to play with the action toys. Whereas most vendors did not want kids in their booths, as they have a reputation for creating disruption, this is exactly what I wanted, since where there were kids, more kids would follow, and eventually parents with challenged wallets were not far behind. The left side of the brain debated the right side, and the verdict was almost always in the favour of the kids, because for twelve dollars, each parent purchased peace in the home castle. The exchange was perfect, in my view; the kids were happy, the parents bought temporary peace, and I made money for helping to orchestrate this fine arrangement.

Conclusion

So there you have it, the story of professional wrestling good guys and villains, wrapped up in a tale of a twisted enigma that plays out in a soap opera, which resembles an audience of the emotionally inebriated. Each week we watched with dedication, since the proceedings were like peeling an onion and looking for a core that lies somewhere in the dimension of infinity, while hopelessly seeking truth and justice. But not all is lost on people like us who watch these wrestling matches, because it nurtures our own inventiveness and plays on our imaginations of discovering our other side, a side that is suppressed in an aimless world that conforms us into monotony and perpetual sedation.

The lessons learned in the epic tale of conflict, which wrestling really is, allow us to harness its teachings in creating our own inventive realities for our everyday lives. Wrestling, after all, is the story of the villain versus the virtuous, much like the Cold War, when we decided to consider the flaws of our Soviet adversaries so we would not have to look into our own mirrors to consider what we had become. It is so much easier for Batman to point his finger at the Riddler, as opposed to considering his own position. It was so much easier to ignore the narcissistic tendencies of Cassius Clay and learn to paint George Foreman as the villain.

But this much is for sure: it is the villain who creates the stage of theatrical drama. It is the villain we come to watch in the hopes of his demise, and it his gift for presenting the horror of the unknown that keeps the audience on the edge of their seats. Without the villain's demise, we could not be granted reason to stand up and applaud the hero!

So, there are a host of lessons that can be learned from the theatre of wrestling and human conflict, which include us having the courage to discover our alter egos, which can be multiple. Perhaps we are all a bit like Walter Mitty, but it is this funny way of looking at things within ourselves that nurtures inventiveness, and it is not one type of inventiveness, since inventiveness comes in science, art, marketing, commerce, politics, commercial design, poetry, mathematics, and much more, leading to the resolution of sorts. Many people do not have the courage to flirt with the seduction of inventiveness, since it unsettles one's sense of self, either perceived or real. But I tip my hat to the inventive storylines of wrestling, in all their pain and glory, and for the dexterity of their off-the-cuff and on-the-fly verbal ingenuity, since they let us come to terms with our alter egos, all without the help of a teleprompter. Not all presents are gift-wrapped, but in some peculiar way, perhaps wrestling gave us the liberation to look within to discover the savage, progress, and civility that constitute the human story in this place we have been hurled into called Earth.

Lifestyle Section

THE RISE AND FALL OF DISCO

Dreams of grandeur, mating calls masked in an enigmatic display of polyester passing through the night, complemented by the beat of tunes spilling out of clubs as the weekend artistry of dance and mystery filled our ears. Words of shallow spoken, drowned by the music and a dance beat that seemed like some type of vehicle to further the object of our desires, as we returned each week and found new and more inventive ways to paint pictures of everything we would like to be, but never would become. Because it seemed that each night, we would come dressed for a play that was ours to create, under the auspicious background of a disco ball.

We knew somewhere deep inside that the illusion of glamour and fame would elude us all, for when all is told, this was the hallucination that protected us from the fatalism of reality. We moved our feet, listening to the sweet sounds of Donna Summer and the Bee Gees as we celebrated the beautiful and gifted days of our youth, never giving much thought to the future. Perhaps we realized that this was just a subway stop to mask the uncertainty of our future, to give us enough time to think of finding ways to make our lives more accomplished as we were subconsciously buying time. But disco seemed to soothe this uncertainty we were to face, and possibly it is this self-inflicted refutation that gave energy to the phenomena of disco, since it was perhaps such an intoxicating denial of realism.

Each night, we went to celebrate life as we thought it should be, while at the same time honing our skill at telling romantic yet distorted truths to unsuspecting young ladies. When all was said and done, disco, after all, was the *"democratization of glamour!"*

A Brief History of Its Origins

Unlike the origins of the universe, which is up for debate between logic-defying theologians and progressive science, we can look with empirical clarity to the true origins of disco.

If the origins of disco are the best-kept secret in all of history, well kind of....it begs the question, when and where is the genesis of this sometimes loved and often despised cultural norm of its day? This is a question worth considering, because back in the late seventies, we never really asked or were not really bothered by such intellectually profound details, since most of us were oblivious to reason or cause and effect. Subsequently, with our meagre paycheques, we were empowering our futures, or so we thought, in long-term investments such as ill-fitting suits and polyester attire, hot cars, cover charges, and wide-eyed girls. Sound familiar?

Disco was the last great pop cultural expression of the Baby Boom generation, and it is in a sense the Boomers' cultural swan song.

Disco's origins are somewhat obscured, but this much we know for sure. Its origins are in New York City, some say Club Arthur Discothèque, which was opened in 1965 by Richard Burton's ex-wife (he had many), Sybil Burton, just after he ran off with Elizabeth Taylor. She had a reputation for drawing celebrities going back to the late fifties and early sixties with the Peppermint Lounge. It was the Peppermint Lounge where Jacqueline Kennedy did the twist and where the Beatles dropped in after their *Ed Sullivan Show* appearances. Many notable celebrities made appearances at Arthur's, including Frank Sinatra, Sammy Davis Jr., Liza Minnelli, Andy Warhol, Bette Davis, and, of course, the very lovely Sophia Loren, to name a few. Perhaps disco glamour was starting to take shape, but the sound was still not born.

The first pre-disco club, the Loft, was opened by DJ David Mancuso in 1970, in New York City. It was a "members only" club, and the underground culture of disco was born. In terms of investigating the musical roots of disco, it can be best explained by the fusion of the gay underground clubs of New York City with the musical influences of funk, Latin, and soul music. But when the truth is examined, this unholy alliance is where the foundation lies of the greatest dance culture ever created.

Some argue that Barry White and Isaac Hayes were performing disco's first songs as early as 1971, and many say that "Soul Makossa" by Manu Dibango was the best early example of disco, which really sounded like a fusion between jazz-infused funk and soul with a Latin beat. Another perspective was once put forth by Fred Wesley, the trombonist for James Brown, when he called disco "funk music with a bow tie."

But it was New York's underground gay clubs in the early seventies, often visited by straights, which nurtured this dance, musical, and cultural phenomenon. The names of these clubs not only included the Loft, but also the Infinity, Flamingo, and 12 West. These and other original clubs fostered the all-night dancing craze of disco during its infancy. The world-famous Studio 54 opened in 1977, during the same year as *Saturday Night Fever* opened on the screens (more on both later), and drew the same type of celebrities that had visited the Peppermint Lounge of early sixties fame.

Any way we looked at it, it was soul music, but at that time disco was still in its formative stage and undefined in its official title, and in my view, the great dance hits of disco did not really come alive, at least as a commercial acceptability, until just before the movie and soundtrack of *Saturday Night Fever* in 1977.

The Enigma of Disco

It is easy to dismiss disco as some passing trend and laugh it off as just another blip in pop culture, but it was much more than that; it was the swan song of the Baby Boomers. It taught a lot of white kids how to dance; it had a beat that made one move. It helped bring out some deeply talented musicians and entertainers and brilliantly written tunes that to this day cannot be swept under the rug by their detractors. It provided very hip nightclubs, a stage for glamour for those who could dance, a counterculture, a place to meet and greet, and in many ways, the setting for the mating calls of this generation. But it didn't end there; it provided a stage for swagger as well as the dress code of disco, far outrivaling the deadpan jeans that hard-core rockers were wearing. It brought some formality to clubbing in the image of more bourgeois attire that included suits and glamorous dresses.

Perhaps it could be said that, members of the techno-culture generation are addicted to social media since they feel a morbid need to display their lives in the electronic universe, in hopes of masking their desperation and loneliness. In some ways, the disco generation did the same thing by going to the clubs and putting on exquisite acts of dance and glamour to showcase its alter egos in this celebration of unsequestered youth, knowing full well that the door of reality awaited. Disco provided the phenomenon for which I coin the term "the democratization of glamour".

So one might ask, what does the term democratization of glamour mean? Put simply, disco allowed people with relatively little means to join this fabulous lifestyle and participate in this ostentatious, if not pretentious, nightclub culture and to be anyone but themselves, just like movie stars, if you will. All one needed was some swagger clothing, a playbook of exquisite verbiage, attitude, and the ability to dance. This democratization of glamour that disco provided was inclusion for the masses and a more even playing field, meaning one could be a rock star without the prerequisite of being a musician. It was this seductive and perhaps inebriated proposition that resonated with the disco generation. It helped define the age while affecting everything around them and expressing the pop culture of the times. Then this begs the question, if you were young in the 1970s and not dancing, what exactly were you young for?

So, Why Disco?

By the mid-seventies, there were two streams of youth segments in high schools when it came to pop music. The first was dance music, which was the cross between soul music and rhythm and blues that eventually became packaged into disco and then naturally flowed into nightclubs. The other was the rock crowd, which would collect the latest albums that were coming out and worship its idols like messiahs, thus the term "rock star." Rock music, after all, had a formidable amount of talent at the time, including such greats as Led Zeppelin, the Rolling Stones, The Who, and the eccentric David Bowie. These and other bands of this genre were still writing and producing their legendary sounds. The Beatles had only broken up a few years back, and their music still dominated the radio.

Some very good Canadian acts played at my high-school dances at L'Amoreaux Collegiate Institute, names such as Rush, the Stampeders, Max Webster, and they even considered hiring the legendary Chuck Berry. I believe that Berry was in the $1,500 range for a performance in 1975, and we had some loose talk on the high-school dance committee of hiring him for one of our school dances. He was one of my idols who influenced nearly every British and American band in the sixties. If James Brown was the godfather of soul, Chuck Berry was the godfather of rock 'n' roll.

I had intimate knowledge of musical trends, since I used to work at many of the school dances (still couldn't pick up girls; that came later), and as a side note, our most prominent member of the dance committee was the late Dan Gallagher, who at a young age was a masterful promoter and organizer. He even created an internal high-school radio station. Dan eventually went on to become a broadcaster on television, including on CityTV, MuchMusic, and the CBC.

It was during that time, when I was in high school in the seventies, that I became unknowingly exposed to some of the early disco music, which to me sounded like a blend between Motown, funk, and a touch of soul. Because we had a large enough black student body, they organized soul dances, and during these dances, my role as a student volunteer was to heat up and serve meat patties at the makeshift concession stand.

As child in the 1960s, I had memories of the R&B Motown sound somewhere in the background of my mind, since my friend Peter's mother would play the records all the time.

But it was at these high-school dances that I really started discovering the very sweet sounds of Marvin Gaye, Al Green, Barry White, the O'Jays with their masterpiece hit, "Back Stabbers," and of course, the Temptations. The sound was very soulful, smooth, and danceable.

I did not realize back then, while I was working at the soul dances, that this fusion of funk, soul, and the Latino sound was laying down the soundtrack for the foundation of disco. But it was this magical fusion that produced the new dance music that would eventually evolve into disco and gave birth to its own national anthem with the creation of the indelible *Saturday Night Fever* soundtrack.

When all this was coming into play, I was coming of age, and I sure liked the sound, plus the dancing was so good. Unknowingly at the time, I was walking down the fork of a road and had to consider two genres of pop culture but out of convenience had to choose one.

Two Roads to Travel

Alternatively, as we became old enough, at around the age of seventeen, we would try to look older to sneak into establishments that served alcohol. This was around 1976, and my rock 'n' roll cronies, who I would often accompany, would end up in local Toronto rock 'n' roll watering holes such as the Piccadilly Tube, Nickelodeon, and the Gasworks, to mention a few. The scenario was always the same: beer, loud music—much of it distasteful, complemented by a crowd who wore drably proletarian attire (meaning clothing that was best relegated to cattle-herding activities). These clubs were decorated with eye-candy groupies who came to adorn the musicians and were in their accompaniment until the wee hours of the morning. And that was the problem with hanging out with this crowd—the musicians were getting the girls, and the fans were going home empty-handed. Eventually, the evening's entertainment cascaded into drunken barroom brawls as the band played on, and the points of disagreement were not exactly debates pertaining to Newton's theories of gravity or calculus as a quantitative philosophy to the rate of change. The brawls were usually started by some inadvertent stare-downs that were the opening act for rearrangement of furniture and pugilistic misadventures. Whereas, I enjoyed the verbal exchanges, the actual rumbles were not my forte.

It eventually occurred to me that I was not going to write *Abbey Road* or displace the Rolling Stones on the *Billboard* charts or do the lead vocals for the Temptations, even though I would have happily accepted this position if it was offered to me. Thus, the current path of peer socialization was going to prolong my virginal status, possibly beyond the second coming! Put differently, being a fan of rock bands was not the road to glamour and was not helping me discover the finer attributes of the opposite sex either. Yes, the band members were having their way; however, many of my cronies and I were not able to seal the deal with the lovelies and were relegated to listening to albums until the wee hours of the night. Going home empty-handed did not achieve the outcome many of us wanted, and at the same time, barroom brawls were not my specialty, since I ascertained that being a lover had finer benefits than being a bar brawler.

Little did we know that the magic of *Saturday Night Fever* in 1977 was to be bestowed upon us, taking disco from an underground movement and hurling it into becoming a mainstream pop cultural phenomenon. There had to be a better way for us to meet girls, and disco was the perfect backdrop to weave some tall tales into the ears of those unsuspecting lovelies, as we broke some hearts, including our own, which of course we would never admit to our bro buddies.

Choices

Disco, after all, was a means to an end—namely, a place and a time where we celebrated our youth and practiced mating calls that were negligibly more sophisticated than sounds of unherded livestock. It was a ritual of fashion, music, and dance that culminated in a celebration of coming together. To help things along, during my last year of high school my family and I moved, so I was no longer hanging out with my rock-head friends and started discovering this counterculture at my new school. It was during this time that a group of kids was organizing disco dances at banquet halls on the weekends.

I remember watching *Soul Train* on TV on Saturdays, but finally, in 1977, I first saw *Saturday Night Fever* at the old Cedarbrae Theatre in Scarborough, and all this came together in a great explosion of pop culture that was felt around the world.

Every city, from Boston to New York, especially Greenwich Village, had clubs sprouting up. Yorkville in Toronto had gone from hippies and beatniks to disco. Every time we tuned in the radio, the *Saturday Night Fever* soundtrack was being played, and the songs were recording masterpieces in their own right. The energy of disco was all around and impossible to ignore.

The music, the fashion, the beat, and the alluring sophistication of the hustle dance steps were incredibly seductive as a lifestyle. Disco had energy and was so alive! So the choice then became very clear: worship rock bands and let the girls slip away, or create your own music every night on the dance floor and hang out at disco clubs until your money ran out. For me the decision was simple!

The rock 'n' roll crowd detested disco, and they had a repertoire of insults that usually ended up with an articulate belching of "disco boy" or "disco sucks." But for them, they were on the wrong side of pop history, and to boot, many of them had love lives that best resembled *Tales from the Crypt*. It did not end there; girls loved to dance, and guess where they were hanging out? At disco clubs and events.

Logically, guess where every astute young male would be hanging out. Exactly!

The cultural rift between disco boys and rock 'n' rollers was very pronounced, and a line in the sand was drawn. Therefore, the choice became clear: either hang out with the fashion- and dance-challenged rockers with the eventuality of going home alone, or dress up like pop royalty, dance the night away while throwing out a repertoire of distorted truths at unsuspecting young ladies and celebrating the culture of vogue.

The Tipping Point

Every trend movement has an igniting point and eventually reaches critical mass; even technology has a special point where it goes from underground to early adoption to the forefront of widespread acceptance. Many incremental and key components need to come together to create a new pop form, some of which I discussed with disco having musical roots in soul, Latin, and R&B. A tipping point, if you will. This was definitely the case with disco, but before we delve into the subject of disco's tipping point and how it went from underground eccentricity to cultural mainstream, it might be quite interesting to see how certain other pop phenomena came about. So let's consider three great forms of pop culture that changed and molded the culture of the day and influenced everything beyond.

Rock 'n' Roll

Rock 'n' roll did not magically appear from nowhere. Yes, its roots are derived from blues, but pre-1955, and it was very hard to define it as a pop norm with youth. The early meaning of the phrase "rock 'n' roll" in black neighbourhoods meant having sexual relations. It had its influences from Americans of African descent, blended with European instrumentation and country music, but this would be a debate for academics and music historians. When looking at pop vogue, things go from formative to normative, and for this to occur, a few things happened in the 1950s to rock 'n' roll, almost by design, or perhaps by chance.

Chuck Berry, who really invented the rock 'n' roll guitar as we know it, hit the billboards in 1955 with his song "Maybelline," which was based on a woman and a car (later he would go to jail for having a female in a car while crossing state lines), which was the prototype lyric for many early rock 'n' roll hits. His genius later included "Roll Over Beethoven" in 1956, "Rock 'n' Roll Music" in 1957, and the gold standard and his masterpiece in rock 'n' roll, "Johnny B. Goode."

Simultaneously, in 1955 Bill Haley and the Comets' song, "Rock Around the Clock," was featured in the rock 'n' roll cult movie *Blackboard Jungle.*

Not to be outdone, the enigmatic and high-energy Jerry Lee Lewis, with roots in country and rockabilly, appeared on the Steve Allen show and performed "Whole Lotta Shakin'," and soon this was followed by Otis Blackwell's masterpiece, "Great Balls of Fire." Blackwell also wrote music for Elvis but was superstitious and refused to meet Elvis in person.

Finally, that guy from Memphis (incidentally, Memphis is the birthplace of rock 'n' roll) shook up the world with his charismatic combination of swerving hips, good looks, and an incredible voice to glamorize and deliver this new medium with a host of hit songs, including "Blue Suede Shoes" in 1955, the quintessential "Hound Dog" in 1955, and the sultry "Heartbreak Hotel" in 1956. "Heartbreak Hotel" was written by Tommy Durden and was about a person who committed suicide by jumping out a hotel window. (Ever wonder why we can't actually open hotel windows and have to smell stale air?) And of course, perhaps Elvis's most indelible performance was in the 1957 movie *Jailhouse Rock*, in which he performed, well, "Jailhouse Rock."

Then, of course, the world had a brief flirtation with Buddy Holly, who had a genius for music and gave us his pop masterpiece, "That'll

Be the Day." He had an audience appeal so diverse that it included him playing and eventually being accepted by a black audience at the legendary Apollo Theater. Buddy Holly was instrumental in inspiring many of the British Invasion bands, including the Rolling Stones and Beatles.

Rock 'n' roll took flight for a host of reasons, many having to do with the urbanization of America in the twentieth century; young people would no longer adopt their parents' music from rural life, where the chance for youth to connect was historically not so pronounced. But America becoming urbanized on its own was not enough to create the phenomena of early rock 'n' roll. It depended on a host of talents and icons to create critical mass, but it was the presence of Chuck Berry, Elvis Presley, Jerry Lee Lewis, Bill Haley, and Buddy Holly that quintessentially defined the sound, energy, and musical grounding that later would influence the British Invasion. It was this fusion, along with the supporting songwriters and cast, that created the phenomenon of early rock 'n' roll and how it defined pop culture in the fifties.

All these things had to come together for rock 'n' roll to create a tipping point, if you will, and reach critical mass. All these artists were separately assembled, but together, much like the solar system, each part moved in perfect symmetry, either by chance or unexplainable design. The end result was to gift the world with what it created…rock 'n' roll.

The Motown Sound
The Motown sound, the genre and style of music that was all its own, had very humble beginnings and actually took some time to go from its roots to igniting into widespread culture. Motown was founded by Berry Gordy, Jr. who had once owned a jazz-oriented record store in the early 1950s that eventually folded. Why? Because it was in the headwind against the next wave of change in pop music—namely, rock 'n' roll. Gordy was caught flat-footed at the time and landed himself on the Ford assembly line in Detroit in 1955. But that all was about to change.

Gordy, an avid songwriter with a remarkable eye for talent, formed his first record label, Tamla Records, with an $800 family loan, and he created the Motown label shortly thereafter. If someone wanted to discuss the roots of Motown, it could be argued that it started in 1959. However, the issue with this line of thinking is that Motown still had no major hits. Yes, the talent had started to walk into 1719 Gladstone Street in Detroit. Just to give a short list: the genius of Smokey Robinson, a jazz act called the Four Aims (better known as the Four Tops), Marvin Gaye, the incomparable Stevland Hardaway Morris (also known as Stevie Wonder). All were supported by some incredibly deep and talented writing teams that included Holland-Dozier-Holland; most credit the 1963 release of "Come and Get These Memories," written for Martha and the Vandellas, for defining the unique texture of the Motown Sound. In 1960, a teenage group called the Primates (better known as the Supremes) auditioned for Motown and were not signed until 1961 (Gordy told them to come back when they finished high school). The Supremes eventually returned and did not have their first Motown hit until 1964, with "Where Did Our Love Go?" and a host of other classics were to come, including "Back in My Arms Again." This was followed up by their appearances on the *Ed Sullivan Show*, which had a reputation for giving airtime to black acts.

In what was about to be the most creative and hypercompetitive time in pop music, which also gave birth to the British Invasion, Motown was about to simultaneously explode. In fact, during their first 1964 tour, the Beatles played much Motown mixed with an R&B sound, some of which included the songs "Money" and "Twist and Shout"!

The momentum of Motown continued, and in 1964, the Temptations released "The Way You Do the Things You Do"; Marvin Gaye sang "Can I Get A Witness"; Mary Wells sang "My Guy"; and Martha and the Vandellas sang "Dancing in the Streets." In late 1964, Mike McLean, head of engineering at Motown Records, introduced eight-track recording, and this led to a higher level of sophistication for the Motown Sound.

In 1965, the Four Tops recorded "I Can't Help Myself." Stevie Wonder was in full swing with his release of "Uptight (Everything's Alright)," and Martha and the Vandellas brought out "Nowhere to Run."

It was perhaps between the years 1964 and 1966 that Motown firmly embedded itself into the normative pop culture, and at a later point took a chapter from the white psychedelic music of the late 1960s and introduced psychedelic soul in the way of the Temptations' album, *Psychedelic Shack*. Later Motown gave birth to the Jackson 5.

Motown produced much more, which is outside the scope of this book, but what is important is that relatively underground trends come to a point of reaching the top and bubble over into the wider culture with an enigmatic combination of energy, design, and chance.

So the tipping point of Motown was more than likely 1964, and it did not really reach critical mass until perhaps 1966. Still, while it was for the most part an all-black sound with a relatively limited audience its gifts were indelible and its sound unmistakable.

The British Invasion

England lost her American colonies in 1776, but the invasion that was to occur in 1964 from the historically largest commercial port of the British Empire, namely Liverpool, was about to shake the world. It was about to pave the way for the legitimacy of pop music, to be spoken in the same breath as Rachmaninoff, Beethoven, and Tchaikovsky. The next tipping point created such critical mass that it still influences everything around us.

If one was a teenager in the early sixties, the lull in American pop music was painfully evident, since there really was no new or cutting-edge sound coming out of the US pop music scene. The exorbitant energy of 1950s rock 'n' roll had come to an exhaustive hangover since some unusual and debatable coincidences took place with many of America's pop icons. Buddy Holly, Richie Valens, and the Big Bopper died in a plane crash; in 1959, Elvis Presley was enlisted in the US Army; in 1959, Chuck Berry was arrested under the Mann Act for transporting a fourteen-year-old across state lines and was incarcerated in 1960; Jerry Lewis married his thirteen-year-old cousin; and in 1957 Little Richard found Jesus.

As the tide of early rock 'n' roll receded, it became painfully obvious that by the early sixties, all the founders of rock 'n' roll had passed into the night without even a tearful goodbye. Perhaps by chance, but perhaps not!

By the early 1960s, all that was left was some Frankie Laine, Frankie Avalon, Chubby Checker, Paul Anka, the Shirelles, Ricky Nelson, and a host of other bubble-gum acts and various other chastity promoting acts. See lists of top hits of 1961–1963:

http://www.musicoutfitters.com/topsongs/1961.htm

http://www.musicoutfitters.com/topsongs/1962.htm

http://www.bobborst.com/popculture/top-100-songs-of-the-year/?year=1963.

So, in many respects, in the early-sixties pop music in America had reached somewhere between watching paint dry to being in a coma. American pop music was rudderless between 1960 to perhaps 1965, and it was the British sound that eventually brought American pop music out of second gear.

In 1964, the time was right for the next wave in pop music; yes, it was still rock 'n' roll, now with roots that blended rock with blues but with an all-British sound. British pop music had gone from a cheesy imitation of American rock 'n' roll to relative maturity, and many of the roots extended from Liverpool, an English city that suffered much hardship during World War II and was adversely affected by England's industrial decline.

With a distinct sound known as the Mersey Beat, Liverpool was the epicentre of the new British sound. Many great bands came from Liverpool, and by 1960 there were hundreds of bands playing the new Mersey Beat sound in the area. I have reasonably intimate knowledge of this, since I have visited Liverpool on business for many years, and my British friends, Phill and Irene, were both hair stylists in the late 1950s and early sixties. Irene did attend the Cavern Club where the Beatles performed on over 270 occasions in the early sixties. She said that people would know you were at the Cavern Club, since back then the club had a certain odour. A little side note: When I asked where the mop-top haircuts came from, they said that they were originally girls' haircuts. Phill actually watched the Beatles perform in Liverpool's Empire Theatre but said it was hopeless, since he couldn't hear anything aside from all the screaming.

This new music was a fusion of Chuck Berry, Buddy Holly, doo-wop, skiffle, and, of course, R&B. Many Liverpudlians claim that there were many other bands as good as or better than the Fab Four, including Gerry and the Pacemakers. However, there is one band that history now remembers best, and before they came to America on November 4, 1963, they polished their lustre by playing in front of the Queen Mother and Princess Margaret at Prince of Wales Theatre in London (see: http://www.youtube.com/watch?v=iWDFuVRWdn4). It was there that John Lennon uttered the famous words, "For our last number, I'd like to ask your help. The people in the cheaper seats, clap your hands. And the rest of you, if you'd just rattle your jewelry. We'd like to sing a song called 'Twist and Shout.'"

But then on February 9, 1964, the four lads from Liverpool with their mop-top haircuts were first introduced to America on the *Ed Sullivan Show* in front of a television audience of seventy million. What many people did not realize was they were watching an historic moment, and it definitely was the tipping point. It was a sound and look that shook the world. The Beatles energized the nation and perhaps let America forget about the slaying of JFK.

The Ed Sullivan Show

The reader might have noticed a fair bit of reference to the *Ed Sullivan Show,* and it might be a good time to acquaint people with Ed Sullivan, since they might be too young to remember the show and how its variety of entertainment touched so many. The cultural impact Ed Sullivan had on Sunday evenings in much of Canada and the United States in the fifties and sixties might be unparalleled.

To appear on this show was a ticket to fame, and many of the greats did: Count Basie, Dean Martin, the Jackson 5, Elvis, the Doors, the Rolling Stones, James Brown, the Mamas and the Papas, the Supremes, Nat King Cole, Barbara Streisand, Ray Charles, Shirley Bassey, Frank Sinatra, yes, even the Muppets, and, of course, the Beatles. On February 9, 1964, Ed Sullivan introduced the Beatles to America, and that moment is considered a milestone in American pop culture, as they played to a record television audience of 73 million, in a country of 191 million. That evening was the spark that ignited the British Invasion.

Subsequent performances by the Beatles on the *Ed Sullivan Show* are a hazy memory to me, although I cannot remember which year I first saw them, since I was very young. What I can remember, though, was that there was a lot of excitement on the part of adults all around, and everywhere you went electricity filled the air in anticipation of the Beatles appearing. Perhaps the only thing as unforgettable to me was the moon landing; one excited us like never before, and the other left us all in awe.

The Beatles took the North American music scene by a storm with a mashed-up sound that seemed to have no American roots, but it did. In fact, John Lennon and Paul McCartney were heavily influenced by Chuck Berry and Elvis Presley. Furthermore, when Mick Jagger and Keith Richards became reacquainted in 1960 at the Dartmouth Railway Station, Richards was carrying the latest Chuck Berry and Muddy Waters albums in his hand. It was at that moment that the Rolling Stones became a group.

The British Invasion was started by the Beatles, but many great bands from the UK were to follow, such as the Rolling Stones, whose first tour was a relative flop, since Jagger and Richards had not yet discovered their song writing abilities. This cultural tidal wave from the UK included Dusty Springfield—who was considered the best white soul singer of that era—the Animals, Gerry and the Pacemakers, Petula Clark, Donovan, the Dave Clark Five, the Kinks, the Hollies, and of course, The Who. The list is much deeper, and one can find out more about the British Invasion on *Wikipedia*.

As a side note, it is interesting to reflect on how the sound of the Beatles matured, and evolved; when they released their *Sgt. Pepper's Lonely Hearts Club Band* album in 1967, it is considered by many to be the first pop album that legitimized rock 'n' roll music as a serious genre. Their music would later be organized into classical arrangements.

The Beatles provided the tipping point, or at least the spark, for the British Invasion, and the bands that followed suit from different areas of the UK provided critical mass and sustainable inertia, as well as incomparable inventiveness. The British Invasion gifted the world without ever intending to do so, and it was perhaps the last great gasp of the British Empire.

As we see, all movements have an igniting point that leads to a tipping point, especially in pop music and cultural trends. Why go through all this information to build up to the story of disco? Because disco, much like all the other genres of musical trends, went through a succession of events to bring it from underground clubs in New York, to critical mass. Staging it this way gives us a framework, both in contrast and similarities to other types of music, and how it all came together.

So now we bring you back to look at the most enigmatic story in human endeavour as we finally mount the courage to discover the cause and effects of the "rise and fall of disco" and how it too shook the world! Because, after all, the epic story of disco needs to be told.

Elvis Presley Jailhouse Rock. 1957.

The Beatles with Ed Sullivan, 1964.

The Supremes early 1960's.

Barry White.

Disco: Back to the Formative Years

Disco did not magically appear from thin air; it had an artistic and cultural genesis that fused a host of sounds that included soul, funk, and Latin salsa. The show *Soul Train* featured some of the early sounds that helped formulate the disco sound of heavy base, but it still was not the identifiable sound that we came to know as disco.

Yes, the O'Jays released their energy-filled masterpiece, "Back Stabbers," in 1972; Don Downing introduced "Dream World" in 1973, which had very early disco overtones; MFSB later introduced the instrumental early disco classic "TSOP." Barry White sang a host of sensuous songs that acted as backdrop music to help many men talk women out of their clothes. But the disco sound was still a countercultural phenomenon played in underground clubs. Still, it had no quintessential sound; it was a story in the making without a clear architectural blueprint.

By 1974, Gloria Gaynor sang "Never Can Say Goodbye," and George McRae performed "Rock Your Baby." Soon, white acts followed with a Euro-type beat, and the disco sound was definitely taking form.

Finally, 1975 was the year that we saw more of a mainstream bent with "The Hustle," a reasonably sophisticated form of touch dancing. Other acts followed such as the bubble-gum classic by KC and the Sunshine Band, "That's the Way I Like It," and the incredibly talented Bee Gees released "Jive Talkin'." And of course there was the very funky Average White Band with their "Pick Up the Pieces" instrumental track. But still, disco did not have the definitive sound and leadership that it needed. If the Beatles and Rolling Stones led the British Invasion, Chuck Berry and Elvis nurtured rock 'n' roll, and the Supremes and Temptations gave Motown its sound, disco was still yearning for someone to carry it on its shoulders and create critical mass, or its national anthem, if you will.

The Lady from Boston Finally Arrives

But wait. There was this other lady from Boston named LaDonna
Adrian Gaines. Say what? Well, here is another clue: she played with a
band called the Crows in the 1960s and released a German version of
"Aquarius" from the 1968 musical *Hair*, as well as sang backup vocals
for Three Dog Night, who themselves featured the incredible voice of
Chuck Negron. She honed her singing skills in a church choir and came
from a devout Christian family, but that did not stop her from writing
songs of sensuality. The first big hit she did, which she had not originally intended to perform, she ended up performing herself anyway. It
is this song that turned into an unforgettable hit in late 1975: "Love to
Love You Baby," which was a simulated orgasm blended into a sensuous and intoxicating melody. But who was this lady from Boston?

In 1976, the tidal wave of the definitive disco sound was about to
take the world by storm when Diana Ross (yes, she was the one Berry
Gordy turned away in 1960 until she finished high school) came out
with her sultry voice, and did an exquisite vocal performance of her hit
single, "Love Hangover," which was written by Pam Sawyer, a London-
born songwriter who wrote a host of Motown masterpieces. "Love
Hangover" had some beautiful musical arrangements and oozed sensuality; this song on its own helped mold the disco sound, yet it still
did not take it to the tipping point, because perhaps the biggest part
of the puzzle that helped create disco was missing.

The tipping point started in 1976, and the year musically belonged
to that lady from Boston, Donna Summer, who was now getting ready
for her coronation. If Elvis Presley was the king of rock 'n' roll, it is in-
disputable that Donna Summer was the queen of disco!

The Queen of Disco Arrives

Perhaps the title sounds campy, but make no mistake, Donna Summer
was a profound talent who had an angelic and divine voice with incredible range that could bring songs alive, along with superb breath

control. This was coupled with the fact that she wrote much of the material herself, along with Giorgio Moroder.

Donna Summer quintessentially defined the disco sound and was perhaps the most important architect of pop music in the mid- to late 1970s. Put differently, she put a whole generation where it belonged, on the dance floor, so people could collectedly discover their hidden ecstasies. Her discography in late 1975 and 1976 included "Could It Be Magic" and "Spring Affair." The story did not end there, as Summer continued to dominate when "Last Dance" was released in 1977, and of course with her rendition of "MacArthur Park," followed by "Bad Girls," and even a duet with Barbara Streisand, "Enough Is Enough," which many a young lady was shadow singing to when being done wrong by the testosterone-driven nature of the young male mind.

She also wrote, or helped write, more of her own music, along with Bruce Sudano, whom she ended up marrying, as well as writing for other artists. She was a phenomenal talent who gave energy to her generation and beyond. What Beethoven was to classical music and what the Beatles were to giving credibility to pop, Donna Summer was to disco. The queen has passed on but is not forgotten. She left us with an incredible discography, including winning the Academy Award for the Best Song in 1979.

The background music of disco facilitated a backdrop for young males of the seventies to learn how to create and paint poems of romantic possibilities for unsuspecting fine females, or was it the other way around? One needed to feel wanted, while the other wanted to feel needed. So, it is this timeless interwoven attraction between the sexes that was facilitated by disco.

Still, this was not enough on its own to spark disco past the tipping point, that place where something becomes the cultural norm, also called critical mass. More elements were still required to create the phenomenon; if *8 Mile* touched a musically deprived generation hooked on rap, *Saturday Night Fever* and the Bee Gees were about to bring disco to the tipping point and beyond by creating an explosion that rocked the Baby-Boom Generation, and any other generation that was around them at the time.

Saturday Night Fever

The actual story of the movie was based on a *New York* magazine article by Nik Cohn titled "Tribal Rites of the New Saturday Night." The movie itself is still a fine example of cinematography that encapsulated dance, music, and the story of a young man on hormonal overdrive who finds himself and learns to live with his ego. The storyline is about a working-class Italian American male (Tony Manero, played by John Travolta) from Brooklyn with a flatlining career at a local hardware store for near minimum wage and a future to nowhere. But come Saturday night, Tony was the man. He had the threads (clothing, or skins, depending what generation you come from); he would show up at the 2001 Odyssey, a disco club, and transform into the man who led the in-crowd. He had it all: the dance moves that were perfectly choreographed, an exquisite collection of "shaggy girls" who were painted all over him, and, of course, the music. And let's not forget the one-liners. Yes, come the weekend, Tony Manero was some type of cross between James Bond, Fred Astaire, and a mack daddy! Like most men, he dreams about the girl he can't have, in this case Stephanie Mangano, who is much too sophisticated for his out-of-the-cereal-box one-liners. She brags about all her Manhattan socialite in-crowd acquaintances, including Broadway Joe Namath. However, Tony, trying to find a way to get horizontal with her, buys some time by making her his dance partner for the upcoming dance contest at the club, in which he wears that iconic white suit with a black shirt, (now etched in time), that helped define the disco look and the commercial success of disco, and especially *Saturday Night Fever*.

Stephanie, exuding female charms, gave hope to Tony that there was a future that was going to be different from just working in a paint store. Stephanie painted pictures in his mind of what could be possible, which, unfortunately for Tony, did not include shagging her, which was up there in his priorities, right behind throwing his future under the bus!

The white-suited dance pose of Tony Manero was one of the most memorable, both liked and loathed pop culture posters of the last forty years. It is as indelible as Marilyn Monroe's skirt-flying pose on the air grates of the New York City subway, James Dean in his leather Jacket, and John-John playing under President Kennedy's desk.

Eventually Tony won the dance contest and considered flirting with a crowd that could assemble a repertoire of more than twenty words. At the end of the film, as he visits Stephanie's place, the film credits start to roll, along with the beautiful piece of ineradicable cinematography as the sun spills through the window and the soft sound of the Bee Gees' "How Deep Is Your Love" serenades the viewer.

This was the escape and glamour that the disco culture provided, haute couture, fashion, refined dancing, nightclubs, and the sexual promiscuity that a pre-AIDS world offered. And of course, who could forget the music with which to waste our youth away? The seductive sound of disco music provided a capstone to a most enticing form of pop culture. Many of us, during our vibrant yet idle youth, unwittingly subscribed to the mantra of Tony Manero in *Saturday Night Fever,* when he was asked about his future and his rebuttal was the famous "Oh, fuck the future!"

A few things get lost in this film. First, the dance choreography was quite good, and John Travolta trained hard and insisted on doing his own dance scenes, using no doubles. In fact, when the editor cut out the areas showing his dance scenes, he threatened to walk off the set—and he was correct, since his moves really helped make the movie. Incidentally, he was trained by dance instructor Deney Terrio, who eventually had his own show that featured amateur dance contestants called *Dance Fever*, which ran from 1979 to 1985, and naturally, every chance he had, he would mention that he was the man who trained John Travolta for his dance sequences on *Saturday Night Fever*. Terrio was a noted narcissist, and addicted to publicity.

Then, of course, there were the fashionistas and nightclubs (more on that later), but what really stood out was the soundtrack music. Because without the music, there was no film, so we could then ask the questions of the ages, "Did the music make the film, or did the film make the music?" or "Did the white suit make John Travolta, or did Travolta make the suit?" The answers to these important questions may affect the continuation of civilization as we know it; it may elude us for another thousand years as philosophers, professional and self-ordained, will debate this and the existence of God into eternity.

The *Saturday Night Fever* soundtrack was, for the most part, created by an English group of brothers who had incredible vocal and song writing talents, first gaining international fame in the sixties. They could have been classical vocalists if they chose, but they sowed their seeds of musical repertoire in the type of pop music that was somewhat aligned with rock 'n' roll but often associated with tear-jerking ballads. They had the type of vocal harmony skills that took the best of the Beatles and Motown and turned it into something that was incomparable at times, with its own sonic texture.

The Bee Gees combined their smooth vocal harmonies with some very unique song writing abilities. In a most creative time of 1960s pop culture, where radio airtime was hard to achieve against the colossus of talent that the era had produced, they had already created timeless pop masterpieces, including "Lonely Days," "How Can You Mend a Broken Heart," and "To Love Somebody," which were all in a league of their own in terms of pop ballads. Incidentally, "To Love Somebody" was originally written for Otis Redding of "(Sittin' on) the Dock of the Bay" fame. Their library of songs continued with single releases such as "Massachusetts" and "I Started a Joke," but by the early seventies, their careers were flatlining, and in reality, the music business is something like living in Los Angeles; you are only as good as your last BMW payment.

Just before *Saturday Night Fever*, they started to move away from their ballad sounds. In 1975, they relocated to Miami and produced the album *Main Course*, which included the very famous "Nights on Broadway," featuring Barry Gibbs's new falsetto sound; the same album also produced "Jive Talkin'." In 1976, they had another commercial success with "You Should Be Dancing," which was featured on their *Children of the World* album. So they already had a disco sound, even before their *Saturday Night Fever* soundtrack.

They went commercial with their new R&B album *Main Course*, with disco overtones that surpassed any marketing successes they had achieved during the sixties in terms of popularity. But what was to take place, either by chance or design, was that they were about to help produce the best-selling musical soundtrack of all time, putting them into superstardom.

It is interesting to note that the original dance scenes in the movie did not feature the Bee Gees' music, and in fact, John Travolta said that he was dancing to Stevie Wonder and Boz Scaggs songs, not the tracks from *Saturday Night Fever*, because the soundtrack had not been recorded yet. In fact, the studio scene with Tony and Stephanie, originally featured their dancing to the song "Lowdown" by Boz Scaggs, but legal issues prevented them from using it, so it was deleted from the scene and replaced with "More than a Woman" by the Bee Gees. Even though the Bee Gees were not involved in the initial stages of *Saturday Night Fever*, this was about to change.

Donna Summer in the recording studio in 1977.

The Bee Gees, 1977.

Guess who in days gone by? Circa 1979.

A Weekend in France

The Bee Gees were given a rough script for the movie by producer Robert Stigwood, and they agreed to lay down a soundtrack for the movie. Barry Gibb later remarked in an interview, "We had no concept of the movie except some kind of rough script they'd brought with them." So, on a weekend at France's Château d'Hérouville studio, they wrote most of the songs for the film. Then, in 1977, the *Saturday Night Fever* album was released.

The album had other memorable tracks, and one that comes to mind was a disco masterpiece by The Trammps, who turned up the heat with their song, "Disco Inferno." Yet it would be hard to imagine *Saturday Night Fever* without the music the Bee Gees produced. The music on this album is timeless.

Some musical purists say that the Bee Gees sold out to disco and to a watered-down commercial realm, but I am not sure this was the case, since all great art forms, when viewed in the context of recallable history, require an appreciative audience, from Picasso to Van Gogh. Music is not different, and in no way did the Bee Gees have to apologize for evolving and re-inventing themselves. Many creative geniuses reinvented themselves, including Leonardo da Vinci. Since the *Saturday Night Fever* album had become the best-selling album of all time to that point and has sold over forty million copies. They were simply connecting with people and made songs that sold. Make no mistake about it; the soundtrack they produced for the film is timeless, inventive, and a masterpiece in its own right that won Grammy Awards, including Album of the Year in 1979.

Disco's Tipping Point

The mass popularity of disco was an amalgamation of events, one inextricably connected with the other. But this much is for sure: without the combination of Donna Summer, the Bee Gees, and the *Saturday Night Fever* album, the commercial popularity would not have occurred, which might be to the glee of many. Each component gave the other energy, and together they intricately produced a critical mass of pop phenomena that shook the world, much like the four lads from Liverpool and the supporting cast from the British Invasion.

I know some readers will turn around and say that I am not paying homage to the rest of the cast that helped propel disco. Yes, there was the energy-filled Thelma Houston, with "Don't Leave Me This Way," and an alternative soul-filled version by Harold Melvin and the Blue Notes. Some credit Barry White, but he was not really disco and only flirted with its roots while he stuck to his knitting, which was to create ballads to help us serenade the fairer sex. True, Gloria Gaynor sang "I Will Survive," which, as mentioned earlier, became the women's national anthem of sorts after being done wrong by males, while the song meant different things to a gay audience.

There was a lot of talent on board; Michael Jackson got into the act, but he was still at the outer edges of Disco; KC and the Sunshine Band helped us "Get Down Tonight," and there was, of course, the first relatively openly gay and unforgettable group, the Village People, who came out with "YMCA." James Brown delivered another electrifying performance with "Get Up" in 1970. Indeed there were a host of other artists who made impactful and profound contributions, but none of the others were essential. What was essential, though, was *Saturday Night Fever*, the Bee Gees, and Donna Summer, since they carried the disco genre on their backs, and forever defined its texture, and gave it its energy, turning disco into an international pop cultural coup d'état.

Some disco purists argue that *Saturday Night Fever*, by commercializing disco, was the beginning of the end. Bill Oakes, who supervised the *Saturday Night Fever* soundtrack, claimed that the movie prolonged disco and did not create the craze; all it did was breathe new life into a dying genre of music.

This argument might have some merit, but the movie, Donna Summer, and the Bee Gees created a quintessential sound and brought epic commercial success to an underground pop culture and dance movement that was begging to be discovered. Together and simultaneously, the film, the church singer, and the boys from England turned Disco into the cultural norm. Disco needed an igniting point, which turned into an explosion that eventually defined the late seventies, and it is this tipping point that provided its rightful place into pop music and dance history. It was this circle that surrounded everyone. Clearly, Disco's tipping point was right during the time between 1976 and 1978, when its influence in popular culture was undeniable, while at the same time it seduced a very wide international audience.

Everyone's Got the Boogie Fever

"We're gonna' come around at twelve with some Puerto Rican girls that are just dyiiiin' to meet you!"

—*THE ROLLING STONES*

To the dismay of rock 'n' roll aficionados, it was only getting worse as they wallowed in tears and realized that staying true to their genre was only sending them to sex-withdrawal therapy. Listening to rock 'n' roll was fine, but the problem was that they had all bought tickets to an empty party, with no real hope of celebrating life with the opposite sex, like disco boys were. Looking at posters of enticing females was interesting, but our quest was to meet damsels in distress, and the hard-core rockers did not quite realize that disco provided a more hopeful setting, as opposed to an empty ticket or some false idol-worshiping. So then, who did you say went disco?

Everyone always remembers, first and foremost, that the first rock-pop group to cave into the enticing allurement of disco was the Bee Gees with their *Saturday Night Fever* soundtrack and *Children of the World* album. Surely this could be swept under the carpet as some type of anomaly and sellout to commercial interests. To many of the rockers, any rock act that went disco was a Benedict Arnold of sorts, traitors to their genre of music, and quite frankly, it is surprising that the drug-infused stoners even took notice that change was in the air. But then, some heavyweight rock acts got into the disco sound, much to the surprise of the world, and the universe in general.

Then the unimaginable happened. Rome fell as the gates of rock 'n' roll perished before our very own eyes when the Rolling Stones, billed as the "greatest rock band of all time" (Jagger and Richards were probably the most underrated pop writers of all time), came out with "Miss You." The Rolling Stones brought a case of wine and belched out the famous lyrics, "Gonna' come around at twelve with some Puerto Rican girls that are just dyiiiin' to meet you!" Oh, my! What has the world come to? Were the Rolling Stones performing disco? To rock fans, this was like *Tales from the Crypt* but worse; this was like Beethoven doing the bossa nova watusi twist. This was perceived as high treason and grounds for a summary hanging. But Jagger, being an astute businessman with an education that included the London

School of Economics, knew a trend when he saw one, understood what it meant to be relevant to each generation, and assumed his own place in timeless eternity, further, Jagger loved to dance from his early R&B influence. For the occasion of disco, they dropped in and contributed with their *Some Girls* album, which was undeniably disco and became their biggest-selling studio album, which to date has gone six times platinum. And of course, it featured their hit single "Miss You," their last number-one hit in the United States and number three in the UK.

Then came a suave cat from Highgate, North London, who played with Jeff Beck and the Faces in the sixties. Once known as "Rod the Mod," Rod Stewart has a well-documented and proud history of being a gallivanting type of gentleman. He went disco in 1978 with his hit, "Do Ya Think I'm Sexy," which to this day has outsold any other single he has ever recorded. Spiky hair and all, he threw another arrow into the already bleeding hearts of rockers. Yes, this was like Hannibal, as he surrounded Rome and its citizens cowered in fear. Well at least to rockers! Without too much surprise, there was the glamor rock group, KISS, led by the insatiable narcissist himself, Gene Simmons (he would have also made a good wrestling manager for some bad guy, but felt being a musician held more esteem). KISS was really a glam rock act, so when they flipped and released their song, "I Was Made for Loving You," it was not entirely surprising.

Blondie never made a complete disco album per se, but their song "Heart of Glass" was played widely in discos in the late 1970s and was originally released on their *Parallel Lines* album in 1978. The band was a new wave act, and after the release of this song, they were heavily criticized by new wave aficionados. To make things worse, the "Heart of Glass" promotional video was filmed at Studio 54, which in the eyes of new-wave rockers was blasphemy of sorts. Her critiques aside, the song established Deborah Harry globally, but when all was said and done, she did what blondes often do: sing, dance, look sultry, and of course, have more fun!

Even Barry Manilow, not a real rocker but a crooner of sorts, got into the act in 1978 with "Copacabana." That was actually a really great and exciting song to dance to.

But disco's energy was in full swing, and another noted eccentric, David Bowie, as late as 1983, came to the post-disco craze with his song, "Let's Dance." Bowie was perhaps one of the most inventive, if not the edgiest of the rock stars of the seventies and beyond. He certainly came late to the disco party, but nevertheless, he made an appearance.

Last, but not least, the Bee Gees, who created the most success-ful disco album of all time, were also considered the greatest trai-tors of all time, not because they were really ever a real hard rock act but because of their commercial success. It was simply that rockers themselves could not ignore the popularity of their commercial suc-cess. Everywhere you turned on the radio in 1977–78, the Bee Gees' *Saturday Night Fever* tracks were all you heard, and this is what worked up rock 'n' rollers into a major lather that would eventually cumulate into the disco record destruction event at Comiskey Park in Chicago in 1979. But more on that later.

Music videos were relatively crude in the 1970s compared with today, but watching the Bee Gees with their disco skins on, sing-ing "Staying Alive" and other songs off the *Saturday Night Fever* soundtrack, really worked up rockers s into a rich and crude agitation.

Yes, their heroes had betrayed them, leaving them in a tearful pool of sorrow and self-pity, looking for answers as to why their heroes abandoned their musical sensibilities and flipped into the realm of "or-gasmic commercial self-indulgence."

However, at the end of the day, artists perform to be recognized, and an artist who is traditionally known for one genre of music has both economic and emotional reasons to do what is necessary to keep a career on the fast track.

Disco Culture

"If I die tomorrow, I'd be fine, because I am so happy."

—BETHANN HARDISON

We were not at disco clubs to write derivative formulas for the Goldman Sachs futures trading desk; we were there to celebrate life with music, dance, and women under a backdrop of translucent lights that spilled onto the dance floor.

Disco was a celebration of life; it simply was a marvellous time to be alive! Disco allowed young people to shed the miserable high-school fashions of the late seventies that best resembled the Beverly Hillbillies and walk into a setting where guys felt comfortable dressing in suits and attire that was relatively well tailored. Considering our lightweight budgets, self-proclaimed haute couture and bespoke tailoring were the calling card for fashion, with a touch of polyester gaudiness, of course.

Disco was glamour and ecstasy wrapped into an enigmatic core that allowed us to transform into self-created weekend stars. After all, according to our thinking at the time, God created weekdays so we could plan our weekends of prevarications and wistful shallowness. It was ecstasy dressed up as dance, music, and therapy for the soul, and a great chance to exhibit some really debonair threads!

Looking back, many of the fashions when I was in high school were so drab, especially for males, consisting really of platform shoes, jeans and a T-shirt. Much of the rock crowd's attire was inspired by the slough-of-mud scene in Woodstock. I remember that many of the guys in high school dressed like they lost a sumo wrestling match with some livestock. At one point, to spiral even lower, they brought in jeans that were denim coveralls; (probably inspired by the workers'

129

revolution march) it was this type of fashion tastelessness that was so sad to watch, and for girls, it was tight, painted-on jeans and a halter top.

Disco allowed a generation to remember why we were alive in the first place, which was to waste our youth away in a nightclub, or so we thought, and a dance culture that was perhaps a dress rehearsal for Facebook, but without keyboards and the "likes."

By the late seventies, we started to see the reintroduction of pleated pants as standard fare for guys, which made a comeback after *Saturday Night Fever*. In the movie, men's pants were still the straight-front, high-waisted, Spanish-type pants. The shoes had some heel but had accentuated points that eventually gave podiatrists a way to finance foot clinics, some five years after we hung up our disco shoes in the early 1980s. Nevertheless, the shoes were excellent for dancing and looked more symmetrical with suits. (Before John Travolta introduced pointed shoes on the screen, guys in the seventies were wearing thick heels, which did not look quite right with a finely tailored suit).

Disco fashion was such a relief from the blue-collar attire worn by the rockers who looked like they were recruits for the people's revolution (as history shows, these revolutions are really old wine in a new bottle). That being said, it must be remembered that back then guys that took care of themselves were stigmatized as feminine outcasts. Axe body sprays could never have gained traction in such a sociological environment. As always, there was peer pressure in high school that taking care of yourself and dressing with style was frowned upon for males, and if you did exhibit style, and if you were a guy, you would end up being relegated to the social gulags.

Today, male teenagers are encouraged to spray themselves with body-spray fragrances like Axe with an unwritten guarantee to get the girls! But this type of conduct in high school social circles in the mid-1970s would have resulted in a barrage of not-so-eloquent insults and perhaps some dental rearrangements for good measure…Certainly, it was a different time, but it was our time!

We eventually broke away from the pressure and got dressed up for our calling card, which was disco. It went further, since disco culture brought back the nightclub culture, where swaggering dress was a prerequisite of mating rituals, and we started to realize that dressing well, especially for guys, was a rite of passage, just like it was for Clark Gable's generation. As cavalier as we were, we were learning to be gentlemen and unknowingly becoming more refined in the social environment, while at the same time, we were unwittingly throwing our futures and education under the bus. But we had solace in the hope that we would eventually be coronated into "Disco Royalty", with pomp and ceremony, which unfortunately fettered out in delusions of grandeur. In my experience, topics of conversations at disco clubs did not include the various philosophies, and we did not much discuss ways to save the Earth from ourselves, (which today is easy to do by creating a Twitter hashtag and presto, the world has changed), or to create statistical modelling theories for advanced regression analysis. I cannot remember much discussion on the finer points of Shakespeare's works in the nightclubs I attended. However, unknowingly, many a male specimen was practicing some reasonably articulate assemblage of the English language, with a touch of equivocation, complemented by flashes of intellect, you might say, to lure the lovely maidens. So then, it seemed that disco did stimulate the intellect on some level.

Their motives were all the same: to find more inventive ways to dizzy and have our way with polyester clad-lovelies, or so many thought, and disco provided the backdrop to accomplish such a lofty goal. Thus, the setting that disco provided was just the ticket, because when all was said and done, what we really just wanted to do was just…

Do the Hustle

Dancing is a tribal expression; it is full of sexual expression, and to actually have a partner with whom one dances in synchronization is an expression of art. We were not Mikhail Baryshnikov or Gregory Hines, but man, some of us knew how to dance the hustle and talk the hustle, which would help us in later life with our careers and spouses.

The hustle had variations from the New York hustle to the Latin hustle, or "touch dancing." Call it what you will, but in the end, its core moves were quite similar. It involved a lot of synchronized dancing steps, turns, and swings, with under-the-arms turns. Some of us became quite good at it, since we realized that dancing was a prerequisite to improving your game on the weekends. At the same time, it was just pure fun.

During my disco days, I met an accomplished dancer and instructor named Cedric, probably in his late twenties, at a Scarborough club called the Aristocrat. The way we met was when he watched me dance one night, and as I walked off the dance floor, he gave me his take on things to the effect of, "Your feet are moving, but your upper body is staying still." I remember that he figured how much I wanted to be to good dancer, and each night I was there, he coached me on dance steps and overall fluidity of rhythm. I never learned to dance by mechanical steps but by the overall flow and fluidity to match the music. I think I learned most of my steps to Barry Manilow's "Copacabana."

As the famous Deney Terrio said, "Women love guys who can dance," so each week I and many of my ilk honed our skills at more clubs with various partners. I became good friends with some of them. I practiced endlessly with Diana, and she was quite patient with me, and thin as I remember her, which made things easier for practicing lifts. I spent a few weekday evenings at the same Scarborough club, working on dance skills. I really enjoyed dancing very much, yet it was at the expense of my down-sloping grades in the final year of high school. At that age, though, gratification was immediate, and we often couldn't see past our shadows.

I eventually practiced with many friends I made, got pretty good, and reached a decent level that enabled me to win dance contests at various clubs in Toronto (I still have some of the trophies). The moves were relatively sophisticated and intricate with the type of dancing we were doing, since it involved dancing with a partner and relatively little solo. This meant that one needed to synchronize steps with the partner and have enough confidence to lead the girl with dance moves. Put differently, one had to be good to touch dance (hustle), since every flaw would be accentuated by missteps. Later, when I entered dance contests, many of the girls wore flowing dresses that twirled when I spun them on the floor, for added theatrical appeal against the backdrop of the dance floor.

When I once went to see professional dancers, I watched their sensuous moves and body relaxation that created flow, which I later incorporated into certain dance routines at disco clubs. Watching ballet also helped with the study of dance fluidity. But I believe many of us learned how to dance by watching *Dance Fever* hosted by Deney Terrio, as well as watching *The Soul Train* show. If one watches shows today like *So You Think You Can Dance*, many of the dancers have a rigid style that creates visual tension and lacks relaxed fluidity.

Later, as I honed my dance skills, I learned how to do lifts and some more dramatic and acrobatic moves. One of my friends, Liam, messed up a lift at the club in the Prince Hotel in Toronto, and the girl ended up with a fractured arm, which I really felt bad about. Oh well! It was all in the name of disco!

Little did I know at the time during the last year of high school, I was too straight and green when it came to the opposite sex, and I did not have the full array of swagger, but then I met a gentleman named Stonewall Jackson. He must have been close to forty, (as we all know that's ancient) was weaned on soul and funk, and in his demeanour obviously understood the roots of disco. I am sure that if I'd gone to his house, he would've played me LPs of James Brown, the Temptations, and Barry White, or perhaps George Benson. He was a bit chubby and dressed in a semi-colourful fashion. He would hang out at the club I did most of my disco teething at. (By the way, I was always drawn to making friends with people older than me, since they had more wisdom and vision.) He always looked conniving and cool as he gauged what was shaking all over the club, and in a way for me he became a fixture there. After some time, we became friends, and one weekend I mentioned to him that I had a girlfriend and stated to him that I felt monogamy was virtuous. That's when he gave me a lecture I would never forget. He said, "Listen up, bubs. You is speaking and thinking all wrong. There ain't no thing called a girlfriend; you call her the 'main lady,' and then you play a few on the side to accentuate the ride!" I said that it wouldn't be right to fool around on her, that in fact, I couldn't live with myself. He then said, "Well, listen up, kid. You will live with yourself just fine, because if she puts the slip on you and you ain't got no backup plan, you gonna' be holding an empty bag while you get played for a fool."

"But Stonewall," I said, "she said she loves me."

He replied, "That just some funky-ass jive talk to keep playin' and bouncing your mind. What you do is love her back, but have a few on the side, man, and start getting a better dig on the playin' field."

So the thought occurred to me that I was young, had no wife or family of my own, and had my whole life ahead of me, like many of my friends. After all, I only wanted to live to the ripe old age of thirty, since everybody over thirty looked so unexcited. So then just maybe Stonewall had a point with his message, which was "to keep a few passengers when driving the bus." Eventually, I called this the "Stonewall Jackson Doctrine," and to me it sounded much more effective than the Truman Doctrine. Every once in a while, I still think of him, which brings an inexplicable smirk to my face.

Disco Fashion, or Should We Say, Haute Couture

Did disco invent fashion, or did fashion invent disco? This is the question that contributes to the reservoir of mankind's unanswerable queries. This is the question that is coiled into a never-ending peel of impenetrable layers in the desperate search for a core that flirts with the truth but in the end only helps to serve as the conundrum that it is. The answer to attaining this truth is as unimaginable as perhaps the origins of the universe. But still, as human beings, we must push on and have the courage to pursue it. So, my chest filled with billowing pride, I will attempt to answer one of the most perplexing questions of all time.

Disco needed one more element to be complete as the calling card of counterculture, and of course, this was fashion. Disco had the complete expression of youthful exuberance, promiscuous sex, music, dance, nightclubs, inebriated idealism, and fatalism, all within a self-indulging mystery.

Disco required that one showed up dressed appropriately in order to play the part. Yes, many of us on proletariat wages used fashion to exude a more bourgeois ambiance toward the opposite sex. Using disco as a backdrop, a young male knew that if he painted pictures to a lovely lady as to what the future held, he had much more credibility, especially if he was dressed in exquisite attire. Costumes of seduction were required to complement the task at hand, which, ironically, was to do away with these costumes if all went well.

In the early 1970s, many guys were indeed dressing like unemployed pimps, with ostentatious attire and oil-based polyester. Remember bell-bottoms, Spanish-style, high-waisted pants and polyester suits? Young men's dress footwear was often elevator shoes, which really helped a lot of short guys. Much of this look changed by 1977 or so as pleats were introduced for men's pants, which was a throwback to the Roaring Twenties. Platform shoes were being replaced by lower-heeled, pointy shoes that were more conducive to a look that complemented dress pants and suits with a more cleanly defined aura, since the bottom of pants was narrowing from shoot-out flairs. Indeed, this was the type of shoe worn by John Travolta in *Saturday Night Fever*, and it was an essential part of the late-seventies disco look.

What often gets lost in this orgy of ecstasy better known as disco is that the materials used were not all polyester. In fact, designers were using natural materials such as cottons, finer wools, and tweeds in jackets, pants, and shirts. Later, I remember some of us were wearing armbands for more of *The Great Gatsby* look. Of course, the introduction of collarless shirts was all the rage in 1977. Fashion styles were also complemented by hairstyles that exposed the male ear. This was appropriate for young men to better hear their fathers' various lectures as to why they were investing their futures in discos. All this, in a nutshell, defined the disco look.

Once this look was quintessentially defined as disco, it could be problematic in some establishments where it was worn because being caught in the wrong place could mean one had to also hear the anti-disco chants, which was an articulate repertoire that usually started with, "Hey, disco boy," and built up to the more Shakespearean rants of "disco sucks," as well as a full à la carte menu of articulate profanity. The brunt of the anti-disco chants were directed at males by other males, and in some cases, as this writer inadvertently found out, one had to be careful where this type of attire was worn.

On one occasion, I showed up in disco attire at a roughneck bar called the Canadiana that was frequented by biker types and a supporting consortium that was in the advanced stages of inebriation. Naturally, after they observed my dress wear, with maroon pointed shoes and gregarious disco attire, including a collarless shirt, the stage was set. I soon noticed I was getting some unwanted attention that led to some less-than-ideal verbal retorts about my outfit, followed up with the promise of pugilistic reconfiguration of my facial structure.

Fortunately, an auto mechanic friend who had brought me there (remember my disco-mobile did need repairs) was a regular and calmed things down as he bought me time. I was grateful for him and the mandatory building code requiring back-door fire exits, for which I promptly headed as I unwittingly challenged the hundred-metre Olympic sprint record in a gallant run for my life. In the background, of course, was a complimentary chorus of "disco boy" chants offered in full harmonic stereo sound.

Getting back to disco fashion, ladies' accouterment did not look quite as desperate a part of the mating repertoire as it is in today's nightclubs. It was a cross between polyester spandex tights and flowing, swirly dresses, some with classical overtones that accentuated the twirls on the dance floor. Make-up was usually quite bold and ostentatious and was used amply enough to ensure that Revlon's share prices benefited accordingly. Ladies' heels were reasonably pronounced in disco mode, but they don't compare to some of the stilts worn by young ladies today that should ensure the growth of the chiropractic profession. Some of the heels worn today are actually taller than the ladies wearing them.

Feminists of the day were bent out of shape, claiming these bodacious exemplifications of femininity were exploitive, but the will of feminists was diametrically opposed to the fashion mantra and what ladies really wanted to wear. Perhaps the die-hard feminists would have been happier if women were asexual and wore burkas and hijabs into nightclubs. But one thing was for sure, feminists were no match for disco, since males and females of those times would have no part of such speak.

But what really stood out in disco days, were the large hair, hairspray, and the use of perms to create a soft, curly look or tight curls. Put differently, ladies' hairstyles were glamorous and celebrated femininity in a way that ensured males of the day took notice. Furthermore, it seemed that the polymers used in hairspray guaranteed that a lady's hairstyle stayed still, despite the conniving young gentlemen who ran their paws through it.

Disco fashion, much like any other fashion, was an expression of sexuality and the emerging norm of the day. Unlike Facebook profiles that are all dressed up with nowhere to go, disco fashion was dressed up with somewhere to go. Each week we came out with a new fashion statement and a host of lines for lovelies in the hope of luring them, better known as sowing our wild oats!

The Disco Clubs

I'm in with the in-crowd
I go where the in-crowd goes
I'm in with the in-crowd
And I know what the in-crowd knows
Anytime of the year, don't you hear?
Dressing fine, making time
We have a whole way of walking
We have a whole way of talking

—BILLY PAGE

Seeing plays on Broadway and at theatres in London's West End is culturally exquisite and quite enjoyable as a means of appreciating art. It is one of the calling cards of being refined, enjoying and appreciating some of the finer accomplishments of human expression.

But we had our own artistry delicately woven into a saga that was an ongoing story as we spun some fantastic tall tales of our own to an unsuspecting audience of exquisitely dressed young ladies who arrived in flowing dresses that nurtured our imaginations. Occasionally they broke our hearts, but in the name of disco, we just stayed calm and carried on. So then, what good would all this music, pillow talk, and dancing be if there were not a vehicle or venue with a roof on it to give a place of celebration called the disco? Thus, the disco club was born to fulfill our weekend desires, or so we thought.

It was the nightclubs that were the setting to help amalgamate the fashion, music, and dance. Disco nightclubs were a place to compare our youth with our contemporaries, something like Facebook, except we did not have electronic anonymity to make us feel like overinflated social media superheroes. How integral was the nightclub to disco? Let's put it this way, without nightclubs to nurture disco, it would be like having gas stations before we invented the automobile. It was like the train without the rails to showcase rail transportation. It was an ecstasy of hallucination, entangled in infinite mistruths, as we became everyone but ourselves. Each week we would show up at the discothèques, weaving some slick dance steps that were eventually complemented by some very smooth and inventive verbiage and tales of dreamy romance aimed at all the lovelies, or at least whichever ones were listening. Every week we would show up dressed in our most discriminating attire, equipped with a new barrage of fabricated tales mixed with some truth, and stretched-out stories that were designed to leave those lovely ladies in a perpetual head spin, to accompany the dance spins that we had masterfully learned to execute.

Perhaps Broadway had extravagant plays with some accomplished actors, but disco culture allowed us to put together some very good acts of our own with little time for intermissions as we tried our best to hide our motives and plots so we would not spoil the ending. Each week the discothèque clubs would provide us the setting to perform on stage in front of a captivating audience of fine young ladies. Yes, we would show up with our life savings, which was often our weekly paycheques, as we made our grand entrances with our gang of associates, each one shallower than the other. Part of the ritual was to shake hands with other males, whose names I cannot remember, as we scouted out the club and feasted on possibilities—against the background of the disco music.

A good friend of mine, whom we will refer to as Mr. Crosby, never to be outdone, would walk in with an entourage of women and during the evening would increase his fan club. He must have been about thirty-two at the time, and he had perfected the art of making a grandiose entrance and creating excitement, confusion, and energy. But his specialty really was working his act in larger clubs, as he would disappear into the crowd and then show up back at our table with more phone numbers. Since we were good friends and believed in being team players, we would keep his date occupied at our table while he gallivanted around the rest of the club. This technique we named "the Crosby shuffle," which was later emulated by many of our associates, with mixed results.

These were the mentors of disco-mania; we were not there to discuss Mesopotamia's effects on civilization, or predict the opening spot rate on the Swiss franc. We were there to celebrate life with music, dance, and women, and not necessarily in that order. Yes, this was perhaps insidious or shallow, but when I look back at it all, it can be credibly blamed on our male psyche and our associated software programming that perhaps needed an update patch, but this was a lot more fun than getting feminized, like the current generation of aspiring males. We had figured out early that mischievous males gave purpose to females who wanted to make it their life mission to set them on the track of hope and civility! On one occasion, I was approached by a fine female I was in the frequent company of, and she asked me a question: "Are you going to spend the rest of your life dancing, hanging out at clubs, and associating with all those misfit friends of yours?"

This was a profound question, which made me think, and after pondering her query for a while, I eventually answered, "Absolutely!"

True, we were juggling balls as we came up with new and even more innovative mistruths that we told to women in discos; we often were not quite sure of what we had said the week before. Obviously, we should have better documented what stories we had woven during the prior week, but I am not sure any of us were in a state of mind to remember the week before. On occasion, a few women would band together and compare notes to dispute our contradictory stories. Subsequently, this would really make it foggy when we showed up at a club, and we were confronted by a hoard of united women who had somehow figured out many of our schemes and tales. What would further amplify it was when they picked up energy with the music of Gloria Gaynor's hit, "I Will Survive," which was becoming the anthem of sorts for women done wrong, since this song seemed to give them united purpose, soulful healing, and energy to deal with our consortium of cronies passing off as gentlemen. Before long, we could see the night was slipping away into a Senate investigation committee hearing rather than the grand disco ball we had hoped for. Sometimes we attempted to rationalize our actions and face the music, but often it was best to cut our losses and slither out of that particular club as our last act of the evening.

So it became our modus operandi that after prolonged frequency at one club, women eventually confronted our consortium of close yet shallow associates, questioning our dubious behaviour. On such occasions, we soon realized that it was time to move our act to another club, where our reputation had not yet preceded us. Of course, we could have defended our honour and said we were prepared to change our ways, but why bother when we could just go to another club seven miles down the road and start our repertoire all over again?

Disco offered hope and change, just like Obama, and we hoped that by frequenting another nightclub, we could enact real, meaningful change in meeting new young and unsuspecting ladies who would listen to our meticulously woven stories. Just like Broadway's travelling shows, we would take our venue to different theatres (discos). So we did exactly that, touring different theatres with the same act, the same characters, and many of the same lines, hoping to find a new audience that would buy tickets to the never-ending saga of *As the Disco Ball Turns*. The only difference between us and Broadway was that our lines were more impromptu and somewhat less rehearsed.

But I personally feel that our biggest nightmare was that soon, Jane Fonda and Gloria Steinem would show up, followed by the camera crew of *60 Minutes*, and we would end up being tried before a feminist tribunal and hung in summary judgment under a spinning disco ball as we were slowly being lowered into the fire with the background music of "Enough Is Enough" by Barbara Streisand and Donna Summer. Somewhere in my mind, this was a possible outcome that not even atonement could resolve. This was the nightmare that made many a male wake up in a horrified cold sweat during Disco-mania! But still we marched on, like all great soldiers.

My parents were less than pleased, as many of my friends and I were starting to throw our university education by the wayside, (in my case plans included university) but we argued the case, that we were studying to complete our PhDs in discology, which we felt at the time was quite the lofty goal that would bring substantial returns on investment. Then again, attaining our PhD in discology was much more intellectually rigorous than some of the academically soft degrees offered in today's universities, which are often designed to keep faculty going, with no reasonable chance of students receiving related employment. Furthermore, when I did come home, my mother advised me that she was not running a switchboard for my social life, while my father took occasion to remind me that I was brought up in a traditional Armenian home that he claimed I was turning into a second-rate motel. But the beat went on, and so did the music!

Incidentally, my initial plan was to augment my precision machining trade with an engineering degree and learn to set up robotic systems. After seeing that his son's education was slipping away as a result of disco, my father barked the following words: "I would personally like to spit in the face of the person who created disco." But still, the disco ball kept turning week after week!

So now, going back to our main story, when all was said and done, it was the disco nightclubs that provided the backdrop for the music and fashion to flourish. It was where we gathered to collaborate on our schemes. It provided structure and set the stage for us to become stars, and it was where the cultural components of disco came together to create the final product. It was these clubs that protected us from the horror of being alone during the celebration of youth. Many will have their own memories, but the centre stage of all nightclubs and the epicentre of the disco universe was Studio 54 in New York.

Studio 54

Right in the heart of Manhattan, the Studio 54 location was originally opened in 1927 as a theatre named Gallo Opera House, then in 1976 it was transformed into a nightclub by business partners Steve Rubell and Ian Schrager. During its heyday, Studio 54 became perhaps the greatest assembly of celebrities in a nightclub since the Beatles dropped into the Peppermint Lounge after their Ed Sullivan Show appearance, or when Jackie Kennedy dropped in to learn the twist. With theatrical lights, disco music, promiscuous rendezvous within the premise, and rampant drug use, Studio 54 was the place to see and be seen.

This is where the in-crowd hung out in the late 1970s, and it soon became the epicentre of the disco world. The list of the celebrities who entered the Studio 54 walls is long, some of the attendees included Mick Jagger, who appeared there with the exquisitely beautiful Jerry Hall, and his ex-wife Bianca Jagger frequented the club. Jagger was also rumoured to be having an affair with Margret Trudeau, who also came to Studio 54 while she was the Canadian prime minister's wife. Jagger denied the affair and said, "I wouldn't touch her with a barge pole," he insisted. "She was just a very sick girl in search of something. She found it—but not with me." Considering that it is rumoured he shagged thousands of women this would be quite a slight; nevertheless, Margret Trudeau was seen at Studio 54. But the A-list for Studio 54 goes much deeper, and it includes the following celebrities and socialites that comprised the "in-crowd."

- Andy Warhol
- Cher
- Dolly Parton
- Elizabeth Taylor
- Frank Sinatra
- John F. Kennedy Jr.
- John Travolta
- Liza Minnelli
- Mae West
- Margaux Hemingway
- Michael Jackson
- Olivia Newton-John
- Paul and Linda McCartney
- Rod Stewart

Indeed, this was where all the beautiful people showed up, along with socialites, rounders, and wannabes that unusually round out the in-crowd, because when all was said and done, they did have a "whole new way of talking and a whole new way of walking."

Remembering Some of the Clubs
Disco's finest hours…

But we mere mortals here in a place called Toronto that had created our own in-crowd, and in many cities in North America, each aficionado of disco could remember the place that helped define their evenings in the mid- to late 1970s.

So taking a walk down memory lane, here are some Toronto clubs that some of us might want to remember—or perhaps not.

- 747 Club Buffalo
- Arvives
- Broom & Stone
- Dinkles
- Falcons Nest
- Heavens
- Le Dome
- Le Tube
- Misty's
- Playboy Club Buffalo
- Ports of Call
- The Prince Hotel

The Decline
The amount of energy it took to club night after night was a hedonistic experiment that had to eventually come to an end. The only thing sustaining it was the raw energy of our youth, which obscured the map of where we were all heading. Disco, after all, was in some way a temporary denial against the fatalism of life.

Many things led to its decline; some may say burnout, for which the disco lifestyle was well known. One could argue that disco music was not able to take its genre and pass it on to a new generation past its 1970s era. The Bee Gees never released another *Saturday Night Fever*–type album, much to the glee of rock 'n' roll aficionados. By 1979, Donna Summer had given all she could give; all her disco masterpieces were already created and performed: "Bad Girls," her studio contribution to electro-beat, "Let Me Love," "Let's Dance," and her wonderful rendition of "MacArthur Park."

Hissy Fit in Comiskey Park

Just like Hannibal circled the gates of Rome, the anti-disco movement circled disco and would accept nothing less than capitulation. Rockers could no longer tolerate their sexual frustration, since perhaps, most of their last years were spent in the company of Sears's mannequin dolls that were decorated with lipstick and wigs, as opposed to lovely ladies clad in bourgeois attire. This was their only alternative to hanging around discos. Their mantra was usually "rock and roll will never die," which was their only collective hope for missing the Baby Boomers' last great craze. But the anti-disco crowd drew a line in the sand, and they were not going to take it anymore. It all culminated into what can be called a "hissy fit in Comiskey Park," Chicago, where on July 12, 1979, Chicago radio DJ Steve Dahl of WLUP organized a "Disco Sucks" event at a baseball double-header that featured the Chicago White Sox and Detroit Tigers.

The way the event was organized was that fans were offered $0.98 tickets to the double-header game on the condition they brought a disco record with them to demolish. The question then became why these anti-disco fanatics went to buy the disco records in the first place, since they inadvertently helped boost disco record sales by bringing them to the ball game. Eventually, the records were collected and brought to centre field between games, a huge disco-record fire was started, and a record-stomping event took place. In fact, some of the record-stompers, with their single-digit IQs, were inadvertently learning some disco dance steps and becoming more fluid in their dancing, and any sort of dancing contradicted their manifesto, but they were probably too drunk to think this deeply. Yes, they did the bossa nova watusi twist and stomped on and burned disco records in what was a form of hoping for sexual emancipation, and the only thing that stopped their freedom march in the seventies was disco, according to their line of thinking. Eventually, this turned into a mini riot as they did their best rendition of rioting English and Italian soccer fans during the European cup.

"Disco sucks" was the slogan that united this audience as they worked themselves into a frothy and collective hissy fit. The anti-disco movement, with its campaign slogan and platform of unrivalled scholarly depth, contained only those two words, with no intellectual reasoning of how and why. Much like a political campaigns, the anti-disco movement had no substance except to polarize the two camps of pop cultural thought. Armed with shallow slogans, followers of both philosophies would be hard-pressed to chew bubble-gum and tie their shoelaces at the same time. The difference, though, was that discologists were in a perpetual state of celebration of sorts. What made it especially alarming was that, in some respects, this collection of young rock 'n roll males had been involuntarily chastised for at least five years, compliments of disco, and Comiskey Park offered their last great hope outside of a house of ill repute to free themselves from this less-than-ideal outcome. Rock fans had, in some cases, become vitriolic toward disco, since their social lives and sense of popular cultural norms were at odds with the times. Put differently, they were twenty-two years old going on forty.

Much gets lost during the late seventies when accessing rock music's progressiveness. Using the world as an example, it was much like the East's bitter disdain for the West; it only serves to mask their own failures and philosophical backwardness. Rock fans had spent so much time in their contempt for disco that they forgot to look at what their genre offered or had become.

The British Invasion passed a decade earlier, and much of what is considered classic rock's finest contributions had really been written by 1976. For example, the Rolling Stones had already produced all their finest singles and albums, including "Angie," "Satisfaction," and "Sympathy for the Devil." The Who had created their finest; Led Zeppelin, by 1978, had created all their masterpieces, the most notable being "Stairway to Heaven." In Canada, the Guess Who had all gone their separate ways (still by far the most inventive pop band Canada has produced), and, of course, the Beatles never participated in the 1970s.

While rock fans had a strong distaste for disco, their genre had changed, and the 1980s gave them a new sound called new wave, which was at odds with what is often referred to as classic rock, because when they took a moment and stopped throwing stones at disco and turned their attention back to rock 'n' roll, their sound was almost unrecognizable. It no longer had the inventiveness it once had; it was no longer the genre of vogue and was not able to breathe new life and pass the torch with flailing hands and give energy to a new generation.

When it could no longer reinvent itself, rock 'n' roll became "classic rock" for a generation of fifty-somethings to pass down to their kids against the backdrop of hip-hop and indie rock music. For much like disco, the candle of its musical masterpieces had passed, only to be remembered. Lacking the clout to define the future, it is left in the conundrum of living only in the past, for the future belongs to those who have the courage to drown out nostalgia and tamper with all the possibilities, insecurities, and unknowns that tomorrow offers.

Some historians like to think that disco demolition night in 1979 in Comiskey Park was the final death knell for disco. Much of their reasoning was that on the day of the disco burning ritual in Comiskey Park, disco music singles still occupied six out of the top ten positions on the US music charts, and by September 22, 1979, disco had no hits on the top ten charts. The story of disco's decline was deeper and more complex than this, because the decline was already in the works, and disco had really given all it could.

There were a host of reasons for its decline; a second attempt in the way of the film *Thank God It's Friday* never came close to producing the energy and originality of *Saturday Night Fever*. Donna Summer exited the disco scene with her last really big album, *Bad Girls*. The Bee Gees were never able to write a second *Saturday Night Fever* soundtrack and did not really participate in disco's incremental evolution. Sadly, all of Humpty Dumpty's men could no longer put back together this cultural phenomenon called disco again, and its pieces now lie in shambles under our reservoir of memories.

By the early 1980s, disco clubs were reduced to cheesy venues within hotels that were catering to social pop laggards who never participated in its original calling card in the first place. Many resort destinations like Cancun, Mexico, had clubs like Christine's, but they looked like relics in 1985, posing as dance clubs for all who never experienced the original magic of disco.

In the end, the fall of disco was self-inflicted, and its manifest destiny was as temporary as life itself. Like some type of giant ball of fire, it burned brightly with vivacity, complemented by incomparable energy, it eventually extinguished itself. But when all is said and done, it left behind a set of cultural footprints that other generations are unknowingly mimicking and owe much to. Maybe disco died, but during its last gasp in 1980, it left behind a dynamic monument called dance clubs, better known today as clubbing. What is less known is that, for better or for worse, disco planted the seeds of rap and hip hop genre as evidenced by the hit *Rapper's Delight* - Sugarhill Gang (1979). Disco was the last great pop cultural contribution of the Baby Boomer generation.

Even today, when we talk of dance music and all the clubs today's youth attend, it is extracted from the legacy disco left behind. Disco has allowed a new generation to mash it and metamorphose it into something they call their very own, without quite understanding the genesis of its genre and the roots of its celebration, because their thin knowledge of cultural history lets them overrate their own inventiveness.

It is disco that provided the phenomenon of the dance clubs that is alive today as a new generation listens and grooves to dance tunes against the shallowness of their techno-culture friendships and doing all the things they will deny one day to their own kids.

So, disco still lives somewhere in that place where we all once played out our dreams, and it is this gift that it gave to the world.

Business & Technology Section

THE TECHNO-CULTURE:
THE TWENTY-FIVE-WORD UNIVERSE,
AND THE SEA OF SHALLOWS

"**W**hat was a starter on a car? What is a steam engine, and when was that invented and who invented it? You keep talking about a typewriter, but I really don't even know what it is. I heard about math, but what do you mean by 'the times table'? And before the calculator, you used a slide rule. Oh! And all that beautiful music was first heard on mono AM stations; how did you stand it? And what is a Sony Walkman?

"I heard that they once had videotapes. Was it true that the best recorded music was on reel-to-reel? Was it better sound quality than digital? You mean that long ago there were genres of music that had lyrics that did not rhyme with *Yo*?

"So connected, yet so alone!"

The false prophets of the blogosphere and related social media platforms exude thoughts of politically correct collective righteousness in their sea of shallows. Like some type of modern theologian, they profess to their followers that the freedom of collective exchange will create a greater whole, but perhaps this will only end up spiralling into a toxic brew of groupthink. Fact and fiction become blurred lines as reporters compete for the race to the bottom by relying on the inaccuracies and hearsay of Twitter, where the emotional carnage of words throws a dagger into the heart of critical thinking.

This a place where intellectual reasoning gets thrown by the wayside into the annals of history, to make way for emotional quips complemented by words of innuendo stirred into a soup of evasive rhetoric, and words are still spoken but nothing is really being said, all in a race for our primal attention. Somehow, we feel that our digital participation will make our lives more meaningful, as we enter the digital twilight zone.

A generation of nocturnal beings is now prowling the earth, many unknowingly celebrating the idleness of their lives by sharing their collective digital irrelevance. There is no need for them to have experience, ability, or training, since their icons have no experience themselves and throw accountability to the wolves. Yet somehow they explain their ineptitude through emotional diversion. Initiatives are started in the name of benevolence, tolerance, and collaboration but quickly degenerate into a digital groupthink that slides into a cesspool of collective and mindless electronic hallucination. These nocturnal beings unknowingly are now drugged into the addiction of the techno-culture, desensitized, with minds ripe for the taking. And the best part is, their minds have been hijacked, and they have no clue that it has happened. It is in many ways the perfect crime! The information age has led them to know a little about many subjects but not a lot about a few subjects.

Unknowingly, they seek a place, a boulevard, a promise for enlightenment and eventually stumble across the digital "Yellow Brick Road." It is here that they desperately try to locate the Wizard of Oz, in order to find that elusive gift—namely, "an attention span"—and *possibly* a personality. It is here that we find Johnny Millennial, as he has been chosen by his peers to represent his generation after much digital bickering. After falling into an unwakeable dream in the Land of Oz, he spends some time walking aimlessly, but one day he is astonished when he meets the lion who, incidentally, has no courage, the tin man with no mind, and the scarecrow with no heart.

"Hi, Lion. I understand that you know the way to the Wizard of Oz."

"Yes, I do," the Lion says.

"Can you please take me to visit the Wizard?"

"Sure," says Lion.

Then Johnny asks him, "Why are you going to see the Wizard?"

The lion sadly says, "Because I have no courage."

Johnny then asks the tin man, "Why are you going to see the Wizard?"

And the confused tin man says, in a confused manner, "Because I have no mind."

Johnny then asks the scarecrow, "Why are you going to see the Wizard?"

And the scarecrow says, in a confused manner, "Because I have no heart."

Johnny is quite impressed, thinks for a moment and then says, "You mean the Wizard can give you these things?"

"Yes!" proclaims the lion.

So then the tin man asks Johnny Millennial, "What is it that you seek?"

Johnny says, "I seek an attention span and perhaps a personality."

Lion ponders for a moment and then says to Johnny, "Kid, you need to join us something awful!"

Days went by as they walked up the digital Yellow Brick Road exhausted and filled with anxiety, fear, and hunger (after all, there are no Arby's, roadside stops, or 911 on the digital Yellow Brick Road), just some witches and occasional shady characters. Since Johnny Millennial has not had to suffer in his sheltered life, these are all new and strange experiences to him, and he is perplexed about how to deal with them. But flirting with the unknown is often how one learns best. After a few more days, horror greeted Johnny when, out of nowhere, the Wicked Witch of the East made an appearance (she probably had anger-management issues and had been out of the dating scene for a while), and

Johnny, without the protection of anonymity of the Internet, couldn't build the courage to trash-talk her as he shivered with fear. He asked Dorothy where entitlement lane was, and she said that it was closed due to road repairs. Quickly, he reached for his smartphone to tweet and send private messages to his even shallower Facebook friends. However, his mommy forgot to get him a digital package that would work in the Land of Oz, since she was too busy driving in her Range Rover to get her nails done, then had to take their dog to the psychiatrist, while she was expanding the outer parameters of her credit card ceiling. Neither Johnny nor his mother ever heard of the new "mobile accountability network" that's required on the Yellow Brick Road, because after all, it was not on Google. His father, on the other hand, had heard of this mobile network called accountability, yet he was too busy taking his male sensitivity classes, spending his time on online dating sites, shopping for earplugs, and had quite frankly become too feminized and ineffective to remember his innate gender role!

Finally, a leader emerged as Dorothy stood up to the Wicked Witch and advised her to shine on, and the witch flew to the moon, or whatever shoebox she crawled out of. You see, Dorothy had natural experiences in life and knew how to deal with such undesirables, unlike the unsocialized Johnny Millennial, who had spent his life hidden in his digital fortress.

Eventually, one day they came upon the Wizard's ostentatious castle. Johnny, being self-centred and never having experienced life outside the comfort of his keyboards and smartphone, cowered in to the front of the lineup to see the Wizard. As the lion and tin man patiently lined up behind him, Johnny Millennial knocked on the Wizard's door. Finally, the Wizard invited him in and asked, "Why do you come to the Wizard's palace?"

Johnny then sheepishly asked, "Oh! Mr. Oz, I need you to give me an attention span and a personality. Oh, and while I have your attention, do you have an extra Apple 16 with a data plan?"

"I would, son, but I can't right now. You see, I am busy updating my Facebook profile, and I am being unfriended, and my fan page just got taken down by Facebook for contravening their usage policy. And Mrs. Oz just found out that I have been visiting dating sites! Now leave me alone, kid, and put your requests up on Facebook like everyone else."

Johnny felt dejected, sad, and cried, but eventually the Wizard called him back, went into his room, and came back out after ten minutes to give him an envelope to be opened only when he arrived back home.

But still, subconsciously, Johnny Millennial wondered and thought that perhaps by being digitally naked, the struggle itself to reach the Wizard was the lesson that uncaged him from his sheltered digital world. He knew he had learned something on the Yellow Brick Road but was still not sure what it was.

When he arrived home, his mother was on the phone trying to get their dog on the Dog Whisperer show, while she advised Johnny she had to go to Saks Fifth Avenue to buy a $3,000 gown for the Feed the Children gala as she did what she does best, talking from both sides of her mouth.

Finally, as the evening came, Johnny decided to open the envelope that the Wizard had given him. It read, "Dear Johnny, I give to you a gift called struggle, and the story of struggle is what builds all greatness and serves as the vehicle to bring out our finest moments. For struggle is the story of humanity's quest to create, accomplish, and be self-made and reliant. Because it is through the opportunity of struggle that one learns to focus and build personality. So, Johnny, I have given you this gift that is often masked in pain, but it is now yours to hold and cherish." (Yours Truly, *The Wizard of Oz*).

With great vestiges of hope, the marvel of today's technology, with unparalleled promises, often serves as a clinic for anger management. It has become an infinite venue of collective intellectual irrelevance in the way of trolls, comments, etc., as they clog the lines of the digital passing lane. It is a glorious time to be alive as humans flirt with some of the greatest technology ever created, both in absolute and relevant terms. This latest dose of inventions fosters economic efficiency, freeing us from mundane tasks yet enslaving us with a type of digital addiction that is defining a new normalcy. It is this great summit of knowledge that our minds are coming to terms with, and how we deal with it is etched in the historical lessons of technological evolution and the Frankensteins that our innovations have sometimes created.

There have always been naysayers to mankind's quest for knowledge; many have said it could not be done, but vision is the commercial process, as much as necessity is the mother of invention, that brings ideas to market. There was a time when medical thinking claimed that if a human were to travel in a car at a speed above twenty miles per hour, they would suffer a heart attack.

Each generation has a unique set of experiences that help define its sense of self and a unified rallying cry, and these collective experiences help define combined purpose. The greatest generation saw the combination of the Great Depression and war, as well as the initial dividends of peace, while somehow they found a way to put a man on the moon. The Baby Boomers' rallying cry was to rebel, create masterpieces of pop music, and challenge the normative structure of society. They invented computer technology as we know it and the Internet, while singing anti–Vietnam War chants.

The Internet generation—millennial, gen Y—has first seen rapid-fire communication technology, the Internet, mind-piercing advanced disruptive technologies that take efficiency and human comfort to a new level, the democratization of knowledge, contraction of the globe, and 9/11. All this in the midst of never-ending perpetuation of undefined wars and conflict with no set of attainable objectives challenging the idealism of their youth.

A BRIEF HISTORY OF THE INTERNET

The roots of the Internet really go back to President Eisenhower's 1958 ARPA (Advanced Research Projects Agency), a military application initiative to create an electronic communication system. This led to packet switching, which was required for computers to communicate the way we know it. By 1969, Leonard Kleinrock of UCLA's engineering school and Douglas Engelbart with his NLS system at SRI International interconnected to the University of California. By this time, this connectivity was really referred to as the ARPANET. Realizing that we have no time here for an academic dissertation on Internet history, so let's just get on with it.

For practical purposes, 1994 is the beginning of the Internet age, since early adopters were on board and the early majority was getting ready to go on stage. By then, Mosaic and the more popular Netscape were coming into the vocabulary, and eventually Internet Explorer became the standard browser. In respect to the Internet, almost anything before 1994 was still in limited use in its teething stage within the military, academia, and technology buffs.

Of course, there were chat boards and dial-up connections with only the most adventurist having access to broadband. Later came a host of peripheral and incremental innovations, as well as enablers, which included affordable broadband and higher-speed processors. As a side note, Apple tried to ensure a closed-end system, meaning that their computer user had to purchase their software to run exclusively with their hardware, which was hardly the hallmark of democratization and consumer choice. Incidentally, this almost led to the company's demise. I realize that there are a lot Apple aficionados who will get worked up into a frothy state if I throw bows and arrows at their beloved, so I might want to be careful with my words. Later, there is a discussion of who invented the graphical user interface (GUI) applications, and it certainly was not Apple. Admittedly, though, the brand affection of Apple is so alluring that it borders on cultish, while at the same time, it now holds the highest economic valuation of any brand in the world, at $98 billion, since it positions itself as technically savvy, easy to use, and a techno-cultural fashion statement of the new in-crowd. Please see Interbrand's site on valuation of brands. It is quite interesting, and of course if you e-mail me with brand valuation questions, I will respond.

A quick look at the Interbrand's valuation of brand equity quickly lets us know the times we live in, what resonates with the global consumer, and how much the techno-culture has affected all this.

Moving back to the evolution of the Internet, Yahoo and MSN became two of the first popular portals and places for digital gathering, while by 1999, Google started to change the way we do research and affected our lives so much that it has become part of our daily essential vocabulary. Today, Google, with its Android, is challenging both Apple and Microsoft in software operating systems, and "cloud computing" is king of the hill in mobile. Once upon a time, *Encyclopedia Britannica*, which was sold door-to-door as well as in stores, was the foundation of all home learning and educational support systems, and one would go through the printed pages to reference a wide scope of topics from science to literature. Then, in the early part of 2002, it seemed the world was moving by too quickly for the static nature of print, as the digital medium was more dynamic, fluid, and real-time.

It was in the early part of the new millennium that another big disrupter came along in the form of *Wikipedia*. It challenged classical library research and fact-checking, and it has substituted the once essential *Britannica*, making libraries as we knew them relics.

It is interesting to note that as late as the 1990s encyclopedias were trying to adjust their game to the new medium of the newly coined "information superhighway" and multimedia (both terms are now a vestige), and offered volumes on DVD discs. Even classical information providers were still trying to sell company databases on 3.5-inch discs for hundreds of dollars as the CEOs desperately tried to keep their companies and themselves relevant in the emerging third industrial revolution.

This is the time before Dropbox, USB devices, cloud applications, Hightail, and the ability to transfer large files over the Internet, unless you had a clunky ftp site. This was the world of a 14,400 bps dial-up that in 1996 was considered new and fast. This was the world of Kodak and Fujifilm, before the digital camera became the norm and put the American icon Kodak into the annals of commercial history. It certainly was the world before smartphones—hosts of endless applications that tell you everything from weather to traffic and even track your loyalty program cards—and certainly the incorporation of advanced cameras in a phone. It was the world of answering machines on tape, and the place before mobile e-mails, rapid-fire texting, and messaging applications that currently keep business phones quiet but other forms of communication vibrant, to oil the wheels of commerce.

Of course, to round things out, Netflix, Apple TV, YouTube, Popcorn Time, and underground downloads came along to strike fear in traditional TV cable providers. As a result of these disruptive changes, many consumers are cutting the cord with cable companies, who also provide packaged data and ISP services, which in turn hurls them into a competitive theatre economists call "perfect competition," better known in practical speak as commoditization, where price is the only differentiator. Simultaneously, Amazon.com came along and started attaining critical mass in the early part of the new millennium; it is currently disrupting the retail model as we know it, with sales of $75 billion, ahead of Target, and over the next few years, it should surpass retailers such as Carrefour, Kroger, and

Costco, giving it the number-two position behind Walmart, which currently has sales of $275 billion per year. Yes, the times are changing, and most retailers in mass market, with the exception of Walmart and a few others, do not have a credible online strategy in place. It is believed that Walmart did more sales on black Friday online than in stores on that same day in 2014.

Shopping mall operators are turning many locations into gathering and entertainment event centres to hold back the online substitutive Godzilla. The jury on the effectiveness of this strategy is still in deliberation as the new young and tech-savvy consumer chooses. Bookstores are now hanging on by their teeth, since they have bloated store overhead that cannot compete with the Amazon.com, which offers both digital and printed books, with a deep list of titles. And the last bastion of "need to try it first"—namely, the religion of women buying shoes—has now gone online, to the dismay of many.

Music now is downloaded and played in transferable formats, from smartphones to computers to modern receivers and USBs in cars, where voice command lets you speak what song you want to listen to in your car. Sync with MyLincoln Touch (please see: http://www.lincoln.com/technology/sync/) came out of the gate first and left Lexus, BMW, and Mercedes in the dust when it came to providing cutting-edge infotainment and voice-activated technology in cars as they teamed with Microsoft. One can even adjust the temperature by voice command.

GPS is almost a must in new cars, since purchasing Thomas Guide in the local gas station has gone the way of watching the best of Lawrence Welk on YouTube, while we have not even started to talk about smart technology. Then again, you can just download a nice GPS program for your Android, buy a $20 bracket for the dashboard, and you are good to go.

Then came the new hangouts for the new digital in-crowd, social media, with a star-studded cast that includes YouTube, blogs,

Facebook, OMG, Instagram, Pinterest, Google, and, of course, Twitter, which completes much of the technological arena today. This has of course been followed up on the various forms of media delivery vehicles, such as smartphones, tablets, and television, which are still being watched primarily by the long-in-the-tooth, while the line between television and computers is now blurred because to the young a screen is just another screen.

We think today is perhaps an unprecedented time of technological change, with incomparable societal impact, and this might be true, but we should not naïvely forget about the first and second industrial revolutions and the rapid-fire innovations that preceded the Internet age. But technology and the speed of technological dispersion is a relative thing, so let's look at some inventions that have changed the course of how we interact as a society; most of which, for the last five hundred years, were essentially American and European in origin. Perhaps then the Internet and its peripheral inventions are not as revolutionary as we all think, in both relative and absolute terms—or are they?

Just perhaps, based on anthropological evidence, and as unfathomable as this sounds, there was a remote chance that there was life on earth before Facebook and even perhaps before disco! So, in the spirit of critical thinking, before we explain the marvels of today's technology in later sections and its by-product, the techno-culture, we should perhaps look at what brought us here historically. It's worthwhile because the stepping stones along the path that has brought us here into this new paradigm called the present is steeped with history, and not understanding our past allows us to be manipulated in the present while not having a clear path to see the promise of tomorrow.

TECHNOLOGY AND DISRUPTIVE CHANGE

We might root ourselves where the wheel was invented, which by most estimations is somewhere in Mesopotamia, or we could argue that Egyptian knowledge of working with bronze and steel was adopted from the Armenians. Or we can fast-forward and discuss Leonardo da Vinci's masterpieces and unparalleled inventiveness that included models of flying machines and even parachutes in the thirteenth and fourteenth centuries.

Change and its difficult reconciliation with the human mind—where the unaccepted is first ridiculed, and then debated, and then finally accepted—are part of the normative process of the human psyche. Eventually, possibility reconciles with reality as the validation of empirical evidence ultimately sobers the unbelievers, and the ones that first ridicule become the ridiculed. This indeed was the case when science proved the earth was round, contrary to the teachings of all three Abrahamic religions.

But getting closer to more immediate industrial history, it seems that twentieth- and twenty-first-century history of technological innovation is steeped somehow in the first two industrial revolutions. So, just before we leap into "we need to talk about now," it might be intellectually prudent to understand how we got here, in terms of technology and its impact.

As humans, we seem to have a rational explanation for the pain of change and often in the initial stages pass off scientific discovery as humbug. Embracing change is not one of our great historical attributes, and ridiculing the new is really a type of denial of the fear that is masked as bravado! Now that we are on the topic of discussing disruptive changes, incidentally, the best book I have read on this topic in terms of commercial disruption is *The Innovator's Dilemma* by Harvard Business School professor Clayton Christensen.

A BRIEF LOOK AT THE INDUSTRIAL REVOLUTION

The first industrial revolution was built around textiles, iron, and steam-engine technologies, while the second industrial revolution gave us railroads, advanced steel/alloy technologies, electricity, the internal combustion engine, and advanced applications of chemicals for industrial use, and the list is just starting.

So, then, perhaps before we get too comfortable or fill our lungs with boastful pride by only considering the current age of technological evolvement, there was once upon a time another incredible era of rapid-fire inventive upheaval that saw more "new-to-the-world" inventions.

The Industrial Revolution, which began in the UK, occurred between the years 1760 and 1840, resulting in a host of "new-to-the-world" inventions that challenged human normative thinking while laying the foundations for the emergence of the middle class. Concomitantly, it fostered unrivalled economic efficiency, lower pricing, consumer price attainability, a relative better quality of life, linking lands by rails while allowing the concept of nationhood to flourish. The Industrial Revolution created a host of disruptive changes both economic and sociological; what follows in this chapter are some of the most impactful, which changed the world forever.

The Textile Industry

While textiles were weaved at home, the cotton gin wheel eventually offered mass production in textile materials by increasing the average worker's output by about a thousand times, thus bringing down the cost of clothing, especially in cottons, to the consumer of the day. Without the leaps in the textile manufacturing industry, disco would never have had its voguish polyester fashion, or better still, mass production of clown outfits for rappers would not have been possible without the Industrial Revolution. Some would argue based on these two points alone that mass production of textiles was not necessarily a good thing. Hence, both forms of pop culture unknowingly owe much to the Industrial Revolution and its repertoire of inventions.

It is the spinning jenny, invented in Lancashire, England, 1764 by James Hargreaves and the advancements in creating lower-cost homogenous weaves that allowed clothing to become affordable. This contribution alone has had economic impact and increased the welfare of so many consumers!

The Steam Engine

Invented in its first commercial format by Thomas Savery in the late seventeenth century, the steam engine touched the human psyche as being the first invention that moved in perpetuity without human intervention, water wheel excluded. The steam engine gave birth to self-propelled automation, modernized water pumping, and was used to power lathes and milling machines, which in turn created consistently precise parts within specifications for the steam engine. It also fostered high-precision parts for other mechanical applications. However, the big breakthrough for the steam engine was that it allowed the invention of something that galvanized and fostered the concept of nationhood as we know it today. What was the technology that linked the concept of nationhood? A gentleman from England was about to change the world's view of travel.

The Railway

"No one will pay good money to get from Berlin to Potsdam in one hour, when he can ride his horse on one day for free."

—THE KING OF PRUSSIA

Perhaps the most awe-inspiring innovations of the Industrial Revolution were the railway and steam engine, and the widespread social implications they delivered could be the context for a thousand books. They were engineered by George Stephenson and Joseph Locke, whose collective brilliance puts them in the league of Edison, and in some respects, Leonardo da Vinci.

I'm not sure what came first, the train or the rail, but the steam engine was a requisite that allowed the movement of the train, as was the concept of machining precision metal parts that provided this mechanization. The rest we can let industrial historians figure out, but this much we know: the first line was opened on September 15, 1830, between Liverpool (the city that later gave us the Fab Four) and Manchester (the great industrial city that probably invented football rioting). Historically, freight between the two industrial cities was delivered by canals, most of which still exist, as evidenced if one takes a trip to rural England between Manchester and Liverpool. As a side note, many of these canals were being promoted as high-flying stocks in the 1790s and caused a stock-market mania that led to a speculative asset bubble that eventually popped. Thus, with more efficient freight movement came more economic efficiencies and associated lower cost that resulted in more competitive consumer deliverables. This resulted in lower cost of goods to market and an increase in consumer welfare.

But the social ramification of the trains interconnected cities and drew large populations from rural life into the fabrication centres of the UK and later elsewhere. Thus, once industries drew skilled know-how, it allowed for an "economic clustering" for certain types of industry. There is much written on clustering by Professor Michael Porter of Harvard Business School in his masterpiece, *The Competitive Advantage of Nations*. In a nutshell, without getting professorial, it means that for industry to thrive, you need your best-related peripheral talent and companies to cluster in a region or a city to support primary operations, and it is this phenomenon that leads to competitive economic advantage of nations and industry groups within a country.

For example, if Lancashire once upon a time had the largest steel industry in the world, it needed a host of peripheral support in the way of skilled labour that understood steel, including metallurgists, engineers, transport facilities, skilled machinery repair people, tooling machinists, and entrepreneurs willing to take risk. In today's world, we can see a modern example in Silicon Valley in way of the IT specialists, entrepreneurs, financial structures, and access to capital, universities, and other related infrastructure to support this type of economic activity. This is the clustering effect that produces competitive advantage.

So, going back to the train, it facilitated relatively rapid and mobile physical connectedness, first for industry, and then for the general population. The railway helped connect towns with cities and paved the foundations of nationhood as we know it today. Once we were able to travel great distances by train for leisure, we started seeing the rest of the fiefdoms until we turned them into nations. Canada itself would not have become a nation without our national railway, and Sir John A. Macdonald knew this. The railway helped to foster nationhood, but still, some so-called nations today are still tribal and in extreme cases failed states.

Even the United States, which really introduced the concept of nationhood to the world, would have lacked the interconnectedness without the railroad to create a unified nation during its inception. The railroad more than likely was the catalyst and structural provider to support the psyche of nationhood.

Advances in metallurgy that centred on developments in smelting steel helped us eventually lay the foundations of skyscrapers in the late nineteenth century, since steel support walls allowed us to build up high, very high indeed. In the Gothic ages, walls were self-supporting, thus putting limits on height.

There were a host of other changes in technology that were the result of British and European ingenuity, including advances in metallurgy that allowed the creation of a machine tools industry that exponentially helped create mechanization, heavy machinery, and a world of precision components and parts that still define the foundations of mechanical engineering. Thus, even today, all modern movement in technological parts, from CNC machines, robotics, airplanes, automobiles, industrial machinery, hydraulics, space missions, to the 3D printer, to name a few, have their genesis rooted in the phenomenon of machine tooling and the related concept of precision scalability of mechanical components. In some respects, this stream of thought helped lay the foundations for the emerging nanotechnology, which means, one day, machines automatically building other machines.

There were mass improvements that the Industrial Revolution delivered, including the advent of improved roads in England, increases in worker wages and conditions, the introduction of sheet glass, efficiencies in agriculture (machines replacing mules), gas lighting (so we could see what our significant others looked like late at night), and chemicals that were used in a host of industrial and consumer applications. Of course, this eventually led to the need for more structured engineering education that took root in the UK and later spread to Germany, which eventually surpassed the UK in many industrial applications. In fact, many industrial applications first invented in the UK were transferred to Germany, and the UK eventually become net importers of these technologies. Before more formal degrees in engineering in the nineteenth century, the design of technology was really dominated by tradespeople, tinkerers, and inventors of various sorts.

Resistance to change is not a new human phenomenon and is really concomitant with all disruptive shifts, and much like the middle class loathing and dragging their heels during the cusp of the digitally driven third Industrial Revolution today, the same held true in the Industrial Revolution as many skills became outdated, but not the worker's will for entitlements. Sadly, disruption leaves behind many workers with dated skills, and this does admittedly create a conundrum that is difficult and leads to many social issues. The First Industrial Revolution, with its relative automation, displaced many craft workers and weavers, leading to a backlash against the new automated technologies. And even though these technologies fostered consumer affordability, offered more for less in the way of personal welfare maximization, increased the quality of life for many, and generally helped chip away at poverty, it came at the expense of a few.

Those whose livelihoods were at stake protested against all this progress, and a movement against this rapid industrialization was born. When vocal protest was not enough, the dissenters turned their efforts to impeding human progress (which, incidentally, does not happen without pain and drawbacks) and started destroying the machines and factories that took their jobs. These people became known as the Luddites, and they planted the seeds of organized labour, in the way of unions, first in England and then the rest of the world.

This sounds uncannily familiar today with the autoworkers and various other militant unions wanting to preserve their way of life against the forces of progress, advanced automation and the competitive dynamics of the marketplace, all the while producing less for more at the expense of diminutive returns for the consumer and marketplace at large. The protection that unions demand from market forces eventually leaves many in poverty, and a good example of this is India, where trade protectionism (Gandhi was a mercantilist who never quite understood commerce) has left many industries in India uncompetitive, leading the consumer to pay more for less, which fosters widespread societal poverty or at least a diminishment in consumer welfare. Unions have never been an ally of progress, since their interests and those of the society are not necessarily of one, and it is no wonder that their psyche is deeply rooted in their Luddite mentality, as one has to admit that historically, poor working conditions have since been resolved, at least in the developed world. There were a host of other advancements born out of the first Industrial Revolution that go beyond the scope of this book, but this much is for sure, mechanization as we know it today was born out of the first Industrial Revolution and later refined in the Second Industrial Revolution. It was perhaps the phenomena of mechanization and automation that had the societal impact of reducing the demand for more than three thousand years of arduous human slavery and repetitive tasks, whether willing or imposed. But I will let scholars and historians argue this among themselves.

Even today, with misty eyes, as we look at the bottom of the glass and long for the good old days, we just might ask ourselves what exactly was so good and bad about the *good old days* in the first place. The Industrial Revolution laid down many of the foundations for mechanization and related efficiencies, while creating a platoon of engineers in Europe and America, which was about to write the story of the second Industrial Revolution that changed the world forever.

Thomas Edison, a giant of technology.

Tesla in 1890, a formidable genius.

Alexander Graham Bell at the opening of the long-distance line from New York to Chicago in 1892.

Henry Ford with Thomas Edison and Harvey Firestone. Fort Myers, Florida, February 11, 1929.

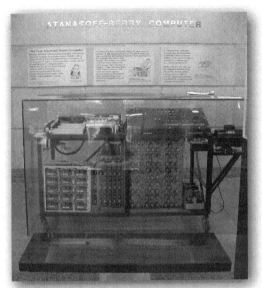

The Atanasoff-Berry Computer, widely recognized
as the first working computer.

The Alto computer by Xerox the first GUI, which they invented and
ignored, choosing to stay with their photocopier business, 1973.

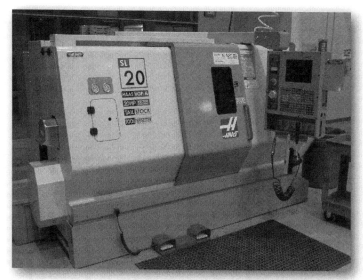

A CNC Turning Lathe machine, the technology that brought out high production and consistently precise parts. It is considered an industrial robot.

An American Family watching Television, 1958.

The IBM Selectric typewriter with the replaceable ball. IBM wrote the book on keyboard ergonomics, which is the basis of all modern keyboards.

An IBM 704 Mainframe, 1964.

Steve Jobs with Wendell Brown at the launch of Brown's
Hippo-C software for Macintosh, January 1984.

THE SECOND INDUSTRIAL REVOLUTION AND THE COMMERCIALIZATION OF TECHNOLOGY IN THE TWENTIETH CENTURY

Depending on what academic school of thought one subscribes to, the second Industrial Revolution happened between the years 1870 to 1914. However, I will extend it to include some of the better-known household names and related commercial applications it bestowed upon us that takes us just past the Second World War.

In the second Industrial Revolution, our imaginations again were about to meet the fruition of reality, which was accompanied by earth-shattering technology that was to forever change the way we interact and spend our days as a species.

As awe-inspiring as the information age is today, with its advanced smart system technologies and so on, it still has not produced something as inventive as indoor plumbing or shattered our core beliefs in allowing us to fly with birds by creating airplanes. True, there have been some incredible incremental inventions such as digitization, medical advances, the Internet, which in some respects is really a telephone on steroids (meaning the base technology of sending information over lines was already there before the Internet), and a host of other incremental efficiencies. However, we need to put things in perspective, since it must be remembered that the computer was invented in 1941, and commercialization by IBM eventually followed.

So, before we puff up with pride about the magical presence of the futures we dream today, it might serve us well to take a brief look at the futures mankind once dreamed of.

But before we go on to a host of other breakthroughs in technology, one needs to consider that inventiveness, either then or today, was not brought about by some socialist stew of utopian thinking of envy, idleness, and mindless egalitarianism with a tad self-inflicted victimization. On the contrary, it was brought about by free-markets, which gives the best chance for incubating human ingenuity and for contribution to flourish both in individual and collective terms.

No other economic philosophy or teaching can deliver or compete with free-markets; true, some of it is disruptive, some of it is painful, but much of it is good. Adam Smith understood this, as demonstrated in his 1776 masterpiece, *The Wealth of Nations*. No other form of economic organization has come as close to diminishing so much poverty, while increasing the quality of life for so many, as has this natural system. As a side note to history, it is interesting to consider that after the British Empire lost its American colonies in 1776, many in Britain thought it was the decline of the Empire. However, now equipped with the philosophies of Adam Smith in its repertoire, the British Empire breathed new life, intellectual energy, and confidence that it could propagate, eventually trading with the United States, while selling a new found economic philosophy.

Later, another British economist David Ricardo, detailed a compelling case for free trade and the diminishment of mercantilism (trade protectionism), where he introduced the theories of both comparative and absolute advantage. Put simply, he posit that protection of industries produces domestically mediocre firms that are held together on the backs of overcharged consumers, and of course, unions are complicit in this by ensuring that a few benefit at the expense of many.

So, going back to the second Industrial Revolution, it disrupted our way of thinking about how we communicate and move, among other things, so let's take a brief look at some of the more noted inventions and the impact it had.

Gasoline Combustion Engine and the First Practical Vehicle

True, steam-engine versions of the car existed as far back as the late 1600s, in the tinkering stage, and there were electric vehicles in different iterations in the late 1800s, but it is generally acknowledged that Karl Benz invented the first practical prototype of the modern gasoline engine automobile in 1885 and mated it with Gottlieb Daimler's two-wheel Reitwagen carriage. Hence, the gasoline driven automobile was born. We now know the origins of the Daimler-Benz Motor Car.

The Ford Model T

> "The automobile has practically reached the limit of its development is suggested by the fact that during the past year, no improvements of a radical nature have been introduced."

—SCIENTIFIC AMERICAN, JANUARY 2, 1909

The genius of Henry Ford was that he created the modern assembly line, leading to a host of societal impacts. It must be remembered that up to this point, cars were only available to the affluent. Ford changed all that when he created the Model T; it was first brought out in 1909 for $850, and by 1914, the price had dropped to $440. Thus, the Model T would cost the average working man four months of wages. Henry Ford gave the gift of mass affordability in an advanced technology. Sound familiar? By 1914, Ford Motor Company produced more cars than all other auto manufacturers combined. His contributions were far wider, since the high adoption rate of cars needed asphalt roads, which were few at that time. Dirt roads were the norm, since the West was still in the horse-and-buggy stage; thus, Ford inadvertently fostered the need for Europe and America to build roads, which were the obvious forerunners of today's expressways.

The story doesn't end there; the Ford Motor Company assembly line really gave the United States systems of efficient and precise standardization that made it the workshop of the world, much like England was during the time of the British Empire. Henry Ford advanced manufacturing systems through the workstation process, where tasks were segregated, while he introduced industrial engineering, a new engineering discipline that involved productivity in the measurement of time and motion with the goal of attaining economic efficiencies. In fact, this is what I started studying before I dropped out of engineering studies, where we would time processes and try to figure out ergonomic positions that would alleviate joint stress, while increasing human productivity. When we look at desk positions in modern offices in terms of layout, and when we look at standardized fast food operations, these processes are all derived from industrial engineering.

Henry Ford wrote the farewell song the for horse-and-buggy and ensured the adoption of gasoline engines over steam and electricity, making use of an unwanted by-product from oil refining, called gasoline.

The automobile substantially interconnected people and fostered further urbanization, offered convenience, and liberalized consumer choice by allowing the masses a time to travel of their choosing, as opposed to waiting for trains. There were drawbacks, of course. This meant that one had to visit the in-laws more often, but whoever said conveniences had no shortcomings?

The medical thinking of the day, as mentioned earlier, was that if a human travelled much past a certain speed, he or she would have a heart attack. Today, heart attacks usually come from auto sticker shock on car prices, but hey, after all, we do need to impress our neighbours.

Electricity

Henry Ford is quoted as saying that mass production would not have been possible without electricity, because it allowed efficient work-flow both for workstations and machine tools. Prior to electrical power, steam engines were used for production, but it could not compete with the missing link that mechanization required—namely, electricity. Mechanization needed electricity as its natural mate to bring it to the forefront as a school of technical know-how. For example, electricity fostered more sophisticated and precision tooling that allowed the lathe and milling machines to build more precise parts.

The invention of electricity is a contentious subject; it is not completely definitive as to when electricity was invented. Some argue it was George Ohm in the early 1800s, giving us Ohm's law. Some argue it was Alessandro Giuseppe Volta, who invented the battery (thus the word *volt*). Others argue that Benjamin Franklin discovered modern electricity. What is clear, however, is that there were a host of chronological scientific breakthroughs, both in Europe and America that brought about electricity as we know it today.

Exhibitions and world fairs were great venues for demonstrating new ideas, and electricity was demonstrated in London in 1881, and then Paris had the first practical use in 1889. However, at the Chicago exhibition in 1893, attendees could see electrified cranes and ride on electric railroads and streetcar systems built by General Electric, which, incidentally, was founded by Thomas Edison. It was in Chicago that the world witnessed the future that was promised.

In 1884, Berlin started using electricity in some quarters, where its brightness was substantially more illuminating than gaslight. Then, in 1886, George Westinghouse, who was famous for buying patents covering a variety of electronic devices, lit up Great Barrington, Massachusetts, for two weeks.

Just like today, it must have been a marvellous time to be alive and take a front-seat view on the disruptive changes that would change our psyches and how we prospered as a species as electricity took the human journey literally out of the dark.

Electricity had a host of impacts. For example, skyscrapers would not have been possible without electric elevators, and elevators would not be possible without electricity. Electricity lit our streets and our homes and provided the emerging industry with structure and controls that brought about advanced manufacturing. Electricity contributed to the progress of mechanical engineering and created the need for electromechanical engineers.

One could write a book on the implications of electricity alone and argue it as one of mankind's greatest inventions, since it changed the world like never before, much like mechanical design. One could also argue that its implications, in terms of pioneering inventiveness, far exceed the Internet.

But what was to come, though, was still unfathomable in many respects, and what followed was a rapid-fire tidal wave of innovation that would awe the world. Some of it incremental, but really much of it was new to the world, and harnessing electricity into a commercially viable technology laid much of this groundwork.

The Telephone

"The latest American humbug."

—THE LONDON TIMES

"This device is inherently of no use to us. We do not recommend its purchase."

—WESTERN UNION, 1876

"It is a scientific toy," said the men of trade and commerce. "It is an interesting instrument, of course, for professors of electricity and acoustics; but it can never be a practical necessity. The telegraph is good enough for us!"

—GERMAN ATTITUDE TOWARD THE TELEPHONE IN 1861

The telephone was initially greeted with skepticism. For example, when Berlin's first telephone directory was published in 1881, it was described as the "book of fools."

Germans consider Phillip Reis to be the inventor of the telephone, since he did develop an instrument that could transmit music in 1861 and just came short of transmitting sound. But he walked away frustrated due to the lack of commercial support for his endeavour, since the thinking in Germany was that the telegraph was more than sufficient.

There was, however, a person who was born in Edinburgh, Scotland, schooled in London, lived and invented in Canada, and commercialized his inventions in the United States. His name was Alexander Graham Bell, and perhaps his impact was greater than that of the wheel, and even mechanization. In many respects, the telephone is the father of the Internet, since it did lay down the lines for communication in analogue format, which somehow sparked the imagination that eventually led to today's digital rapid-fire communication.

The first example of clear speech, as we know it, was made between Alexander Graham Bell and Thomas Augustus Watson, in March 1876, and the first long-distance demonstration was in August 1876, between Brantford, Ontario (home of a pretty good hockey player named Wayne Gretzky) and Paris, Ontario.

Some early detractors posited that the telephone would diminish the art of lettering in the society at large (much like texting and other forms of high-speed communications are being blamed for the abomination of the English language today).

Penmanship did not diminish due to the advent of the telephone, while computers, especially word processors, allow the writer to reconfigure words and sentences into more pliable rhythm, thus, saving on ink and erasers. In fact, word processing allows one to ponder and massage sentences like never before. It can therefore be argued that word processors increased the quality of the English language.

Much like the train, what the telephone actually did was eventually connect people on even a deeper level, further bonding the evolving concept of nationhood while creating efficiencies and new formats in which to argue with your significant other.

The telephone created efficiencies both in commerce and people's daily lives that were unfathomable compared to the Pony Express and telegraph, and much of communications technology today is a derivative of the telephone. The telephone made news travel much faster than any technology before.

The Airplane

"The aeroplane will never fly."

—Lord Haldane, Minister of War, Britain, 1907

Mankind's fascination with understanding the majesty of flight, even after studying the magnificent abilities of birds, is as old as the human species itself. Since the beginning of dawn, the puzzle of flight had eluded us, as it seemed that our imaginations and the reality of flight for so long and by so many could not be reconciled.

This was about to change. So then, where do we start? When someone watched paper or leaves fly away or kites being attached to humans in China as far back as the first century, do we consider the models of the aircraft Leonardo da Vinci designed to be the blueprints for the modern aeroplane? Some of them included a parachute, a human tied to a machine, and even a helicopter. Or do we consider that, in 1781, the first manned flight that had humans aboard took place in a balloon over Paris? The first airship that was to have commercial potential was a nonrigid airship, commonly referred today as a blimp, and the first most successful attempt was by a Brazilian, Alberto Santos-Dumont, who combined the gasoline engine with an airship blimp for a thirty-minute flight over Paris in October of 1901. There were visions of commercial travel by nonrigid airships for both passenger and commercial applications that never really came to fruition as a practical form of transportation, and so blimps saw limited use.

The Italians used airships in their first bombing application during the Italo-Turkish War in March 1912, and in the early stages of the First World War (the one that was to end all wars...hmm!) the French, Germans, and Italians deployed airships for reconnaissance and tactical bombing. But near the end of the war, their use as a military weapon became painfully vulnerable, since they were quite easy to shoot down.

The Germans still felt there was commercial application for the nonrigid airships, which offered intercontinental flights for passengers, including destinations from Frankfurt to Recife, Brazil. Zeppelin, a German airship company, expanded its offering by starting a passenger service between New Jersey and Germany, which ended in a horrific crash in May 6, 1937, in front of cameras and live radio broadcast that captured the horror and played it in theatres the very next day.

By the early 1900s, the seeds of change were sown, even though it was not evident to the unperceptive mind that the emerging technology—namely, the airplane—would be victorious.

Unpiloted, engine-driven flight was pioneered by Samuel Langley as early as 1896. Even with funding of fifty thousand dollars, which was a handsome amount of capital at the time, still Langley could not produce a manned, engine-driven flight. The problem was that he could not master the human controls required for flight stabilization.

That was to change, as the Wright brothers had experimented with and solved the problems of power and controls. However, what really gave them the other missing link was having their own skillful mechanic, Charlie Taylor, who built a lightweight aluminum engine, and for those who know the history of aluminum engines and the metallurgic challenges and advantages they provide, this was an achievement in itself. What's also interesting was that many of these skillful people were engineers in their own right. Even in the late 1800s and early 1900s, it was still a developing discipline.

Then, on December 17, 1903, mankind's parameters of thinking were changed forever when Orville Wright made the first documented engine-driven flight in Dayton, Ohio, that lasted a whopping twelve seconds. However, the local *Dayton Journal* newspaper would not publish the story, saying the flight was too short to be of importance, even though it was captured in a famous photograph. Thus, the media really missed out on that date, perhaps the greatest technological achievement in human history, and probably the most liberating. But then, the media has always had a history of discussing topics from the outside looking in.

In 1904, the Wright brothers greatly improved on their endeavour and flew the first complete circle in what today we refer to as the engine-driven airplane, covering 4,080 feet in under two minutes.

Even as late as 1908, French media questioned the legitimacy of the Wright brothers' flying machines but would later have to eat croissant, with no butter, when the brothers later flew over France. Thus, the era of air travel was born.

Concomitantly, the era of aeronautical engineering was born as a result of what the Wright brothers accomplished against the headwind of occasional human backwardness.

Of course, airplanes first advanced in military applications, equipped with machine guns, resulting in famous World War I dogfights. The first commercial flights were technically offered in 1914 by a company called the Tampa Airboat Line, founded by Glenn Curtiss, which offered a twenty-three-minute service from Tampa Bay to St. Petersburg, Florida.

Then we saw the first practical commercial flights in the 1920s, and flying became more comfortable in the 1930s, when higher altitudes were accommodated by pressurized cabins and in-flight comforts, including a trained crew of stewardesses. The first stewardess was Ellen Church, a trained nurse from Iowa, who was also a trained pilot; though she was turned down for a pilot job at Boeing Air Transport, the predecessor of United Airlines, Church was hired as the first stewardess when she proposed that trained nurses would calm the public's fear of flying. She embarked on her first trip on May 15, 1930.

As head stewardess, Church hired a team of trained nurses, better known as the "sky girls," and thus the role of the flight attendant was born. Today, United Airlines recognizes Ellen Church as the world's first stewardess on airplanes, however, the first flight attendant was German Heinrich Kubi, who in 1912 served on the Zeppelin airships.

The Germans invented jet-plane technology in the latter part of the Second World War, with the world's first jet-fighter aircraft, known as the Messerschmitt Me 262 *Schwalbe,* which was later followed by the world's first jet-powered bomber aircraft, the Arado Ar 234.

However, commercial travel was ushered in by the British with the de Havilland DH 106 Comet series of jet planes in 1952, the first production commercial jetliner. It made the earth smaller, offering a customer-friendly, quiet cabin and reducing travel from New York to London to eight hours. The Comet, being a pioneering technology, suffered from safety issues that led to a host of tragic crashes, damaging the brand and reputation, which then made room for the late entrant.

The Americans introduced the practical Jet Age by way of the efficient and safe Boeing 707 and captured the world market for commercial jet aircraft. The Jet Age had arrived, and the world became a smaller gem to bounce around, along with the glamour and romanticism that Pan Am Airways provided. This was of course complemented by a bevy of lovely stewardesses that offered passengers much visual aerobics.

It is this period, starting in the 1950s to 1960s, which is often referred to as the golden age of air travel; travelling stars and celebrities of the day were referred to as the "jet set," since they had the financial means to travel in the early days of the high-speed Jet Age. Many of these shining stars and socialites were the people who flew to Paris for the weekend or dined in Rome, with the paparazzi in full tow. It was a thrilling time to be glamorous; on the other hand, it is almost always a thrilling time to be glamorous. But then again, for those who want to pretend to be glamorous, they can upload their lives on the social media in the hopes of having some type of recourse to disposition.

Interestingly, unlike other industries, passenger jets have only marginally increased their speed since the late 1960s, and the concept of supersonic passenger travel never quite materialized, except with some flirtations with the Concorde, which has since retired. So, if Moore's law states that microchip processors would double in speed every two years, which has held true in the digital revolution, this has certainly not been the case with commercial jet travel.

In closing on the implications of airplanes, it could be argued that it has changed the human story of technological revolution more than any other breakthrough. Consider then how much the human psyche has changed since man's quest with flight. For example, if we had an airplane five hundred years ago, and it landed in a crowded city in front of thousands of people, they would be so awed and breathless that a new religion could have started. But today we consider the once impossible notion of flight to be normative.

This much can be said: mankind's ability to master flight provided an unexplained confidence into all that was possible by humans, both glorious and tragic.

From Still Pictures to Film

The world we see today of easy digital video uploading to YouTube owes much to the past, since there was a succession of inventions that changed the world and have now delivered us into the third Industrial Revolution we are seeing today.

Let's start with still pictures, which we take for granted today. Consider what our sense of documented history would be like if we'd had still photography two thousand years ago. Would it show a victor's history or that of the fallen? Would organized religions be held accountable to support assertions with visual documentation? What did our ancestors really look like? What if we had captured in pictures Beethoven's moments of creating the sonata?

At best, before the 1800s, we relied on critical history, which the Greeks first gave us, supported by romanticized paintings of our fallen icons and indelible moments in history, both in savagery and glory, as our values evolved.

The first documented attempt to create still pictures, although it ultimately failed, was by Thomas Wedgwood, around 1800. Then in the 1820s, Nicéphore Niépce, with relatively crude results after several days of exposure, created the first known pictures. But it was Niépce's associate, Louis Daguerre, who refined photographic images, better known as the Daguerreotype process, which required only minutes of exposure and was commercially introduced in 1839. It was in that year that practical photography was introduced.

Eventually, a farmer from Cambria, Wisconsin named Peter Houston came along and invented the roll-film camera in 1881 and licensed this patent. Then George Eastman came along, better known for his affiliation with the iconic Eastman Kodak Company, and as a result amateur photography was born. Ultimately, by the early 1990s, digital pictures came along and allowed our moments to be shared at warp speed.

But once upon a time, Eastman Kodak ruled the high seas of the photographic world with a near monopoly on photographic film industry, and this American icon now fades into memory.

So then the question is, what impacted the world more, Instagram or the invention of photography? What would Facebook be without instant photography and the compulsive and sometimes-narcissistic need to visualize the minutes of our lives for the whole world to see? Without photography, what would we be sending out on our smartphones? This much is for sure: today's instant makers of visual gratification in the way of Instagram, Pinterest and the likes, perhaps do not realize it, but they sit on the shoulders of inventive giants and the earth-shattering innovations of pioneers that created pictures and then moving film, as we are about to see.

Motion-Picture Film

"The cinema is an invention without a future."

—*Louis Lumière*

We take for granted going to a film and the gargantuan amount of video, television, and online choices available on YouTube, Popcorn Time, Hulu, and Netflix, to name just a few. Perhaps it might be a lesson in humbleness to step back and peel away the layers of progressive technological film history to discover the true genius of the advent of the motion picture.

Motion-picture film was a "new-to-the-world" invention, and the first relatively crude version was a device patented in 1867 by William Lincoln in the United States that showed animated pictures or movies. The technology involved moving drawings or photographs that were watched through a slit in what was called the "zoopraxiscope".

However, it is Louis Lumière of France in the late 1800s who gets credit for the portable motion-picture camera, because he and his brother put together modern motion pictures by mating three separate technologies—namely, the motion-picture camera, moving film, and the film-processing unit.

But it was Thomas Edison in 1896 who showed the first commercially viable projector in the United States in the way of the "Vitascope" projector. However, there is a wide body of evidence that shows that Louis Le Prince had shot horse-drawn and pedestrian traffic in Leeds, England. Le Prince is regarded by many film historians as the father of motion pictures, having made pictures years before Edison and the Lumière brothers.

The Nickelodeon was the first film theatre that showed only films and was opened in Pittsburgh in 1895.

Films in this period were only a few minutes long, but early theatres would play enough of them to create a thirty-minute or more viewing as a paying event. Eventually, thousands of Nickelodeons sprouted worldwide.

It was from the advent of film theatres that silent films like *Keystone Cops* and the Charlie Chaplin era came. Sometimes there would be a commentator in the theatre who explained the scenes or an orchestra accompaniment supporting the film. The concept of sound in films came about relatively late because of technical audio-synchronization issues, but finally in 1921, Warner brothers released *The Jazz Singer,* ushering in what was then known as *talkies*, meaning film with sound.

Then came colour films, which surprisingly were in the pioneering stages in 1899 by British cinematographer Edward Raymond Turner. The technology evolved by the 1920s to Technicolor, which is a term many of us remember. Even with the support of perhaps the most famous film ever made in colour, *Gone with the Wind,* released in 1939, technology did not usher in the change to colour film, as one would expect, or create the tipping point for colour film production.

That would come later; as history shows us, the diffusion of colour film was a long, drawn-out process when we consider that by 1944, only 12 percent of American films were in colour, and by 1954 the number rose to over 50 percent. What changed this was television, since by the 1950s it started to be broadcast in colour. This alone was the end of the monopoly on expensive Technicolor.

It is also interesting to note that 3D movies were available in theatres in the 1950s, and before the Second World War, there were various home-movie cameras on the market, although not relatively cheap. However, what really made taking homemade motion films practical and easy was the advent of the camcorder.

The first camcorder originally ran on analogue tapes, and the first VCRs were introduced in 1971, soon after the great war between Sony's Betamax (1975) and JVC's VHS (1976) took place. Many, including my friend, John McAulay, a professional filmmaker with whom I did occasional work for in the 1980s on film sets, widely acknowledges that Betamax was a superior format. When I spoke to John in respect to this, he sent me the following comment.

"Sony was able to capitalize on the demise of Betamax as a consumer format by introducing its professional format in 1982 (intended primarily for news-gathering at the time), which utilized a slightly modified and upgraded version of the Betamax tape cassette, as well as higher resolution recording and playback electronics. It was this development that eventually led to the advent of the integrated video camera/recorder combination that became known as the professional "camcorder" and was subsequently also introduced in lower-resolution form using VHS, 8mm, and eventually digital cassettes, as a consumer format."

As we all know by now, the undisputed heavyweight championship in terms of consumer adoption was eventually won by the VHS format, even though Betamax was a superior product.

The video format spawned a video-rental industry that is now generally defunct, while putting an end to adult-film houses that widely proliferated in the early 1970s, since people were watching adult films at home on VHS.

By the 1990s, the DVD began replacing VHS, which is now relegated to the history of industrial design. Still, we have Blu-ray players in high definition that give us mind-blowing visual and sound quality, only to see 4K Ultra HD TVs pushing the technological goal line even further.

Finally, it should be noted that more than likely, digital film is the game-changer that has allowed social media to gain legs when it comes to visual motion, since one no longer needs a clunky digital camcorder. Thus, it is because of digital film and pictures that the in-crowd can upload pictures on Instagram and the likes as the privy events of our lives are willfully shared. The digital film quality of smartphones, although not as good as video cameras, has increased by leaps and bounds, making a business out of catching our lives spontaneously. At the same time, it is perhaps the phone video that has captured indiscretions and outright criminal acts, leaving many defense lawyers to argue to the jury that age-old phrase, "Are you going to believe what you see or what I am telling you?"

It was film that first allowed us to see how we collectively thought of ourselves as a nation by watching our society for the first time in recorded motion picture on the big screen, so as to have something to compare our lives to. It was film that perhaps galvanized nationhood, much like the train and radio, and it was film that made way for television. Television would not have existed without film, and that would mean a world today without YouTube.

Perhaps it is film that to this day romanticizes our senses, gives us escape, and lets us drift off from the trials and tribulations of living in the modern-day fast lane.

So then, one might ask the question, what was a bigger technological breakthrough, in absolute and relative terms, YouTube or film? And what impacted the world more? I propose the following boulevard of thought on this, in terms of comparison. Motion pictures gave us the shock of moving pictures, to see as how we look in our natural movements of the human body. Filmmaking also allowed us to see how the rest of the country lived in real motion. YouTube, on the other hand, is the democratization of film.

For more reading see these sites:
http://en.wikipedia.org/wiki/History_of_film_technology;
http://en.wikipedia.org/wiki/History_of_film;
http://en.wikipedia.org/wiki/Movie_theater.

The Pioneer versus the Emulator

Commercial history is littered with pioneers that were later taken over by a more analytic incumbent who moved up the learning curve by studying the pioneer's mistakes during market introduction. So it might be a good time to briefly examine the topic of pioneers, analyzers, and late entrants, since examples of this are quite abundant in the history of technology section. What is certain is that the rewards for a new-to-the-world innovation are a mixed bag. As we saw in *The Airplane* section, Boeing employed this strategy against the very innovative de Havilland Aircraft Company, when the Comet jet plane's safety issues were studied and rectified by Boeing as the late entrant. Hence, Boeing eventually came to dominate commercial jet manufacturing.

The story continues with a host of examples. Consider the story of the computer, which was first introduced as the Atanasoff-Berry computer (ABC) in 1937. The industry was later dominated by IBM and Burroughs, just as diet cola was first introduced in the 1950s by Cott but was later taken over by Diet Pepsi and Tab. And, of course, there was the handheld calculator, first introduced by Bowmar, as well as one by Canon, but that market was overtaken by Texas Instruments. Turning the clock forward, complex scientific and business calculators are now available on apps for Android and Apple smartphones, so we might be saying our farewells to handheld calculators soon. The plight of the pioneer continued when the videocassette machine was first introduced by Motorola and then dominated by Sony. Finally, the first wireless phone was by Motorola (most of us remember those big clunky things), and that market is now dominated by Apple and Samsung. And of course BlackBerry, which brought the first smartphones to market, or at the very least, introduced rapid-fire mobile communication as we know it, is now a virtual relic.

The story continues. Take, for example, the Honda Civic, which was originally a Japanese iteration of the very cool and inventive British Austin Mini, while very few people who drive a Honda today are aware of this fact. The Japanese perfected this technological science of incremental engineering through a technique known as Kaizen, a continuous improvement philosophy that has helped make Japan an industrial powerhouse, and now the Chinese are continuing this Asian tradition of emulation at the expense of Japanese industry. They lack Japanese quality standards at this time, but nevertheless, they are creating havoc in Japanese industries.

Henry Ford did not invent the gasoline engine but sold the most automobiles in the world for many years. Later, General Motors, led by Alfred P. Sloan and his brilliant designer, Harley Earl, took advantage of the Ford Motor Company's shortcomings by offering various colours, designs, and scales of cars that caught Ford flat-footed. Sloan said the famous words, "a car for every purse and purpose." Thus, it was General Motors that introduced the marketing concept of segmentation, so that we now know where the term "market segmentation" comes from when taught in business schools.

Commercial history is filled with lonely inventors, first movers, pioneers, and romantics that never made it financially, and their stories lie in the dustbins of the history of commerce.

The Wireless Radio and Broadcasting
A Partnership in Dance

"I do not think that wireless waves will have any practical application."

—HEINRICH RUDOLF HERTZ (THE FIRST MAN TO PROVE THAT TRANSVERSE FREE SPACE ELECTROMAGNETIC WAVES CAN TRAVEL OVER SOME DISTANCE)

Much of today's wireless technology, including smartphones, smart homes, hot spots, Bluetooth, streaming, and various other applications centered around the Internet, has technological roots in radio. And the first practical demonstration of wireless would fall back into the lap of Alexander Graham Bell and Sumner Tainter, who in 1880 demonstrated the world's first wireless telephone message.

In 1891, Nikola Tesla started to research radio, and in 1893 he gave a demonstration in St. Louis; in 1898 he demonstrated in Madison Square Garden a radio-controlled boat in a pool of water. Previously, he had proposed that it might be used in telecommunications. This alone, in many respects, created the foundations for robotic controls, torpedoes, and spaceships controlled from Earth, while lending energy to the concept of smart cities. In 1894, Indian physicist Jagadish Chandra Bose demonstrated the use of radio waves publicly in Calcutta.

However, it was an inventor and electrical engineer, Guglielmo Marconi, who was able to achieve long-distance and relatively practical wireless transmission. His company, the Wireless Telegraph & Signal Company, was formed in Britain, and in 1897 he transmitted wireless sound fifty-five kilometres from Salisbury Plain to Bath.

Without arguing who was the inventor (since inventors have to assemble prior knowledge and bring it together, like a symphony of music that creates the totality of new sound), this much is for sure: in general, there seemed to be a host of inventors and tinkerers that incrementally made progress on the manifestation of radio as we know it. In fact, this was the case in the late nineteenth century to early twentieth century, when so many new-to-the-world things first came into our daily lives and manifested incrementally, and, in many cases concomitant knowledge that eventually resulted in a final and glorious invention. This is evidenced by the record of application of trademarks and patents in the United States, the United Kingdom, and continental Europe. It is also fair to say that nations with strong trademark protection laws have a history of being the most inventive, since intellectual property is protected, which leads to commercial rewards.

Wireless technology found its first use at sea in the military, and eventually on commercial ships, including the *Titanic*, which signalled its distress calls using wireless technology.

Radio

Often called "the most prolific and influential inventor in radio history," Edwin Armstrong created many of the practical components of the radio known today. Armstrong combined prior inventions, just as George Westinghouse did, into practical and consumer-applicable uses. For example, Armstrong patented wideband frequency, better known as FM, giving the listener a static-free experience with higher fidelity sound and the receiving technology of the super heterodyne principle.

This allowed listening to the radio without headsets, ushering in the social event of the family sitting around a radio as part of an entertainment ritual. In fact, before television this was the cultural norm, as people listened to news, propaganda, events, and radio theatre, which incidentally perhaps exercises all of our five senses. Expanding on this, radio obviously touched our sense of hearing, but other senses as well. For example, it helped us imagine the sight of the characters introduced in radio theatre, and let us consider what those people looked like. For example, how do we visualize villains? So, one could argue that we could literally touch things that we conjured in our minds on radio, like the soft feel of her lips. Did radio play on taste and smell? Absolutely, to this day, we are encouraged by radio to visit restaurants and taste their menu, which leads us to better discover our senses of smell and taste. But perhaps in a world of radio, not television, it allowed us to exercise and meld all our five senses into being better in touch with our sixth sense, which is perhaps the ultimate form of awareness and intelligence.

Radio was the first practical manifestation of wireless transmission of sound through airwaves. And it was radio that further helped cement the concept of nationhood, since it reduced distance, while nurturing our imagination.

Much like the GUI interface, radio needed to be consumer-friendly, and it was this gift of the imagination, among others, that Edwin Howard Armstrong left to the world.

Radio Broadcasting

Early radio broadcasts go as far back as Christmas Eve of 1906, when Reginald Fessenden broadcasted to ships at sea from Massachusetts. By 1912, the US government required licensing for broadcasting, which they have not done with the Internet as yet.

For practical purposes, radio stations, in virtually all corners of the world, simultaneously diffused in the 1920s (a marketing term for consumer brand adoption). Radio stations started to appear in the Netherlands in 1919, in Canada, the United States, and Argentina in 1920, the UK in 1922, Germany in 1923, Egypt in 1925, Africa and India in 1927, and Qatar as late as 1968. A more comprehensive list is available at: http://en.wikipedia.org/wiki/History_of_radio.

Radio provided news, propaganda (which is a natural by-product), music, and entertainment in general, while changing our social lives and further fostering the type of connectedness that helped build nationhood.

When radio was introduced, it featured free music, and many predicted that the demise of record sales was not far behind. Eventually, stations paid artists for the right to broadcast their music, and in the end, the irony was that it was the radio stations that ultimately helped promote music album sales. In fact, digital downloads are creating the same royalty issues today with iTunes, helping to solve the dilemma for music creators.

Open-ended entertainment was broadcast in America, where the story continued and manifested itself in an endless web of human glee and tragedy. Some of the first included *Painted Dreams* and *Clara, Lu, and Em*, and with the primary audience being housewives. The sponsors were soap makers such as Proctor & Gamble, Lever Brothers, Colgate Palmolive, and Dial. Thus, it is the golden age of radio that gave birth to the phenomenon of "soap operas."

In 1931, 40 percent of American homes had radios, and by 1938, that number grew to 80 percent. Radio gave people instantaneous entertainment value with the switch of a button, much like the Internet today. Radio was perhaps the first medium that allowed us to compare the state of our lives with those of others, to ensure that others scored higher than us on the misery index. In many ways, it opened spontaneous family and community debates on a host of issues that touched our lives, from war and politics to morality, while shaping our sense of collective righteousness.

Radio was the medium where we first heard our nations' leaders, from Churchill's defiant speeches (he wrote his own speeches) to the comfort of knowing that Roosevelt was steering the American ship, even while he was lulling America into a dreamy socialist manifest of the New Deal, which incidentally deepened and prolonged the Great Depression.

Radio created its set of on-air stars, most notably Orson Welles and his masterpiece *The War of the Worlds*, as people were certain that we were being attacked by aliens, only to find out it was a play. But radio's greatest gift was possibly the nurturing of our imaginations as we listened to plays and broadcasts of every kind, endlessly trying to visualize the participants and the expressions on their faces. In fact, in the 1970s, when I was in high school, I listened to the American playhouse theatre on radio, to imagine and relax in the evenings while studying. It's interesting to note that this is when I discovered Larry King on radio, well before he had a television career on CNN.

But with a view of ensuring that we do not turn this into a Harvard debating club, this much we know is true: radio had a host of incremental inventors that gave us the gift of travelling sound.

The visualization of our imaginations, however, was soon to come in the way of a visual and moving British invention known as television.

Television Broadcasting

> "Television won't be able to hold on to any market it captures after the first six months. People will soon get tired of staring at a plywood box every night."
>
> —J.W. RIDGEWAY, CHAIRMAN, RADIO INDUSTRY COUNCIL, UNITED KINGDOM, OCTOBER 1950

Social media, smartphones, and our digital society are not the first attacks on our attention spans, since television did this with regular broadcasting starting in the late 1940s in America.

In 1911, Boris Rosing and Vladimir Zworykin created a crude television system, but the images were not of moving quality, even though film had already been invented.

Television is not an American invention; it is true that electricity was needed first, but the inventor of the television and first practical broadcasts came from a very inventive place. That place was Scotland, which, along with the rest of the UK, had technological pioneering roots dating back to the first Industrial Revolution, combined with an outstanding academic system that brought us engineering know-how and that timeless economic philosopher, Adam Smith.

On March 25, 1925, John Logie Baird revealed the transmission of moving pictures with a public demonstration in a London department store. It was still relatively crude, under twelve images per second, which is the benchmark required to give the appearance of motion to the naked eye. Baird vastly improved on this when he gave a demonstration in his London laboratory in January 1927, and later that year, he transmitted a long-distance television signal over 438 miles (705 km) of telephone line between London and Glasgow. Eventually, his company produced a broadcast that in 1928 made the first transatlantic television transmission between London and New York. Subsequently, his company, the Baird Television Development Company, was really the world's first television broadcasting company.

In 1936 the BBC was the first regular broadcasting service with three hours of programming a day, and during the Second World War, it was taken off the air due to concerns about German fighter planes using its signals as guidance. Another interesting fact of technology diffusion was that the UK had fifty-four thousand TV sets versus forty-six thousand in the United States in 1946. Though this was about to change.

The shock to the human psyche of watching a moving broadcast in our homes was earth-shattering both in relative and absolute terms, especially when we compare it to the Internet. As glorious as the Internet is, it is still an incremental invention compared to the television, and it certainly comes second in shock and awe compared to the invention of broadcasting.

Put differently, television and broadcasting was new-to-the-world and was a giant step both sociologically and technologically, as it changed the economics of the advertising industry because radio and television were the first threat to print advertising, much like digital media is eroding the market share of all of the above.

Television, contrary to predictions of the day, did not signal an end to radio, since each medium has its own intimacies.

Radio nurtures the imagination more, since it is sight-deprived, and television allows us to let our hair down and plunge into the thoughtlessness of a push media, while being entertained and hypnotized, making us feel like we can live forever.

Television broadcasting, much like radio, further connected the concept of nationhood while molding public opinion. For example, it helped determine the outcome of the 1960 US presidential election, when radio listeners felt that Nixon won the debate, but the television audience thought that John F. Kennedy won; he looked poised in contrast to the unshaven and gruff-looking Nixon.

Television was the messiah for the visual side of the human mind, and advertising soon followed in a three-network American universe. What's interesting to note is that in the late 1940s and early 1950s, each show had one sponsor, and this was the launch pad for some very famous brands, including Tide laundry detergent. Tide, which is by far the best-selling laundry detergent in North America and goes under the Ariel name abroad, was the first synthetic laundry detergent. First introduced in America in 1946, it was the three-channel universe in the fifties that allowed Tide to be featured on P&G's soap box shows, and with little audience fragmentation (and as mentioned earlier on radio broadcasting), the term "soap operas" moved from radio format and was parachuted into the television medium. Here is one of Tide's commercials from the fifties:

http://www.youtube.com/watch?v=tMICBp4k-Z0.

Many once-famous haircare brands, which are now off the market, were first launched in the fifties and sixties, shampoos that promised women hope, including Prell Shampoo, White Rain (still a top seller in the discount segment in the US market), Halo (now only found in dollar stores), and Head and Shoulders, which is still a top seller. Below are some commercials of note:

http://www.youtube.com/watch?v=2L7fojO25c8;

http://www.youtube.com/watch?v=QGffuvCr9xA;

http://www.youtube.com/watch?v=gKe4bslwrVw;

http://www.youtube.com/watch?v=4WzAx0c7Z5g.

In fact, many of the famous "consumer packaged goods" brought their brands to mass market via the three-network American universe of ABC, CBS, and NBC. Or perhaps you might be interested in going to the dealer to purchase a brand-new 1957 Lincoln with power seats and door locks, see: (https://www.youtube.com/watch?v=-ca5VN-CyQ4).

American TV shows of that era included the *Texaco Theater Hour* with Milton Berle, *I Love Lucy*, and the *Ed Sullivan Show*, with usually one sponsor owning the complete show and advertising rights, and with only three networks, audience captivation was relatively easy.

It was this type of captive audience, in a non-remote-controlled world, before the billions of websites and social media channel fragmentation, that advertising agencies such as Saatchi & Saatchi operated in. It is this world that is depicted in the *Mad Men* series, with dreamy jazz sounds of the early sixties permeating the background. The advertising techniques, inventiveness, and jingles from that era are still the building blocks of all advertising because even in the digital age, with the advent of social media and major portal platforms, we still need enticing and well-designed billboard ads, banners, content for YouTube commercials, strategies for Facebook display ads, strategies for Google AdWords, pre-rolls, and, of course, we need something resonating to say in sponsored tweets.

In essence, brands still need creative, but what certainly has changed is the platform, along with the hyper fragmentation for consumer eyeballs and minds. It is then fair to say that advertising sophistication and delivery has evolved in digital and social media, but the content development was really pioneered on the medium of television. Because, when all is said and done, Facebook "likes" do not necessarily translate into sales for a brand; *cool* does not mean they will buy in the world of digital shallowness, but incredible media campaigns, compelling advertising content, and great products, do help.

Television, it could be argued, was the fabric that kept us connected once upon a time. There are many indelible moments it delivered. It gave the first news magazine and documentary series, *See It Now*, from 1951 to 1958, featuring the very inquisitive and intellectual Edward R. Murrow, who eventually debunked the Red Scare and Senator Joe McCarthy. Television gave the first great news broadcaster, Walter Cronkite, referred to as the man who Americans trusted most, his chance to report on the times. It was television that brought then Vice President Richard Nixon's famous Kitchen Debate with

Khrushchev. In Canada, our hockey heroes went from the imagination of radio to visualization. It was the medium that brought the end of idealism, with Walter Cronkite reporting on President Kennedy's assassination, and America found a way to heal, as the world was introduced to those four fine lads from Liverpool. Television allowed the *Ed Sullivan Show* to introduce the greatest entertainers of the day, and in many cases the greatest entertainers of all time.

Broadcasting turned the tide of the Vietnam War against President Johnson in the 1960s and awed mankind forever with the 1969 moon landing.

It was this public lens that showed the anguish of a resigning president leaving the White House, as the nation questioned its confidence in government. Television brought images of the fall of the Berlin Wall in 1989 with the demise of the Soviet Empire, delivering us a lone superpower with the long-awaited promise of hope, peace, freedom, and a new age of enlightenment. But sadly, we saw this opportunity lead us into a new age squandered in the suffocating hypocrisy of the victor. And finally, it was television that brought to life the horror of 9/11 and the endless war on terrorism, which does not have the courage to define the enemy.

Mainframe Computers

"I think there is a world market for maybe five computers."

—*IBM CHAIRMAN THOMAS WATSON SR., 1943*

The history of the mainframe computer makes for an interesting story, and as mentioned in *The Pioneer versus the Emulator* section, inventing a technology while bringing something to commercial reality often represents two separate schools of thought. The German inventor

Konrad Zuse in 1941 created the first programmable working computer and is often regarded as the inventor of the computer, but it was still an electromechanical device. The British made significant contributions with the Colossus computers that were used for code-breaking in the Second World War.

However, American know-how gifted the world the first fully electronic computer with the ABC, invented by the team of John Vincent Atanasoff and Clifford Berry, hence the Atanasoff-Berry Computer (ABC). It was conceived in 1937, with a working model showcased in 1941.

But then J. Presper Eckert and John Mauchly created the ENIAC at the University of Pennsylvania's Moore School of Electrical Engineering between the years 1943 and 1946. They eventually had a dispute with the university over patent issues and formed the Electronic Control Company, which brought to market the pioneering UNIVAC I mainframe computer. Later, through a series of acquisitions and mergers, it evolved into Burroughs Computers, a name not well known to millennials but versed still in the memory of Baby Boomers.

Thus, the first commercial sale of a mainframe computer was the UNIVAC I, which was first delivered to the US Census Bureau in 1951, and later IBM, as the late entrant, joined the competitive theatre. The customer list of first mainframes makes for an interesting read.

Date	Customer	Comments
1951	US Census Bureau, Suitland, MD	Not shipped until 1952
1952	US Air Force	Pentagon, Arlington, VA
1952	US Army Map Service	Washington, DC. Operated at factory April–September 1952

1953	New York University (for the Atomic Energy Commission)	New York, NY
1953	Atomic Energy Commission	Livermore, CA
1953	US Navy	David W. Taylor Model Basin, Bethesda, MD
1954	Remington Rand	Sales office, New York, NY
1954	General Electric	Appliance Division, Louisville, KY. First business sale.
1954	Metropolitan Life	New York, NY
1954	US Air Force	Wright-Patterson AFB, Dayton, OH
1954	US Steel	Pittsburgh, PA
1954	Du Pont	Wilmington, DE
1954	US Steel	Gary, IN
1954	Franklin Life Insurance	Springfield, IL
1954	Westinghouse	Pittsburgh, PA
1954	Pacific Mutual Life Insurance	Los Angeles, CA
1954	Sylvania Electric	New York, NY
1954	Consolidated Edison	New York, NY

Source: Wikipedia

It should be noted that these computers were much more predictive of the 1952 US presidential elections than CBS, since the computers predicted a Dwight D. Eisenhower landslide, much to the dismay of CBS, which had it the other way around.

But when it came to the commercial refinement and applicability of computers, it was a company that some might know as International Business Machines. Eventually IBM became the market leader, regardless of Chairman Thomas John Watson Sr.'s lack of vision on the mainframe when he made that famous quote in 1943: "I think there is a world market for maybe five computers." History passed him by. However, his son was much more receptive to the technology and better saw the future and its commercial application.

Even though IBM did not incubate computer technology and started out of the gate quite slow due to Thomas Watson Sr.'s non-support of the technology, it eventually started its march toward market domination with a host of market offerings. Some notable ones included the IBM 701 in 1952, and in 1959 it launched the IBM 7090, with a then-blistering capability of 229,000 calculations per second. It was put in the shopping cart by the US Air Force. The rest is pretty well history.

Today, with the advent of robust servers, the mainframe is relatively obsolete when compared with the scalable environment of cloud applications that include accounting and advanced Management Information Systems (MIS). Expanding on this, the story of substitutive threats goes on today with cloud computing, in the way of Microsoft's Office365, which has many of the features of a server but is maintained by Microsoft online with multiple personal device synchronization, eliminating the need for an in-house team required to maintain it. Some of the very first victims of this change are going to be the livelihoods of the many server technicians, who now find less work in the classical server environment. The story of the cloud is much wider when we consider that Android, Adobe, security software, and backup systems are cloud-based. Now that we are on the subject of backups, it is my experience that many small businesses back up once a week, if that, assuming the data was backed up properly. Subsequently, if they lost their data due to a flood or fire, they have no catastrophe plan. In today's business world, this could mean that enterprises in over 50 percent of instances would go out of business in a few months due to permanent data loss or the hundreds of thousands of dollars in lost productivity costs. You have been warned! Like it or not, we upload our critical information to the cloud, including e-mail accounts, bank information, our personal lives on Facebook, and of course, those digital pictures of the minutiae of our lives we can't help but show the world via Instagram and the like. Being inundated by downloading hordes of software to maintain on our personal computers (PCs) is diminishing, since it becomes evident that cloud computing is one of the great disrupters of the 2010s.

GUI and the Personal Computer

The story of the graphical user interface (GUI) is one of a lost opportunity of a market leader, Xerox missing the next big thing. Here are the facts: GUI was not invented by Apple or Microsoft or IBM. A critical mind could argue that Microsoft and Apple refined and commercialized the GUI and mouse as we know them. There is nothing wrong with this line of thinking, since as proven in other sections, history is littered with first movers and pioneers who fell flat on their faces in terms of commercial success.

The story of the personal computer started in 1970 when Xerox spun off an R&D division in Palo Alto, California, named PARC (Palo Alto Research Center) Incorporated. A team of very talented individuals innovated there (away from the politico of corporate culture), including better-known names such as Larry Tesler, who later moved to Apple and left indelible footprints there. Hence, it was PARC that gave birth to the Xerox Alto computer, which was the brainchild of Butler Lampson and was for the most part designed by Chuck Thacker. A Xerox commercial from 1972 of the newly minted personal computer named the Xerox Parc—Office Alto that showcased the "first graphical user interface", as well as the concept of electronic mail. I highly recommend watching this commercial that's available on YouTube, since it peeks into the future with uncanny accuracy that apparently the senior executives at Xerox could not see some forty-plus years ago:

(See http://www.youtube.com/watch?v=M0zgj2p7Ww4).

Panasonic once exclaimed in their marketing jungle, "way ahead of its time." And this phrase is the best way to describe the Xerox Alto. So, when all is said and done, the Xerox Alto computer commercial envisioned the future of desktop communications technology and gave hints that the Internet existed.

Unfortunately for PARC, Xerox at the time was still enjoying its patented exclusivity of photocopiers, which was a great invention unto itself, and its East Coast management team, led by Xerox president Archie McCardell, who was an accountant, could not wrap their heads around computer technology, and neither could his cronies of former Ford Motor Company bean counters. This is not surprising for a host of reasons, since not only did Xerox enjoy patent on photocopiers, as mentioned earlier, but the brand itself was associated with the only legitimate voice of photocopying. In fact, once upon a time, you did not ask to photocopy things; you asked to have it "xeroxed," much like we do not ask for a paper tissue today but a Kleenex.

It is this type of brand recognition that Xerox had, coupled with a monopoly that drove its corporate culture and its strategic decision-making process, as it had become, in some respects, a hostage of its own success.

The photocopying industry party that Xerox had going on was the model of selling or leasing copiers and then obtaining perpetual residuals on ink, supplies, and the likes. Xerox, as an organization, was a money-printing machine, and it is such an incredible sense of strategic inertia that led to the inebriation from which the hangover of missing the next big thing had not even been considered. Many corporate leaders then lacked strategic vision, as is the case now, but it was the success and patented protection of Xerox that set them up for the failure of missing out on the PC and GUI. Sadly, confidence often leads to arrogance, which then acts as a barrier to stop one from learning.

So the story of Xerox missing the PC party because of the photo-copier gala shows us again how many company leaders just cannot see the future. Considered in a different perspective, if the Xerox management had been Ed Sullivan in 1964, they would not have booked the Beatles to play in front of America.

Eventually, the IBM PC dominated and really brought hardware systems to the personal computer market in the 1980s, and in the early 1990s they tried to mate it with their software, a version of Windows called the Operating System 2 (OS2). Even though their hardware system became the standard, their software system could not compete with the dominance of Microsoft Windows.

Microsoft, of course, ended up dominating the GUI market with its system that was not close-ended, meaning that Microsoft made its software compatible with an IBM personal computer platform, which also included clones, while staying clear of the hardware business. PCs becoming a commodity through the advent of IBM clones changed the market, but few saw that hardware was to become a commodity (economists call this "perfect competition"), since at first, PC hardware was perceived to be an intricate assembly and creation process that always had room for differentiation, as well as technical and brand barriers to entry. Eventually, IBM itself got clobbered by IBM PC clones and spun off its PC business to Lenovo.

As people buy their iTunes, play them on both their iPhones and iPads, (incidentally, the music purchased from Apple, is played on Apple products, unless of course, it's converted), and buy into a company that is making a statement for many of the norms of the techno-culture, we need to understand that Apple did not in any way create the democratization of computers. In fact, even though Apple had and still has a very intuitive and functional graphics interface, coupled with a near-cult following of its brand, it almost went out of business when they felt they it could force people to buy its software and hardware together, meaning that their software only ran on Apple's hardware. This close-ended system engineering strategy was in itself was a gross misread of the market. Further, this line of thinking inhibited technology diffusion.

Additionally, Apple computers unintentionally promote business illiteracy in the sense that basic programs such as Excel have different patterns of usage on Apple. Once high-school and college graduates come into the workforce, moving from Apple to IBM PC requires a learning curve, which has associated economic costs for firms. I realize Apple aficionados might get worked up into a frenzy about the preceding comment, but the fact of the matter is that even though Apple has the highest market capitalization of any firm in the world, its computers are not compatible with network-based accounting systems, such as ACCPAC, Simply Accounting, Sage Business Vision, or ERP applications such as SAP, to name a few.

But in making a case for Apple, it is true that Steve Jobs invented the concept of techno-cool by creating a visionary industrial design and functionalism with the Macintosh, iPod, iPhone, iPad, and most recently the Apple Watch. The story doesn't end there since Apple is the preferred format for the music industry as well as graphic design. Just as a side note, musicians recently forced Apple to make their software compatible with Sonos. But, when all is said and done, Steve Jobs left the world this gift and legacy as he turned industrial design technology into a fashion statement, without the stitching.

However, this being said, Microsoft came out on top with Windows, since it veered clear of the PC hardware sector and stuck to its knitting, which was MS Windows, in an open system. Still, some consider Microsoft to be the corporate boogeyman or long in the tooth, but this has to be balanced with the fact that what Microsoft really gave to the world was a standardized operating system for user diffusion, meaning that one could work one's software on any computer. And in this respect, Apple with its close-ended systems, was simply undemocratic, and if it had its way it would have led to a diminishment of consumer choice.

It can be said that if Henry Ford gave the world the modern assembly line and affordable cars, then Bill Gates gave the world the gift of product standardization in respect to operating systems, while heralding in the PC era, first in the way of Microsoft operating systems such as 3.11, Windows 95, 98, XP (let's skip Vista), and then Windows 7 and Windows 8, and now Office365 cloud. It was also Microsoft that allowed the MS Office Suite that contains Excel, Word, Access, and PowerPoint to be the workhorse of modern business offices. So, on a global scale, it can be credibly argued that Microsoft standardization of PC platforms is what helped the PCs flourish, both at home and especially at the workplace. It is the MS platform that exponentially increased the adoption of the computer age, fostered affordability, and created great productivity gains that allowed economic "lower-cost inputs," while substantially making firms and households more productive, leading to a considerable increase in consumer welfare. If the world had fragmented operating and office productivity software systems, it would have heterogeneous ramifications for global efficiencies, while not allowing consumers or firms to go up the learning curve, promoting segregated software illiteracy.

Some More Inventions

Of course we are going to eventually steer our attention to the phenomena of the Social Media, but there are some other inventions of note that need to be considered so we may compare the plethora of technology today in relevant terms.

So, just before the social media experiences its long awaited roasting, which comes later in the book, I respectfully ask you for just a little bit more of the most important thing we can all give, and that is your time. Just put your feet up and ignore those texts and e-mails, Internet surfing, job offers for staying home at $500,000 per year, your daily cash that you have been rewarded by some benevolent spammer, or perhaps how Kim Kardashian has just been hired as a quantum physics consultant at NASA…

In my personal life, I had the good fortune to be trained as a high-precision machinist when I grew up in my father's machining business. He was a master of master technicians of machining and mechanical things, and his skill set was not only out of this world, but some parts he made in 1969 ended up out of this world, specifically on the *Saturn 5* that helped take the first man to the moon. In fact, he was one of many of highly skilled types that increased the quality of Canada's capital stock, and it is no wonder. We were building some of the finest aircraft in the world in the 1960s and literally had an army of skilled engineers, technicians, and craftsmen that defined our inventive and manufacturing prowess as a nation. Economists call this the quality of the capital stock, and it is sad to see the future without updated manufacturers based on high levels of automation and the peripheral skills required to maintain advanced automation. What is perhaps even more alarming is seeing our youth Twitter their lives away in the latest trendy café with little chance of meaningful employment.

So, getting back to myself for a moment, when my father first opened his machine shop, I spent my summer as a twelve-year-old canvassing doors for new business, since I had learned this skill for my newspaper routes. Hence, I guess I was his de facto director of sales at that time. Then again, I was the only salesperson, with a remuneration package that consisted of lunch and a chocolate bar. I also was the director of floor-sweeping at my father's small business and then worked my way up to chief machine cleaner. Hmmm! At the same time, I was threatened with dismissal on at least a hundred occasions. I am quite sure that my father's relative must have been general George Patton or perhaps General MacArthur, but this much I knew for sure, he had great respect for Henry Ford. Either way, I begrudgingly learned work ethic, self-reliance, and discipline through him, which is more than a son can ask for from his father. Later, I had also taken engineering courses that gave me a solid foundation in blueprinting, industrial economic efficiency, metallurgy, and CNC programing, so this just might give me credible background to discuss some of the following technologies.

CNC Machine

For those that have not been exposed to machining, it is the process of making high-precision steel parts for mechanical applications. Classically, a skilled machinist would make these parts using either a lathe or milling machine, or a host of other metal-conforming machines. Hence, the process was labour-intensive, even though automation existed on some level, including automatic feeders and tracer systems. Still, they delivered relatively inconsistent parts in high-production manufacturing runs. These parts are required for engines, transmissions, pneumatic components, aircraft, space arms, medical devices, and so on.

Thus, once upon a time, when luxury autos like the 1956 Lincoln Mark II was built, Lincoln picked the most accurate parts that came out of their machining bin and compared them to their blueprint drawings specs for accuracy to use on their flagship brand. Hence the term "blueprinting" an auto engine with the best parts available from many, leading to a finer end product.

As an interesting side note, the 1956 Lincoln Mark II was primarily built by hand, priced at $10,000, as it positioned itself against the Rolls-Royce, which sold at the same price point, and in 1956, it offered air conditioning and power windows and seats. Few were made, about 1,300 per year, and a customer list that included Frank Sinatra, Elizabeth Taylor and Elvis Presley. It is considered a masterpiece of industrial design during America's golden age of automotive excellence. More can be learned about this car and its development at:

http://www.youtube.com/watch?v=BeKCc1hSV-I.

Since we now know where the term "a blueprinted engine" comes from, meaning the most within spec parts of a production run, we have a better understanding of the variations and relatively slow productivity in human-made parts on traditional lathes and milling machines, but this was about to change.

The CNC machine, in many respects, is a close cousin of industrial robots that has its roots going back into NC (numerical controlled) machines in the late 1940s to early 1950s, which ran on punch tapes and was invented by John Parsons. By 1959, the NC evolved into what is currently known as a CNC (computer numerically controlled) named the Milwaukee-Matic-II, the first machine with a tool changer.

Without getting into an engineering dissertation, what the CNC does is automate and produce high-precision steel components in mass production, with limited labour, far more accurate and often with fifty times the output of traditional lathes, complemented by less variation between parts. This is because the CNC uses a computer-driven system to change spindle speeds, tooling changes for different processes, and cooling liquids during the steel-machining process, augmented by pneumatics to exert force where necessary at the right technical exertion. From a mathematical point of view, the technology is based on three-dimensional x-, y-, and z-axis movements.

For example, disk brakes on cars are produced on CNC machines, and a host of engine parts, spindles, transmission components, as well as aircraft and military applications. Put differently, it has many robotic characteristics.

Historically, CNC machines cost over $500,000 in the 1980s, and setup times were sometimes days and were performed by highly skilled technicians and engineers at quite a high cost. So unless someone had a large production run, a firm could not justify amortizing the setup cost against the variable cost of parts produced. Today, entry-level CNC machines can be purchased at about $10,000, and more serious ones in the $50,000 range, while the setup time is in hours and more user-friendly due to the advancement of GUI and various other built-in developments.

Today, everyday cars have mechanical components machined to relatively consistent and exacting standards, while being cost-efficient, largely due to CNC lathes and milling machines. Separately, we have seen gains in metal stamping and assembly processes, which are all required for computer parts, smartphones, etc.

Robotics

"Bill" Griffith P. Taylor showcased a relative crude prototype of an industrial robot in the March 1938 issue of *Meccano Magazine*, using one electric motor that had five-dimensional movements and was able to grab parts. However, the first practical robot for industrial application was conceived in 1956 at a meeting between inventors George Devol and Joseph Engelberger, who together helped create the industrial future with the first industrial robot, named the "Unimate," that was first showcased in 1961.

This first industrial robot, Unimate was installed in 1961 at the General Motors New Jersey factory at a cost that in today's money, factoring in relative inflation, would be in the millions of dollars. Robots started performing tasks that included utilizing six axes with the capability of welding, gluing, tighten bolts, handling materials, and paint-sorting, to name a few of the functions.

And oh! Did I mention that robots today are used in assisting surgeons in hospital surgeries? Their present and future are becoming very clear as tomorrow becomes undeniable even for hard-line Luddites. Interestingly, even though robots were an American invention, for a host of reasons the Germans and Japanese later dominated the manufacturing of robots, which is an important part of a nation's competitive architecture. Now, however, the tide has changed back to American and German manufacturers that include Rockwell Automation, and the Japanese are no longer necessarily the market leaders.

Thus, it is these robots that will help bring manufacturing back to North America, in a much cleaner format than it left. Those economists who, incidentally, believed that a service economy would reap great benefits for developed economies, are greatly mistaken. Since much of the service industry has become commoditized, nearing perfect competition, and the imitation gap has closed in software skill sets as well as a host of other talents, it is no surprise that when we phone for tech support, the specialist is often somewhere in India or the Philippines. Yes, our service industry is now being outsourced abroad, and of course politicians are clueless about how to bring back robust middle class jobs. Furthermore, much of the service industry is facing further substitutive threats by the emergence of artificial intelligence that can literally run accounting and legal planning functions, to name a few. With a view of getting a deeper perspective of what is around the corner, I strongly suggest watching the documentary "Humans need not apply" that is available on YouTube.

Today, industrial robots can be purchased from Rockwell Automation or Kuka Robotics of Germany in the range of $27,000; this is what could help pave the way for the renaissance of North American manufacturing. Just ten years ago, these same robots could cost upward of $500,000, while at the same time, these newer robots employ advanced optical technology that has been adopted from smartphone cameras.

If an organization purchases these robots for their assembly operation and amortizes the cost over three years, they are looking at wages for the robot of $4.25 per hour, and the robots cannot go on strike, unlike union employees who have bullied firms demanding higher wages that are diametrically opposed to the tenets of marketplace competitiveness and consumers who get affected in the way of higher prices.

The factory of the future will be loaded with highly trained engineering and associated skilled technical types in the front office, with fewer people in the plant, and those who are in the plant will not be wearing those dirt-covered overalls that we associate with heavy industry. Much in the same way robotics takes away jobs, they have the ability to make North America competitive again, and this is what will drive high-paying careers, not politicians with no real commerce or manufacturing experience. So it might be wise for today's youth to study the sciences and related applicable manufacturing manipulative technologies, since without manufacturing, a nation loses its inventiveness, and in fact, the pilferage of manufacturing in the UK was a major reason for the British Empire's commercial decline. Perhaps North America should quickly learn this sad lesson from Britain. That way we can perhaps spend less time on societal entitlements and more on competitive enlightenment.

I posit then, that unless we want twentysomething and thirtysomething year olds to be idle debaters on social media against the backdrop of having flourishing careers as baristas, we need to perhaps now create the most high-tech skilled workforce in the world. Higher wages for the middle class do not come through entitlement and self-righteous government redistribution of wealth, but through complex and difficult-to-learn advanced skills. This is what will create well-paid and intellectually inquisitive jobs for the future of tomorrow, not shallow speeches and political rambling from industrial illiterates, and not the mediocrity that comes from protected markets.

As mentioned earlier, robots no longer cost millions of dollars each, and the technology is becoming quite attainable to the start-up and smaller organizations. It goes then that the implementation of these advanced and related technologies, including nanotechnology engineering, is the West's last great hope to create fertile grounds for inventiveness and upwardly mobile, sustainable careers.

As much as politicians would have one believe they can save a $70,000-per-year GM assembly line job with six-pack Jack and his relatively low skill set, they cannot, and these types of jobs will not be coming back anytime soon. So, then, if I were twenty- or thirty-something today, I certainly would put my smartphone down for a little while, cool the idle debating and associated intellectual diarrhea of social media for just a bit, polish up my math and left-brain skills, go to college, study as a robotics technician and/or engineer, and create the future of tomorrow. The factory of the future will belong to those that are setting up and maintaining these plants where twenty people work in the office and three in a meticulous plant. With these types of skill sets, there will certainly be much to like on one's Facebook profile.

Okay, so enough of this professorial ranting, but just before we leave the section, I have included a list of other inventions that changed the way we live, some perhaps not as impactful as Stevenson and the railroad:

- Air conditioning, 1902 (American)
- Insulin, 1928 (Canadian)

- Sunglasses, 1929 (American)
- Helicopter, 1939 (American)
- MRI, 1979 (American—Dr. R. Damadian)
- Transistor, 1953 (American)
- Nuclear technology, 1945 (American, as a result of the Manhattan Project)
- First space flight satellite, *Sputnik*, 1957 (Russian)
- Video games, 1958 (American)
- ATM, 1967 (American)
- Pocket calculator, 1960s (American)
- Polio vaccine (American)
- Video game console, 1968 (American)
- Arpanet, 1968 (American)
- First man on the moon, 1969 (American)
- World Wide Web, 1990 (American)

A FAREWELL TO THE TWENTIETH CENTURY

So there you have it; there once walked some incredibly inventive people, just like today on this place called Earth, with limited tools but overflowing at the seams with romanticism, and perhaps this is the precursor to inventions and commercial promise. These inventions and more changed the world but especially the human psyche of how we saw ourselves in both the nineteenth and especially the twentieth century. Many of these inventions had disruptive implications that forever would change how our lives would be lived and challenge all that was possible.

Innovation and romanticism are dreamy bedfellows, and perhaps it was curiosity that fostered technological earthquakes that certainly shook our world, perhaps even more than the Internet, in at least relative terms, and in some cases, absolute terms.

By now, we have all gone into various stages of comatose listening to how marvellous all this new technology we are seeing is, primarily joisted on software, the Internet, and its related offspring. But most of these words sound tired because the future is now, and it can be said with some confidence that technology developed in the first Industrial Revolution and advanced into what we have now, has been responsible for a higher quality of life and the democratization of knowledge.

We sometimes forget to appreciate the present, since without all this technology, our tasks at work would be more mundane and repetitive, while we would quite possibly be riding a donkey to work. Imagine a world without cars, not having a chance to see the world without the jet, not reading under light, no advanced life-saving medicine that has increased the quality and duration of life, no indoor plumbing, no affordable products that factory efficiencies provide that has helped diminish poverty, and then imagine a world where we could not do simple things like phone a friend to give them comfort. It is this world I present to you, without e-mails, texting, and the convenience of Google, without YouTube, the fluidity of *Wikipedia*, and all the apps on smartphones that both free and enslave us, depending on one's preference.

The only problem is that many don't know how difficult it was to create all this new technology that the West gifted the world, and many take it for granted. Most of us today cannot remember the world before social media and how effortlessly we send information across this planet. Because before this, the best speed we had was the telex, then radio, and then as newspaper reporters like Walter Cronkite fed information through the wire, that evening or the following morning, the papers would interpret it. Often this is how the journals of our times were created, which helped create the newspapers of our lives.

What we do with this magical knowledge should be at a higher level than idle digital debating and social media narcissism. Its seems that freedom and its by-products of democracy and technology should together be delivering us elected officials in every corner of the world (though one wonders at times if some people are even qualified to vote). The problem is that all this calling for a new age as we learn to better harness this technology thing isn't translating into freedom, and a good example is the Arab Spring, since they just can't seem to get this separation of religion and state thing that America has been dancing to since 1776. Paradoxically, we should respect that many other nations, and not just in the Middle East, just might need an iron-fisted leader with a touch of benevolence to make them feel loved.

Of course, it is frustrating for the West, which has delivered nearly all the imaginable freedom, progress, technologically and otherwise, that we could think of in the last five hundred years, so then, why is freedom being sent back by much of the world, like some cheap "made in China" shirt bought at Walmart, and all they want is a refund? This is the same type of phenomenon that Richard Nixon struggled with in his book, *1999*, in which he discussed the Vietnam War and was perplexed that American norms of freedom were not being embraced by the Viet Cong. But then again, democracy is not necessarily good for everyone, especially when considering (with much salivating emotion, chest-beating, and little logic) whom we sometimes collectively vote for in this psychological state I call "collective misguidance!"

However, sometimes the intoxication of self-indulging oppression is more enticing, since it inoculates one against the unimaginable. Freedom does not come to everyone, because with freedom comes responsibility, discovery within, the price to acquire it, and the constant nurturing to preserve it.

THEN AND NOW

So, then, in this book we have so far answered what was thought the most perplexing question ever presented to civilization—namely, "Is there life after disco?" But now we have to gather the courage to ask and then answer the most enigmatic question ever presented to humanity, even more profoundly important than the origins of the universe: "Was there life before the Internet?" The answer has now emerged that there was indeed life before the Internet, since there is a wide body of archeological evidence to support this theory.

So far we have had the courage to address other perplexing issues that have dogged mankind: Do heroes need villains? Is Kim Kardashian a budding quantum physics professor at MIT? Who was the greatest trash-talker of all time? What will rap music do when we run out of words that rhyme with *bitch and yo*? And can Yahoo journalists write articles that would appeal to anyone with a lower triple-digit IQ? And of course we dealt with the attention span dilemma of Johnny Millennial.

Somehow, the world was here, and there is enough documentation to support the fact that humans on this planet existed before 1993; we even put a man on the moon with the computing power of a calculator in 1969. We can start in 1993, which really is when we started seeing the widespread adoption of the technological marvel riding on the connected world that has catapulted us into the arms of the third industrial revolution (more on this later). Then it might be interesting to revisit this world and create this place that was in some ways the good old days but in other ways was not!

Stock Trading

The tracking of stocks before the early 1990s was done by reading the stock columns of a newspaper the day after trading, unless one was a stockbroker. This applied to both equities and futures listings. If someone wanted a live quote as late as 1995, they would call their broker for the latest information on the position of his stock, the Dow, as well as other indexes. When one wanted to do research on a company, one's broker would fax or mail a write-up about the organization, including things we take for granted today, like the stocks, financial statements, trailing earning, and beta risk rating, and so on. Put simply, perfect information certainly did not exist for most equity holders, and the stockbroker's positioning power was strong.

By the early 1990s, there were some portable stock trackers that made watching the stocks all day quite possible, but this practice was not the norm, and stock research was still always in the hands of the stockbroker. Information was only for the few and privileged, but this was soon to change, as certainly the democratization of stock tracking had yet to arrive. It becomes hard to fathom today, but to sell a stock, one had to phone the broker, put in a sell or buy order at market or limit, and the broker would phone back, letting the person know the stock was transacted.

Younger stock traders in today's world cannot fathom this type of relative inefficiency, but this was the world we lived in; information was held in the hands of a few. Today, we execute trades online for as low as nine dollars per trade and we get live market data from our online brokers, be it TD Waterhouse or E-Trade. If one wants a wealth of knowledge on equities and stocks, Yahoo Finance is probably the deepest and best free site for equities research in terms of trailing earning, PE, research reports, bid-ask spread, and relative pricing of industry competitors, with side-by-side metrics that include market EPS, EBITDA, enterprise value market caps, and a host of graphs to analyze, until one turns blue with information overload. You may try this link for an example:

http://ca.finance.yahoo.com/q/co?s=FDO.

None of this comes without a cost; people will now find out for themselves just as their brokers did that rarely, if ever, will one be able to consistently outperform the major indexes, such as the FTSE 100 Index and Dow Jones Industrial Average through individual equity purchases, but then that would be a topic in itself, which is outside of the scope of this book.

Today, for example, Yahoo Finance and similar sites provide live information for firms to watch the trading of currencies, which facilitate the purchase of foreign currencies at spot rates, forwards, and other hedging vehicles in order to stabilize the organization's foreign currency accounts payable and accounts receivable, thus smoothing out earnings in a more predictable way.

As a side note, if one really wants to attain a rich knowledge of the markets and drops out of Facebook and tunes into that *haute couture* look that never goes out of style called "making money," my recommended readings would be *Barron's, Financial Times, The Economist,* and of course, the *Wall Street Journal.* Incidentally, none of these sources are free because, simply put, the quality of their financial reporting and critique is worth paying for.

What we now take for granted was not available as recently as fifteen years ago, and the ease of information we attain at our fingertips should never be underestimated, as it is a marvel of human achievement, while promoting relative egalitarian access to financial knowledge. Then again, what we do with this financial knowledge is quite another matter.

Newspapers and Business

The speed of disruptive change has affected a host of industries but most notably the classic newspaper as it tries to create an economic model that works. But in limiting ourselves to the business reader's viewpoint for now, one of the great rites of passage for businesspeople was showing up at work with a business paper under the arm such as the *Wall Street Journal* or the *Globe and Mail.* It was in some ways a complement to business attire and indicated to one's boss that you meant business.

The ritual was then to browse through the journeys and misadventures that capitalism offers, trying to take in the news of which company reported its earnings, changes in key management, mouthwatering acquisitions, along with closing quotes on stocks and futures, the economy, and so on. Not all the articles were dry; often they were written with humour and incredible insight that showed us how certain business activities would have societal impacts that were not only economic but would touch our lives. After all, economic activity perhaps affects our lives more than anything else.

The business paper is a time-honoured tradition, and its etiquette is changing, since print is static when compared to digital media, and its delivery is cost-prohibitive when compared to digital delivery that can come to the subscriber's desktop, laptop, tablet, or phone and give the reader the latest and greatest by the minute.

Today, one gets his quotes, business news, and spots rates on currencies, equities, and futures online with a host of sites, including Yahoo Finance, Marketplace, and blog sites. Today, one can read what people and analysts are saying about a company's stock and management at will.

We are all used to getting most things for free on the Internet in the name of this egalitarian democratization thing that is being rattled into our heads. However, when it comes to writers online giving away their labour output for free in the name of benevolence, that's not fair, of course, and would defy the tenets of self-maximization. "So, give it to me for free, while I am not willing to work for free," is the enigmatic hypocrisy that dogs us all and is perhaps the new inebriated cry of the digital proletariat.

So without starting the biggest debate since the Big Bang, if one has to produce worthwhile business journalism with "crème de la crème" articles that give unique and empirical insight, it is therefore logical that papers have to hire something more than interns who are still affected by what their left-leaning professors taught them, with, of course, their hypocritical market-driven salaries they collect along with four months off a year.

To create something called excellence in business journalism, for that matter, requires that the writing team is compensated well for its efforts, and the collective output is worth paying for.

A partial list of business publications that are truly world-class and can therefore charge for their product through pay walls includes, but is not limited to the following:

- The *Wall Street Journal,* which gives us the daily journal of American and global enterprise;
- The *Financial Times,* which gives a very British and worldly view of business;
- *Barron's*, probably the finest-written weekly magazine on the stock markets, which includes insights on equity valuations, interviews with fund and company managers, and a market laboratory that contains a host of economic indicators;
- *The Economist*, a British magazine weekly that focuses on business news and international politics.

I Need a Job, 'Cause Blogging Don't Pay

So what else has changed? Once upon a time, résumés were mailed after responding to help-wanted ads in newspapers, and people used to phone to find out the status of their applications, to the point that companies implemented policies of, "don't call us; we'll call you". For the most part, help-wanted sections in newspapers have gone the way of the bossa nova watusi twist, since job sites such as MonsterBoard. com, Workopolis, and the like have displaced them.

Today, résumés are sent electronically but are still filled with exaggerations or selective reasoning; I guess some things never quite change.

But just as the electronic job boards found their footing and declared themselves king of the digital job board jungle, this new thing called LinkedIn came along to knock job boards off the mountain. LinkedIn, in a nutshell, gives a member the ability to display a résumé for the whole world to see, and the site also acts as a business networking site. Companies can create a page, and to boot, LinkedIn has dug into the market share as well as threatened the foundation of electronic job boards. In many ways, LinkedIn has become the Facebook of the business community, but with more selectivity. At the same time, many people who post their *curriculum vitae* online and exaggerate their credentials in front of a world stage do so at the expense of committing digital perjury.

The story doesn't end there. Personnel agencies, which have always prided themselves on taking something blasé and presenting it to firms as the "next great hope," are now fighting competitors on two fronts—namely, job boards—but more acutely, LinkedIn. However, it helps them poach key personnel and *re-giftwrap* them to other firms. So, in many respects, their days are numbered, except perhaps for the highly specialized personnel executive recruitment firms, aka head-hunters.

The Last Flight of Travel Agents

Another thing that has now passed us is the profession of travel agents, who once had years of experience and knew all the nuances of the airlines, how to arrange connecting flights, and how to book the traveller into a nice hotel for a reasonable rate. Does anyone remember the days of going to a travel agent or spending endless hours planning that perfect trip? I am sure many under thirty-five don't.

Simply put, travel agents built a reputation by diminishing travel risk, and did I mention that they had a monopoly on access to information with the airline driven reservation software systems, while the only thing the paupers had was word of mouth?

Wide-eyed young ladies who were going to travel the world in search of glamour, discovery, and adventure felt the allure of becoming travel agents. Travel agents were paid commissions by tour companies, hotels, and airlines to sell their inventory, and once upon a time, it was a really great way to make a living and see the world at the same time.

Traditionally, the travel industry's MIS were Sabre, PARS, DATAS, Apollo, where they had exclusive access to trade information, just like real-estate agents. Some built great reputations for putting together trips with nice accommodations; some just sold knowing that the client really did not know much about that hotel in Mexico or Chicago.

If, however, the travellers really wanted to make sure they booked decent accommodations, a travel book on their destination country's hotels could be purchased—for example, to ensure that they didn't end up at a dive—and then sometimes they still did, as often the digs one ended up in were not exactly like the books or brochures described them to be. Countless hours were spent with agents, hotels, or airlines directly to put together travel plans, such as accommodations, car rentals, and airline tickets.

Today, of course, we can get on Expedia that seems to be a relatively simple task, and book our tickets, compare rates on airlines, car rentals, buses, cruise vacations, trains, and hotels, and have our boarding passes e-mailed to our smartphones. All this and more is now available, as the final curtain on the travel agents' careers, as we knew it, has been drawn.

TripAdvisor.com is also available as a research tool, which provides a host of firsthand, hopefully unbiased reviews, written by travellers about their experience of a place, while Expedia, Priceline, and Cheaptickets.com offer near-perfect information, allowing the travellers to find everything they need to arrange their travels at the click of the mouse.

When we think for a moment of the convenience this disruptive change has provided consumers via the Internet, it would be "so yesterday" and inefficient to make travel arrangements like yesteryear, when we had no access to all this information, but it was the *modus operandi* of the travel world just a few short years ago. Technology is delivering what academia terms as "perfect information," and certainly this is almost the case with the travel industry.

Snake Oil Salesmen and Asset Bubbles

So, then, looking at some more disruptive changes, we have to naturally turn our attention to those willing accomplices of booms and busts, namely, real-estate agents. Currently, the low monetary policy in Canada is fuelling distorted asset prices, which can be best described as a bubble. And historically, as with the tail end of all bubbles, rational evaluation and empirical accountability falls in deaf ears, as is the case with all manias. Leading the choir ensemble is none other than the self-indoctrinated prophets of information hoarding, the various Canadian Real-estate Boards, as the supporting symphony that includes real-estate agents, mortgage brokers, appraisers, and inspectors. Oh, and did we forget the CMHC? More on that in a moment!

What is especially interesting is when the government calls for a soft landing, which means they think they can predict the outcome of economic peaks and valleys; the only problem is that they never predicted the 2008 meltdown. The bottom line is this: there has never been a boom without a bust, and it is unlikely that perhaps the world's most underpopulated country as a ratio of land size will defy this, considering we have enough land to build fifty countries.

Real Estate Boards publish monthly statistical analysis that paints a healthy picture of an overbought market. Take, for example, some new and poorly built condominiums at $600 per square foot in the Greater Toronto Area and technologically dated 1,500-square-foot homes from the 1950s fetching $800,000 to $1,000,000. Of course, when one presents the empirical economics in terms of consumer household debt, which is higher than the United States just before its real-estate crash, this rosy line of thinking is rebuffed as fact getting in the way of emotional inertia. When mentioning this evidence to real-estate types, they go into emotional hissy fits and make claims that homes are affordable based on twenty-five-year amortized payments (which means the home buyers will never be able to pay off their home); this seems to be the new *modus operandi* of the purchaser.

Then, in the case of Toronto, they claim that a hundred thousand people a year move to the area, and this is driving demand along with dubious offshore money laundering schemes. That's fair, but are there reliable statistics with which to support their individual economic position, while at the same time, are we producing a hundred thousand jobs a year in Toronto to accommodate this? When faced with this question, the real-estate orchestra starts pulling out its finest arrangements that usually include some oldies but goldies, for example, "When compared with New York, our prices are cheap;" or the hit musical single that everyone is listening to, "It could never happen here," is a sure sign that Toronto and Vancouver are in a bubble. But their best hit single that is always played during asset bubbles is "This time it's different"! This sounds like a recovering alcoholic romancing the bottle again.

Much of this can be attributed to economic euphoria and groupthink that has evolved into a type of national narcissism, which claims our real-estate sector is made of Teflon. On the contrary, it is made out of outdated wood materials, mud and homes that are technologically dated at least fifty years. So as the bubble grows, we now recite Canada's latest anthem, "Canadian Exceptionalism."

Simply put, people are buying payments, not home prices, and agents are hoping enough affluent immigrants and young people who have never seen a real-estate bust, are naïve enough to keep overpaying for real-estate. Another *caveat emptor* for consideration, is that while older people are watching in glee their asset prices increase, their offspring will not be able to afford homes, at least in the GTA, and what this leads to is a socio-economic problem that I term "intergenerational poverty." The other issue is, without reasonably priced real estate, how then do we attract a skilled workforce to the area? Hence, as a result of this, cities with high economic cost-push factors become uncompetitive.

Then of course, their favorite drum players (aka various real-estate boards) come out and say that homes are affordable, in light of the low interest rates, and call for a great year ahead, in spite of the fact that economists have said that household cash flows are in danger of default. This, along with the fact that the IMF, the Bank of Canada, The Economist magazine, and a host of rating agencies are calling Canadian real-estate twenty-five to fifty percent overvalued. Better still, proponents of real-estate claim that the US housing meltdown cannot happen here, despite the fact that the CMHC (Canada Mortgage and Housing Corporation) is on the hook on behalf of the taxpayers to the tune of about one trillion dollars in liability exposure in Canada, while about seventy-five percent of mortgages in Canada are insured by the CMHC, because many are highly leveraged. All this is starting to make Freddie Mac look financially prudent in comparison.

As a side note, realtors and mortgage brokers become quite ruffled every time the government tightens the mortgage rules, or the feds signal the end of easy money. Then again, interest rates remaining low might be out of government control if the bond market downgrades government debt and interest rates go up due to the required return on risk. The real-estate industry gets further worked up into a lather when CMHC insures less mortgages, since they are on the hook—or should I say taxpayers are—for highly leveraged loans, and now CMHC will not insure homes worth more than a million dollars. CMHC might eventually be the Canadian government's next Frankenstein, and they can take family pictures together with their close cousins in the United States, namely, Fannie Mae and Freddie Mac.

Any government that takes away this unsustainable yet perfect storm of the CMHC and easy money from the real-estate cartel, will go down as the biggest villain since the Grinch who stole Christmas.

One could write a book alone on the unscrupulous behaviour of many real-estate agents and the like who make a living out of pimping out overvalued homes, at least in Canada.

It is imperative that as a prerequisite to show up at the party, real-estate agents come armed with their Photoshopped pictures, as they do their best rendition of a Hollywood red carpet event. The ritual commences by showing off their darlings, which in this case are their home listings, and of course, mounting their real-estate signs in front of their new listing, which usually includes their picture on the "for sale" signs. But these signs on the lawn should not be taken lightly, since they are a form of marking their territory.

Then comes the plot that eventually reveals itself like a Barbara Cartland Harlequin romance, as everything unravels to show clearly the true meaning of the story. Eventually, people willingly line up to purchase these homes like applauding lapdogs, as real-estate pimps step up into their role by meticulously yet manipulatively preparing the incumbents for bidding wars. The end result is that the bidders have now unwittingly become their Johns. Exhausted and dejected, since they are looking for love in all the wrong places, these buyers feel they are pursuing the works of Picasso, but end up with the one that couldn't get the date for the high school prom, as they are ushered out to walk the boulevard of broken dreams. Eventually, the real-estate agent prepares for his or her next carnival show, perhaps more entertaining than the last. But hey, it is business, so let the wheels turn, and perhaps your lucky number will come up.

Of course, the industry as a whole has made a business of ensuring imperfect information is fed to the consumer. This is complemented by low interest rates supplied by the Bank of Canada. And as expected, as long as we have low monetary policy, this industry will believe in God, and if interest rates go up, they will all turn into atheists. It is no wonder then that the Competition Bureau went after the Toronto Real Estate Board (TREB) and its monopoly on hoarding information, which TREB still does in many respects. They are such a powerful organization that they won a case against the Competition Bureau in April 2013, still, they withhold historical sale prices of homes and days on market claiming they are protecting the consumer.

The plot thickens as they applaud the Bank of Canada's historically low monetary policy, which support their overvalued real-estate-asset carnival show that is currently going on. And naturally, when low-interest-rate addiction is pulled out of the equation, the corrosion of the housing market will be exposed, like the last act of a burlesque dancer, but then again the earthquake can occur even in a low-interest-rate environment, as was the case in the United States and Japan. The overinflated labour costs are due to no foreign labour competition and dated building techniques and inefficiencies further inflate home prices.

When the asset bubble of this economic euphoria finally bursts, or at least cools, the real-estate industry and consumer reaction will most likely be blaming the Bank of Canada and the federal government for the slide in real-estate prices. But this will be like the drunk blaming his alcoholism and woes on the liquor store, only to wake up with a hangover when the party ends. As quoted by Eric Rugley in the January 25, 2014, issue of the *Globe and Mail*, "The best cure for high prices is, well…high prices!"

This being said, sooner or later the monopoly of information these real-estate types hold will come to an end, as disruptive technologies aided by the consumers' insatiable thirst for perfect information will acutely change the dynamics of the marketplace. Today, information is much more accessible through www.realtor.ca, and one can get a pretty good idea of what is available on the market, and of course in the United States there is Realtor.com, which offers US homes for sale with deeper analysis than is available in Canada.

The question then becomes what will be the tipping point where free information flows to the next level, where real-estate agents go the way of the Peppermint Twist and the Berlin Wall? It could be a combination of an asset bubble bursting and technology democratization, making people realize that only the very best of agents will survive. In fact, they very well could end up in the same plight as the travel agent. The signs are there, and we are starting to see this with www.propertyguys.com, and the like.

Perhaps we need to consider that flipping real-estate assets with a groupthink of infinite asset appreciation is not nation building; it is the symptom of a country suffering from strategic inertia. It is the by-product of a state that is too intellectually exhausted, perhaps lazy, and lacks the energy to innovate and create the next Avro, space arm, insulin, or Blackberry.

Banking

Moving to online banking; just seven years ago, this was a struggle because the technology and the ISP pipes were still relatively crude, while our mindset was suspicious of transferring our financial information online. At the same time, it never occurred to us that banking face-to-face all those years could have been just as dangerous with the information that the teller had. Alternatively, all the sensitive information on the client could be forwarded to a fraudulent credit card creating organization, which is commonly referred to as *a takeover*.

For businesses, getting simple information like balances, transaction printouts, stop payments, bill payments, wires, other financial inquiries and directives was a time-intensive telephone-and-in-person world. Today, all these things mentioned can be done at a click of a mouse.

BACK TO THE OFFICE OF DAYS GONE BY

For those of us over forty (and this can happen to the best of us) can still remember the business world and its communication devices before the information and computer age. However, in terms of finding a practical beginning, and without getting into an academic exchange, the widespread use of PC computers and the Internet as a symbiotic necessity, did not start becoming widely adopted until the early 1990s.

While large corporations in the seventies had green-screen terminals hooked into mainframes, mainstream computer use was still not into our cultural folklore, and of course I realize that everyone's mileage on this will be different. By the 1980s, the IBM AS400 midrange mainframe was in the norm at many organizations that had the size and requirements. Personally, when I started my career in the early 1980s, I had an excellent vantage point in office-related technologies, since I worked for a company in Canada that handled some of IBM's equipment, which included their classical Selectric typewriter series, which are probably the finest typewriters ever made, as well as some of the first word processors that were being marketed. Prior to that, I had also worked for Lanier Business Systems, where we sold high-efficiency dictation pooling systems and some quite complex word processors. And I suspect that I have evolved into a wannabe information technology whiz!

What I can tell the reader with some confidence is that these early micro- and word processor computers were quite a challenge to use, since they were DOS based, with a set of sometimes-unforgiving commands we had to key-in. In other words, these computers needed operators who understood a library of prompts and commands, especially in a non-GUI environment, and having computer skills of any sort was an exception. In fact, I specifically remember that on major sales calls downtown, we had to be supported by what we called MSRs, marketing support reps, to make it look like these machines were easy to use, when in fact they were quite a nightmare, especially the one called the WordStar, which was, well, a word processor.

What I unknowingly was doing by selling these machines was helping to usher in the computer information age, but to me it was a job to support the irrational exuberance and associated lifestyle of short-sightedness that comes from youth. At the same time, I had the good fortune to train many lovely secretaries on the finer points of these new technologies, which made it a dream job of sorts. So it is for these reasons that I humbly sit at the table of legitimacy, having applied experience in this area and subsequently a good bird's-eye view to legitimize myself as a reasonable student and authority on this subject.

I certainly remember selling office equipment, including crude desktops, into the downtown Toronto and Mississauga areas, where I reluctantly honed my cold-calling skills or lack thereof, which I first learned during my newspaper days. One afternoon when introducing a word processors, I remember a receptionist ushering me out, saying that people like me were taking jobs away; this must have been around 1983. It was this mindset that I and many others had to often deal with, since fresh thinking and the status quo rarely are natural bedfellows.

Change eventually comes once we let the genie out of the bottle, but it takes time for many to accept that the next train is here, as evidenced by a prior chapter on the history of invention. Sometimes, when progress is slow, such as the adoption rate of electric cars, we like to subscribe to conspiracy theories as to who is impeding it, when in reality, it is the market forces at large, including consumers.

In some respects, when we romanticize about the good old days, they were not as good as we might all think. True, offices were filled with smoke, liquid lunches, and attractive secretaries, with very few of the human-resource types to spoil the party and make everyone walk on eggshells.

Much of the culture of business was not really that far from the world depicted in the *Mad Men* series, and offices during the sixties right up to the eighties were quite different from today—some good, some bad, but then again, that in itself could be a book. However, one of the most interesting things in watching the *Mad Men* series is not just the striking fashion and dress formality but seeing the industrial design of office technology being employed in the 1960s and its evolution over a tumultuous decade. No ad agency today could survive without PowerPoint, but somehow they did in the sixties and beyond by employing storyboards.

When we focus on the employment of technology and associated rituals, especially when taking a step back into the 1970s to early 1990s, the business communiqué and its host of inefficiencies is unfathomable today.

The office that once was might give us a perspective of how things have really changed in the rituals of commerce. So with chests puffed with pride, I present this section to somehow bring back to life what was, while framing it in contrast to the office and business world we now might take for granted. But perhaps I can give the reader the gift and clarity of perspective.

The Sales Call

Every type of business deal commences with some form of communication utilizing a device of some sort, or perhaps a chance face-to-face encounter. Today, there is a wide array of ways to reach customers to solicit new business. Some of these include the telephone (still)—although e-mail has replaced it as the primary form of communication—and then there is texting, but this is primarily between friends and business colleagues. Some people try to connect with decision-makers through LinkedIn, while webinars and practical vehicles for one-on-one video conferencing, such as Skype and Lync, are becoming the norm.

Others, especially web designers and SEO (Search Engine Optimization) operators, send rather shallow e-mail spams with little knowledge about the business or industry they contact, hoping that if enough mud is thrown at the wall, something will stick. This is a bit old-school, but since many are fearful of telephone rejection, (especially these days), it sure keeps one's sense of self intact. I call this the broad-brush approach as they promote themselves as the messiahs of knowledge in terms of how they are going to help your business without first understanding a business. This in some ways is no different than the door-to-door aluminum siding salesman of the 1950s using a blanket approach (see the movie *Tin Men* with Richard Dreyfuss), but at least the salesman had a visual on the house, seeing the wood siding had rotted and needed replacement.

Going back to techno-culture norm of soliciting, these types believe a blanket approach will yield results, and it might not occur to them that crafting a targeted individual e-mail and researching understanding the basic business model, while coming up with strategies of how their services might yield better results, might have some commercial merit and lead to a face-to-face meeting. SEO hustlers are quite notorious for this, saying that if we are found, the *Promised Land* will follow.

So then it might occur to broad-brush techno-marketing types that they might have to study the business they approach and come up with some original thought and clever insights to get the potential customer to the altar so that a dialogue of some sort can begin. This might even show that one has enough respect to genuinely care, and nothing can beat being genuine.

Many organizations today are using a combination of phone calls, e-mails, and classic in-person cold-calling, which requires some thick-skin when it comes to getting turned down and in many cases being thrown out of offices. But then again, this is the type of experience few people had when I started my business career, and fewer have today, since being told "no" in person is enough to send someone to call Dr. Phil to have a shoulder to cry on. Put differently, being turned down on the phone is like being turned down for dates thirty times a day; for many, this is devastating, but for highly skilled sales practitioners, it is part of the ritual.

Currently, a lot of sales teams are at crossroads with their methodology to market. Many are led by old-school types that have pictures of General Patton or maybe Rambo on the back wall, and charge up the troops into a rich and bubbly lather and ask them to do what they did, which was to make cold calls and get the decision-makers on the phone, or arrange a meeting in person. This has merits but drawbacks as well, since one has to train the team at prospecting and appointment-arrangement techniques. Thus, many sales teams are in disarray, since many of the techniques that worked in the past are becoming challenging to reconcile with the multiple communication vehicles that are available today, against the backdrop of the five-second attention span. The deployment of technology and its symbiotic relations with human interaction in the modern sales force are still a work in progress.

At this juncture, it might be wise to step back in time to the seventies and part of the eighties, where you had to get past the switchboard and then the decision-maker's executive secretary, but then you were "In Like Flint".

Then came the more widespread use of tape-driven answering machines, and then digital answering machines that allowed people to hide behind them. Add that to the fact that they now can ignore e-mails and that most companies have receptions that are like a fortress just in case Osama bin Laden's protégée shows up or an employee goes postal, and one could see that getting through Fort Knox might be easier.

With the phenomenon of the techno-fortress as an aspect of our modern society, meaning, we are usually in our comfort zone of protective technology, it is no wonder that most are too uncomfortable to pick up the phone and get slam dunked, since we find e-mails less intrusive and less likely to elicit a response that will deflate the average ego or pierce thin-skin.

When the telephone replaced the telegraph, it created a disruption of the tradition of business etiquette of arranging appointments and meetings, either by classic mail or through the telegraph. During the 1800s, arranging business meetings meant formal communiqué of back-and-forth letters, combined with the use of the telegraph. At the time, this method was the normative chain of events to get an audience for a firm's products and services.

Once the meeting appointment was established, a horse-and-buggy, train, or later, the first cars took the salesperson to the meeting. Once telephones were adopted into more widespread use in the early 1900s, people called for appointments on these new devices to sell. Subsequently, the deployment of this technique was considered, at the time, lowbrow or not of proper etiquette.

Before the use of e-mails, you left a phone message with the secretary when reaching out to a business contact if they were out, or they would transcribe it on a memo pad and leave it on the person's desk. Alternatively, you would leave a message on their answering machine, and when they returned to the office, they would have an array of messages to go through, both written and voice from answering machines. They would then call you back, maybe later in the day during the time you were out, and they in turn would leave a message; when you came back to the office, you would call them back and they could be out or occupied on the other line. Sometimes, this cycle could go on, and the total time lost in this dance called "catch me if you can" could last for a few days, maybe longer.

If we broke down the time on this back-and-forth messaging and did an economic, quantifiable efficiency study, we can see that this costs firms in terms of lost productivity.

Today, if people want to engage in a business telephone conversation, they contact each other by e-mail for the most part, and they set up a time that they can both be available to talk. Needless to say, this is a more efficient use of scarce resources; however, the human skill of impromptu conversation is being affected.

Video Conferencing and Getting the Troops Together

Traditionally, when management got key personnel together from different offices in design, engineering, and sales, it usually involved the coordination of getting ten people to fly to the location of the head office. Usually, the office manager or secretary would be on the phone coordinating airline tickets, hotels, and venues of entertainment.

Furthermore, the coordinator, just ten short years ago, could not go onto Expedia or Hotels.com or the like and was thus forced to employ the services of a travel agent on the phone for days to coordinate the big powwow at the head office, which usually ended up as a yawner anyway. Today, if one wanted to have a multilocation team meeting in person, this could be easily coordinated by e-mailing each participant their hotel and airline reservation—accomplished in two hours or less.

In terms of cost to the firm, let's look at crude accounting numbers of the cost of gathering ten people at the head office. It would be at least $20,000, without including lost time, and then if the lost time is added, this could lead to another $20,000, for a grand total of $40,000.

This is not to say that face-to-face meetings of the intelligentsia of an organization do not reap rewards, because they do; however, today's firms can employ myriad affordable cloud-based technologies, including video conferencing. Providers that come to mind include GoToMeeting, WebEx, Join.me, TeamViewer offering video conferencing and webinars for under hundred dollars per month, or firms can always opt to go Skype for Business conferencing or invite team members via Microsoft Office365 Lync.

In the 1970s, only large organizations with deep pockets could afford video conferencing, and it was rare to see it in smaller firms. Today, we have the democratization of this and so many other technologies that we might take all this for granted, forgetting the efficiencies they deliver.

The Office Memo

We can still find office memo templates on MS Word, and how much it is still used is up for debate. But not long ago, if you wanted to give your staff a memo on a certain subject, you would have it typed up on a typewriter, print up a hundred sheets for a hundred people, and then have an assistant or mail clerk physically distribute these to everyone's desk of physical in-boxes. As one can appreciate, this was not exactly immediate communication, and the implication of the time to photocopy, the cost of paper, and the environmental footprint was cumbersome, to say the least. Furthermore, it was not exactly instantaneous.

Also, if you just wanted to send a quick message to six colleagues, you might have used a memo or have the secretarial staff arrange a quick meeting, or left a voice message on each of their respective answering machines, which compared with today would be an inefficient deployment of resources. The first attempt to change this was in a commercial for the Xerox Alto in the early 1970s that introduces the concept of e-mails and the GUI, which in many ways drew out the future with uncanny accuracy, please see: http://www.youtube.com/watch?v=uY3I-tbpFGA.

Of course, as mentioned earlier, Xerox and its bean-counter culture at the time missed the boat on the biggest thing since the Twist, but what makes this Xerox commercial interesting is that you can hear all the typing and associated clatter of offices of yesteryear in the background.

Calendars and Appointment Books

One finely remembers the days of print calendars, which are still in existence (I still hang one on my wall) and the appointment book, which has almost evaporated since once upon a time making business appointments usually entailed that you phoned, or your assistant did, to arrange an appointment, and this was transcribed in both your assistant's and your own appointment books.

Of course, many a time, appointments were inaccurately transcribed, coupled with the fact that the amount of time deployed on this task was taxing. There are some people who still keep an appointment book, but these are more than likely older people, hairstylists, and doctor's offices, (the worst technological laggards most of us know of).

Today, Outlook Calendar organizes your schedule with meeting invites that get confirmed electronically. Some people use Android for appointments, but it's difficult to sync with Microsoft Outlook. Hence, if you want to be taken seriously in business, use Outlook and stop acting like you left college yesterday. The good thing about electronic calendars is that it's all in writing and confirmed.

There are other benefits to using Outlook, since you could put your future to-do list on the calendar as well as share your calendar with colleagues, create tasks, and so on, all at your fingertips, not to mention organizing your e-mails. Of course, you can have all these functions synchronized to your smartphone.

E-mail and the Swan Song of the Classical Letter

The 8.5″ x 11″ classical letter is certainly not what it once was; true, it is still employed in law firms and ends with advising one to govern oneself accordingly, (visiting the in-laws gives us much practice with this) but is relatively thinly used in businesses today. Not too long ago, it was the norm of communication. The process of crafting a letter usually started with the secretary coming into the boss's office to take short-hand notes, the success of which, they will readily admit, had much to do with the executive secretary's skills. Then the shorthand would be typed into a letter, which required that the typist had impeccable grammar and spelling skills (remembering there were no spellcheck tools at the time). It was then presented for the writer to review and sign, and if it required anything more than minor revisions, the letter had to be retyped from scratch.

Method II was the manager leaving a microcassette that contained voice directions for various letters, referred to as "dictation," on the secretary's desk. Then a transcriber machine with full foot pedals and a headphone to listen to the voice instructions would allow the secretary to slow down the voice and stop it in order to transcribe the letter using a typewriter. Law firms and doctor's offices still might employ this method, but it is now transcribed via word processors. But once upon a time, it was the *modus operandi* of the business world, and I used to actually teach executives how to give dictation.

The skills of typing structured, aesthetic, correct letters; filing; grammar; shorthand; and dictation were taught in colleges and some grade-school courses to meet the demands of offices, and as a result there was a battalion of executive secretaries to support management. Today, most of us depend on the *spell-check* and *grammar check* that are available electronically to get through life, which is quite cool, while universities produce some graduates who are functionally illiterate yet somehow are allowed to graduate into the unsuspecting arms of commerce. But then again, universities and colleges are quite skilled at marketing courses based on false statistical probabilities of employment. However, in Canada, as long as they can get offset funding, the train rolls on. A couple of good examples are court reporters and travel agents, who have slim prospects of employment in today's technological savvy market.

So, getting back to dictation, when I worked for Lanier Business Systems in the early 1980s, we marketed dictation equipment as thought-processing systems. The sales pitch was that by carrying a handheld dictation machine, you could capture some of the thousands of thoughts that go through a person's mind in a day and then capitalize on this. This led me to have the opportunity to train lawyers, assistants (who were usually more pleasant to look at), and other professionals as part of the post-sale process of these dictation systems. At that time, some of the first word processors came to market and into the workplace, meaning the typist now skipped the typewriter and went directly to the word processor, although typewriters were still used as a printer with the more advanced IBM Selectric series. This, of course, signalled the beginning of the end of typewriters.

Our sales-speak was that the dictation systems were just as applicable as ever, since voice went directly to word processors, as opposed to typewriters, and this was true for the most part. But the robust nature of word processors allowed the secretary to delete, replace, copy, cut, and paste, and that eroded some of the advantages of dictation systems. With the exception of the legal profession and a few other stalwarts that still use dictation systems, we are seeing little use of this method, and in terms of letter writing, a vast majority of our correspondence is done electronically, often with poor format. Why bother formatting a letter when today's workforce, for the most part, does not really understand visual proportion, layout, and the positive effects they have on the receiver's psyche, be it electronic or in a classically printed format?

In sales departments just five years ago, one would send a short letter that accompanied product samples, but this is being replaced by the printed copy of the correlating e-mail that probably includes the price quote, (these are often now in the body of the e-mail) so the receiving party can just relate the samples to the e-mail and make easy sense of it all. It seems that our attention spans are not what they once were.

When e-mail was really coming into the cultural norm in the mid-nineties, there was still a wide array of older executives who had their e-mails prepared by their assistants. The reason these executives could not type their own letters was that they never took typing courses as I had the good fortune to do so, and to be taught typing concepts such as home base, which trains a person to type with two hands. This has changed, since, for the most part, everyone writes their own e-mails, especially when communications are so rapid-fire, and e-mails that are just sent out are received and responded to by the other party, even when he or she is out of the office, with the capability of smartphones. Colleagues can even text each other while they are travelling.

Without being functional in these areas of rapid-fire communication (what is considered the basic skills today), one can be considered functionally illiterate in the current world we live in.

Going back to letters for a moment, they still exist, and most managers who need to write letters work with their assistants to create a draft copy, massage it by moving paragraphs and making corrections, and then submit it to their assistants to give it a professional look that includes justification, grammar, layout, etc. Still, a classically printed letter has merit in the business world and shows that the writer has a sense of respect toward the recipient, taking time to communicate in a more traditional way, and it might touch them; on the other hand, in a time-impoverished society, it just might not. So then again, it might be best to romanticize what was!

However, if a classic letter is deployed cleverly in our current techno-culture, we can still mail a person a formal request to meet him or her, which is exactly what travelling salesmen did in the 1800s, and who knows, this just might be effective, since showing respect, thoughtfulness and tradition can sometimes soften up the hardest of people.

The world of electronic mail creates incredible efficiency through its fast-moving communications technology; the advantages are so overwhelming that it would be a topic for a paper on its own, succinctly put, one can receive an e-mail, consider a timely and balanced response, copy others to keep them into the loop, and respond to e-mails late in the day to greet overseas associates just as they wake up.

Other Changes

It is this digital world that allows us to send or share pictures electronically, through social media, including Facebook, Instagram, and the like. We send electronic forms that were once mailed or faxed but can now be stored easily on servers. In art departments, design used to be physically presented for approval and then sent back for revisions, which was costly and unnecessarily dragged out projects; today, any small changes can be e-mailed back and forth at warp speed and approved just like on *Star Trek*. If the file is large, it can be sent through a cloud-based FTP link such as Hightail, even translation of letters are sent out and given back in soft copy, while commercial photo shoots that once resulted in the photographer presenting the sample prints for approval have changed now with the instant gratification that comes from digital photography.

E-mail has facilitated all this and then some. For example, just ten years ago, brochures were mailed to a prospective client; and then a follow-up phone call would be employed to see if the client got the brochure, and if he hadn't, another phone call added to the client's workload and intake of calls. These unnecessary calls contributed to what I term "sound stress and aggravation."

Today, as people are talking to a business associate, they can send a digital brochure that is received in ten seconds, and this is especially significant when dealing with overseas communication. Just ten years ago, when a brochure was mailed to an out of town client, this hard-copy brochure could not be instantly shared with twenty colleagues at the press of a button. So, in business today, ensure that your digital presentations have visual resonance and look completely professional, because this is the new "first impression."

There are other stunning benefits to the digital world, some of which include typing a search word on Outlook, and the required e-mail can be found instantly, instead of searching through physical correspondence. And of course, escalation of anger can probably be better harnessed by e-mails, where one's angriest letter can sit in the draft box, never to be sent, but at least one had the satisfaction of writing it without the imprudence of sending it.

But now the keyboard is going to be more practically threatened by voice-recognition software; yet what can be extrapolated from the old world and brought into the realm of electronic communications are basic courtesies, such as opening an e-mail conversation by writing, "Good day," "Dear Sir or Madam," or a simple "Hello" instead of "hey there!!!!"

Keeping certain enduring things from the past, such as respectful etiquette, shows that our culture is confident enough about its foundations to propagate it to a new generation. Hence, crafting electronic letters should be done showing that one is cultured, thoughtful, refined, has *savoir faire* and has progressed past the Neanderthal stage.

Accounting and ERP Systems

Accounting is the economic reporting system that is often described as the language of business. The first records of the double-entry system were created in Florence in the late eleventh century and widely adopted in Venice in the early 1300s. In fact, Italy had such strong knowledge of accounting and finance that it resulted in Edward II of England bringing in financial types in the early 1300s from Lombardy,

Italy, and giving them land in London to facilitate their expertise. Today, we know this area as Lombard Street, which is still one of the great centres of world finance.

Accounting is still taught in colleges by ensuring students first learn the T accounts as a debit or credit, depending on which side of the accounting equation it falls on. They then transcribe them into journal entries, building on this into the trial balance and finally making their way into the general ledger, making special adjusting entries where needed in between. These, of course, are still the building blocks of all accounting software today.

Larger and more sophisticated organizations had mainframes that ran their computerized accounting programs from as early as the 1950s, and one of the first practical accounting software systems was the IBM 9Pac, upon which many of today's accounting packages are based.

Not too long ago, for small- and even medium-sized organizations, accounting was still done manually, where entering information into the general ledgers was mathematically tedious, and if inaccurate journal entries were transcribed, it would ensure that a linkage of other related entries would have to be all reversed in order to accurately reflect the economic activities being recorded.

The IRS and Revenue Canada had strict rules on keeping the general legers in a fireproof safe or a second record, for the reason that if they perished, so did the recordings of the profit and losses, balance sheets, and the supporting journal entries. Hence, as we all know, governments get quite worked up if they don't have firms and households to collect from, because after all, governments need money to squander while they sell the idea that they are doing this for the collective good—at the expense of individuals, liberty, and of course, justice.

Getting back to accounting, inventory systems of old were kept on cue cards in perpetuity, reconciled with accounting systems by recording the individual sales purchases and opening and closing inventories to ascertain a true cost of goods. Just like today, many firms never really had or have a handle on true cost of goods. Of course, this leads to mistakenly thinking that the company was making a profit during the year, when in fact, the books were bleeding money.

Perpetual inventory purchases and sales record-keeping was copious, while not up to date by the minute, meaning a firm's real record of inventory lagged behind for days and weeks, resulting in undershipping to customers, often referred to as stockouts, leading to lost sales, while at the same time, at a press of a button, management could not have an accurate inventory number by day's end. In fact, this is how retailers operated, and some still do.

Purchase orders were done manually and were difficult to track and put into the general ledgers in a timely manner to be actionable by management.

But the story gets juicer. When employees could manually generate the inventory cards, load up an extra few pallets of goods on a friend's truck, lo and behold, it became difficult to track the inventory count on the firm's manually driven perpetual inventory records. At the same time, the accountant would only adjust the discrepancy with a simple journal entry as shrinkage, or even better, he could be a part of this unscrupulous game.

Often this type of inside larceny usually went unnoticed until the lost inventory grew too large (greed does leave behind large footprints), or until one of the firm's customers came around and said he was offered some of the products at thirty cents on the dollar, but by then the horse was usually out of the barn. Thus, the last great hope was to call detectives Columbo, or Horatio from *CSI Miami*, only to be disappointed to find out that they only handled homicide cases. The firm also had the option to call in a forensic accountant; however, he might charge more than the cost of the theft. So the wheel turned until someone noticed that something needed fixing.

These were the antiquated dilemmas many firms had to deal with before accounting software became the norm, and it was a world that is unimaginable to those who never experienced the manual systems. Put differently, paper-and-pencil journal entries were tedious and required a very high level of skill and an eye for meticulous detail.

Accounting software for small firms today is no longer cost-prohibitive. Starting with entry-level programs such as QuickBooks, which is sufficient for a one-person show, and then going up the scale grade, we see Accpac Simply Accounting and Sage accounting ERP systems that could network hundreds of computers and handle both small and midsize firms, even in the cloud computing, since it acts as a formidable MIS (Management Information System). Incidentally, these software programs are not compatible with Apple.

To go to the Maserati level of Management Information Systems, one would have to get into an ERP (Enterprise Resource Planning) system such as SAP, Oracle, PeopleSoft, or Great Plains Software, but these systems start in the hundreds of thousands of dollars and can cost millions of dollars to implement corporation-wide. However, these ERP systems provide a set of deliverables that could run everything from manufacturing processes, human resources, inventory auto replenishment, accounting, and then some, all within one software platform.

The implementation of these systems often results in a suffocating number of committees and endless departmental meetings; political tug-of-war ensues as to which department hoards, (a soft-power type of bullying) and what data information each department controls. In the computer age, people with specific skills and a stranglehold on the old system information get worked up into a lather as the new system erodes their political powerbase. New MIS systems expose the inefficiency of the old systems, as well as some departments.

Today, one can purchase popularly priced accounting programs in one package with available third-party add-ons (similar to apps on your smartphones) that seamlessly integrate functions, which include but are not limited to the following:

- Accounts receivable
- Accounts payable
- Inventory
- Order entry
- Purchase orders
- Full general ledgers/income statements/trial balance/balance sheets
- Payroll
- Manufacturing, including bill of materials (this gives a break-down of components required, including direct-cost labour to manufacture a finished good, while giving perpetual inventory counts before and after)
- Sales and purchase analysis
- Forecasting and inventory management
- Managerial reports
- Special note areas for all customers, vendors, and processes
- Budgets and forecasts.

Not too long ago, all these business processes and economic functions were done by pen and paper. This method was not only tedious and labour-intensive but also left room for much human error and was inefficient, to say the least, while collecting all this information into a central depository was a nightmare.

This was the reality Baby Boomers and gen-Xers were hurled into, and when we look back at it, we wonder how we got through these times. But then again, to make up for all the information know-how we did not have then, we had to be quite good at other skills, such as math and accounting, a comprehensive knowledge of the English language, having phone numbers memorized, adding complex numbers in our heads, and so on.

Unfathomable as this may be to gen Y and millennials, it was the world they had never been exposed to and were saved from, which in retrospect is quite a blessing, even though it could be argued that having all this information makes our minds lazy in some respects. But the world of accounting before the computer age becomes a faded memory for future historians to write about, since this generation will never have the opportunity to be without and feel it on their skin.

Perhaps having all this information at our fingertips is the reason people are buying brain-training games such as Lumosity to help with attention span and memory.

Collateral Material

Traditionally, collateral material has been in printed format for companies, brands, services, ad campaigns, and so on. Information was printed by offset printing that could provide exemplary quality output. Some firms would photocopy this information, but the real slick stuff was done by printing press, much like it is done today.

Copywriters of collateral material would prepare all this, and layout artists would assemble the information into a final presentation and then gave the printer mechanical artwork. Eventually, by mail or in person, a sales rep would present to the potential client a professionally designed printed corporate folder that had enclosed information sheets for the customer to consider, and much like today, the information was just too much to digest for the end recipient.

Of course, after last print was prepared, the firm might have introduced a new product model, which often meant that an insert would have to be added into the company brochure or wait until the next print schedule. It seemed that the print could not keep up with the pace of business, and there was a divergent separation between the lag of print and the dynamic nature of commerce. Obtaining pictures for the company's brands, as well as lifestyle pictures, required that the firm hire a professional photographer or had companies that would offer royalty-free pictures via a catalogue they would send by mail. The person in charge would then go through the stock pictures to pick out the images to support the collateral material. For example, the brochure might require a picture of trees, the ocean, a smiling person, and so on, as part of the componentry to assemble the final visual look.

Further, after the pictures of products or places were shot, the firm had to wait a few days to get back proofs to select from, and often the people in charge wished they had made changes to the props, lighting, or shooting angles, but they could not see the mistakes until they reviewed the proofs, and by then it was too late. It was not instant gratification, whereas nowadays, one can see the photographic mistake right in the studio by reviewing digital pictures on a large-screen computer on the fly. Often the plan for the photo shoot and the resulting outcome were at divergence, and this did lead to reshoots adding costs to the firm and instigated turf wars with the agency or photographer, or sometimes both, as the occasion allowed.

Some layout artists understood the mechanical process of printers, and they would create the final artwork for offset printers, which was a painstaking task that required extensive know-how and acute skills. Of course, if there were typos on the material, it would result in the political blame game that would rival a cardinal sin.

Today, in contrast, an artist can send artwork in digital format ranging from *.jpeg* to Adobe Illustrator or *.pdf* to a client for approval in ten seconds, without a face-to-face meeting. Feedback can then be given via phone, instant message, or e-mail, and if necessary, changes can be drawn by markup tools to direct the artist. This of course, not only increases speed but collaboration as well, and in the Wiki world, teams of designers from around the world can work on the same project around multiple time zones and countries nonstop.

It is interesting to note that we are now seeing low-resolution screen grabs of graphs and computer screens in books, collateral material, and other print material. What this means is that these are not the high-resolution print format that is required to have vivacious print quality, and of course has resulted in the reduction of the communicative deliverables of the collateral material, which in fact is often the brand. For those that are perceptive, pick up a recent book and see the faded picture with weak resolution within many books.

Collateral material needs a host of components to turn into a resonating marketing presentation, including, but not limited to, copy, layout, illustrations, typography, and, of course astounding pictures. In days gone by and before iStock Photos, one would have to go through extra picture catalogues that agency firms would collect, from fashion models to landscapes to lifestyles, to make up the photographic elements of the firm's collateral material for the art department to work on.

Today, for example, when we look at all these happy families on new subdivision billboards for homes that look quite enamoured of their new digs, they are, for the most part, extracted pictures from sites like iStock Photos, Fotolia Stock Photos, Getty Images, and the like. What this means for the uninitiated is that the art department can literally scroll through a million pictures by category and pick up a pictorial asset to use for what amounts to lunch money. Just ten years ago, this was impossible, but the evolvement of digital pictures and online brokers of these pictures has made this possible.

Digital collateral material, especially in Business-to-Business (B2B) communication, is a key threshold of differentiation, at least in order to foster first-look interest, such as sending a compelling digital brochure to a potential customer. However, it is surprising to see how so many organizations and so-called consultants cannot assemble a stunning electronic brochure, or at least have a professional create it for them. What is especially concerning is that most sales departments send out PowerPoint slides that are laid out in a format with improper use of typography, proportion, and grammar, with weak pictures and branding that looks more like a grade-school project. The marketing team could help by looking over all PowerPoint presentations internally to ensure they meet the corporate brand dress for their communicative output to customers.

One should remember that most of us are visual, and a digital repertoire that is minimalist and voguish, while it exudes *savoir faire*, is one of the key elements of branding. This is especially true in the digital age, since after all, we are not that different from the caveman and are still in many respects innately driven.

Collateral material and compelling subject lines are the new battleground in much of the B2B, as well as B2C communication, and literally the first impression in the digital economy is paramount. In comparison, when one has not experienced the old way of mailing brochures and following it up for feedback with endless and often fruitless follow-up phone calls, today all the digitization that is available to us now, can easily be taken for granted. But that was the world sales and marketing departments played in once upon a time. However, in the presto-digital age, one can talk to a client on the phone and e-mail him or her a brochure for real-time reference on the fly.

The Era of Fax Machines
The death knell for the telex was definitely the fax machine, which allowed for more practical two-way communication and was more easily

documented. Assuming that a firm liked keeping a mountain of papers for record keeping of correspondence, which was fine, however, if the fax ran on thermal paper, it would be just like old soldiers, and "just fade away" over time.

The fax machine became popular in Canada by the mid-1980s. This particular technology really changed and disrupted office communications more than we might give it credit for. The first ones in practical use were based on using thermal paper that came in rolls, and when the roll finished, a replacement would be put in the machine. The older ones had no memory, meaning that if the roll ran out on the weekend, the sent message would not be received, due to a lack of paper, and of course, this would mean a missed sales order. Certainly, this was not the only problem with thermal paper, since after some time, as mentioned earlier, the print would fade out and would play havoc with documentation in various offices, engineering firms, medical and legal settings.

To overcome this dilemma and minimize loss of information, staff would photocopy the thermal on 8.5″ x 11″plain paper. This would be viewed today as unnecessary waste of paper, leading not only to cost but environmental footprints and mundane task of labour deployment, two relative inefficiencies by today's standards.

At the higher-end of fax technology, commercial art firms had faxes that could send and receive in colour, reducing the time it took to approve artwork for ads, labels, etc.; there will be more on that later. The more advanced fax machines that developed later ran on inkjet or laser technology, used regular copy paper, and the printing output lasted a lifetime. Out-of-paper memory became a thing of the past. Then again, it almost seems embarrassing to admit that some companies today still deploy a fax machine. To overcome this antiquated system, faxing has now been incorporated into computers, where the computer can receive and send faxes, which is a relative leap forward, but still, staff seems to have this innate urge to print a received or sent fax to show the boss that something worthwhile is being accomplished at work. Then again, what is worthwhile becomes a topic on its own.

To give practical insight in the world before the use of faxes, customer orders were either mailed after they were painstakingly typed by the secretary and the salesperson picked-up the purchase orders, or as in many cases, the orders would be taken verbally over the phone. Of course, what was said and what was transcribed by the order-taker were often subject to discrepancies.

Today, because of e-mail, we receive numerous spams every day from stock tips, encouraging us to purchase shares on negative-equity companies, or perhaps Viagra or unsolicited dating advice. But the story does not end there; e-mail or banner ads are filled with opportunities to make twenty million dollars in a Nigerian business venture that will probably end up in a kidnapping ransom situation in Lagos. Then again, we might get offers from digital messiahs such as SEOs that offer top search rankings on Google for your business to make up for the fact that the business might not have a credible go-to market sales strategy. Then of course there are offers, or e-mails, supposedly taking you to your bank to update your information, but it really is a digital phishing site where you input your personal information so someone can draw credit cards in your name to entertain his lovely Russian mistress. The flow of degenerative offers is endless in the cyber world, and I could delve further, at the expense of abominating the English language.

Then and even now, we receive faxes broadcasting ads for "leaking basement fixer-upper services" to people who live in condos, "accounting and insurance services," as well as a host of other offerings because the last great hope for advertisers of intruding in the office was the fax machine. In the social side of office humour, faxes were sent back and forth to other companies of the latest dirty jokes, and of course, this made for great entertainment to lighten up the day.

Faxes were not too private, so if it was to be discreet, the recipient had to phone the sender to make sure he or she could hang around the fax machine like some type of idle office squatter, until the message arrived. Of course, back then, accounting departments got their own separate fax numbers, so the rest of the staff would not know that they were paying their bills past ninety days.

The fax allowed a significant revenue stream for telephone companies, since the fax required a dedicated phone line. Much of this has changed with the introduction of VOIP technology, playing havoc with telephone companies' traditional profit centres, such as fax and long-distance. As much as the fax created relatively breakthrough communication leaps and displaced the telex, there soon would be a new kid in town, around 1993, called electronic mail.

Today, organizations still have fax machines, knowing full well that they have really sung their swan song, as they hope someone will come take them away to the museum, to be humane and to put them out of their misery.

Typewriters

The go-to typewriter in the 1960s, until their relative demise in the 1990s, was the IBM Selectric typewriter. For those under thirty-five years old, it might be a term they have never heard, but the typewriter was once the standard individual bar mechanical type that would jam when a fast typist would hit keystrokes in succession too quickly. These were still in existence in the early 1970s. The market then went electric, and later electronic. But it was the IBM Selectric, with its ball-based mechanism and electromechanical design that ultimately captured seventy-five percent of the US market. Eventually, IBM introduced a memory component in the Selectric series variation in 1973 called the IBM Mag Card II typewriter that offered a whopping eight thousand characters. This meant that the typist could prepare four different form letters and merge them with the customer base. Primitive as this may sound, it was one of the first relatively crude word processing and publishing applications. Oh! And a person who typed had to have a comprehension of the English language, including grammatical structure and spelling (I was a lousy speller, so computers really saved me), which is becoming a rarity in the digital age.

IBM Selectrics had automatic erasers, using the backspace button that replaced correcting inks and ribbons. Before the advent of practical and cost-attainable word processors, one could not just copy and paste into sentences. Modern word processing programs have illuminated the structure of language because of copy-and-paste capabilities. Incidentally, the typewriter had one type of font, perhaps Times New Roman, and of course, IBM had options of changeable mechanical balls that could be replaced if a different font was needed for different documents. This was considered quite the cat's meow when it first came out.

Simple things we take for granted did not exist, like changing the size of a subtitle or italicizing, massive mail merging, access to five hundred fonts, and the full array of the CMYK colour universe. Of course, spell checks did not exist, and if the secretary or administrative assistants typed a draft letter for the boss, any notable changes meant that the letter had to be started from scratch.

Later, the IBM Selectric typewriters were mated with various first-to-market word processors (I sold many of these) and were used both for inputting data and as a printer before the commercial advent of inkjet and laser printers.

Just before we say farewell to typewriters, another noted design on the IBM Selectric series was its ergonomics, in terms of how the keys felt on the fingertips, with recessed cups on each key. This was IBM ingenuity and studying the customer at its best, to understand the sense of feel during usage and how it created comfort, both physically and emotionally, for the user. I call this ergonomic productivity. The curvature on keys created output efficiency because of the ergonomic engineering. Today's keyboard ergonomics used on various computer devices are based on the IBM Selectric keyboards and owe much to this long-forgotten breakthrough.

The Japanese employ this method of building around the user, and what comes to mind is especially car design, where they ensure parts not only fit correctly but sound correct, from the buttons to the sounds exuded when closing the door. The reason for this is simple: upon first impression, it means exacting standards, refined engineering, and as-sembly know-how.

The IBM Selectric was so popular that there was a complete in-dustry on its own of refurbished IBM typewriters for sale. This was the office setting when it came to word processing that once existed not too long ago, filled with both romanticism and inefficiencies that are unimaginable today.

While You Were Out and Telephones

How can we discuss all this miraculous technology without the mention of smartphones? Long ago, when you were out of the office for a field call, you would wonder exactly how many calls you missed and how you would follow up on your missed calls after returning to work.

Typically, you would come back to your office and ask your assistant how many calls you got, or perhaps a team member left a tear-away paper message on your desk. Then, of course, this was in addition to listening to your answering machine playback tape messages that were often more long and winding than a Fidel Castro speech to the United Nations. While you were listening to your answering machine play back your messages, more calls would come in, and if you worked in an era where the car phone or wireless handheld were not yet in use, the resulting tasks upon your return would pile up like a Hong Kong traffic jam.

Simply put, you were without communication when you travelled (unless you were James Bond). To replicate this era that really existed up to the end of the last century and perhaps beyond, conduct a self-experiment and see if you can handle the feeling. For example, turn off your computer and your smartphone for two days, and then go about your business, if you can. To those brought up with this technology, it would feel like you were lost in the forest and became a digital orphan, but once upon a time, this was how the game was played; inefficient relative to today, yes, but this was the game.

So once you compiled a list of all your missed calls that had to be returned, the added challenges of dealing with multiple issues that arose during your absence was quite overburdening and often required you to put on a fireman's hat, trying to put out a host of fires.

Enter the smartphone world, and you will find the ultimate communication device for talk, e-mail, texting, and its endless apps, which include anything from social media, GPS, maps, contacts, digital airline tickets, even a retail flyer app named flip, (which is playing havoc on retailers, since it does price comparisons), to streaming movie apps to the TV, such as Popcorn Time, Netflix. Today, many of the programs of a desktop are on the smartphones by way of apps. Subsequently, it is perhaps the ultimate game-changer, and even Captain Kirk and Batman would never have left home without it!

As a result of the smartphone, workers can compartmentalize their work while they are on the road, dealing with e-mails or texts and addressing many of the tasks that come up when out of office. Some e-mail items that need a more thoughtful response can be contemplated while travelling, and travellers can then give a more thorough reply at a time of their choosing by utilizing their laptops or by phones if they like to tap.

In old school days, many of us remember returning important calls, only to receive another important call as we tried to catch up while five lines were on hold for us; this alone was a daunting task!

The phenomenon and the widespread use of the smartphone has only really been more widely adopted in the last six years, and the way it organizes people and creates business efficiencies should not be taken for granted. At the same time, the way it addicts and dumbs down a generation should not either, but more on this later.

Another area that deserves notable mention is the evolution of business phones and how they are used and integrated into modern communications. Today, the business phone is still relevant. Years ago, the phone ringing off the wall generally indicated that you were a busy and successful company, but now the barometer of activity has changed from phone calls to e-mail inquiries. Thus, company phones can be relatively quiet, while the indicator of how busy they are is measured by e-mails. Consequently, this has created a generation gap of senior managers in the over-forty range that like the warmth of a phone call versus the millennials who find they are more efficient via a combination of e-mails, texting, and instant messaging. And let's face it; it would be a bit traumatic for many millennials to crawl out of their digital fortress and initiate phone calls, perhaps because two-way fluidity of conversation has gone from mostly audio to textual.

We should not really pit the phone against e-mails and other forms of digital communication, since they all have individual merits, but a combination of all offers an incredible totality and has its place. This is why millennials have been encouraged to get on the phone and make cold calls to customers, which is a lost art and requires thick skin, while it promotes rapid-fire wit and intellectual fluidity. An interesting article in the August 30, 2013, issue of the *Globe and Mail* discusses this in the Careers section. But in reaching out to the millennials, this much is for sure: the boogeyman will not come out and get you if you pick up the phone. Subsequently, if a potential customer slam-dunks your pitch, you have choices that include chalking it up to experience, calling your mama, or ranting about it on your smartphone, Facebook app, or blog. Decisions, decisions!

Some Final Words on Business Processes

The future that was promised by *Star Trek*, the Xerox Alto computer, the moon landing, and our imaginations is here today, and to truly appreciate its splendid awe, we should perhaps contrast it with yesterday, since perspective comes with time and allows us not to take things for granted. Sometimes the good old days were not quite as good in many aspects as our faded memories imply.

Then, to take more of a macroeconomic approach, it is fair to say that today's firms, if saddled with the technologies of yesterday, would have a cost structure that would put it in the red because of dated inefficiencies that could no longer compete in today's dynamic global marketplace.

Efficiencies delivered by all this technology have tamed inflation (even though governments publish biased low inflation numbers) while creating structural unemployment, meaning that the jobs are there but the skill sets are lacking. Either way, the technology the West has brought to the world in the last six hundred years has gifted the human story.

The technology we have today, both good and bad, has mostly been brought about by the infinite curiosity that commercial forces offer, and certainly not brought about by the hopes of creating jobs with resounding speeches of government leaders.

Thus, it can be said that market economies spawned almost all of this technological inventiveness, while increasing consumer welfare and eradicating much poverty.

As a side note, perhaps this claim of free-markets needs explaining. First, competitive products and services offer the consumer more for less, not less for more, which allows consumers to be able to afford and acquire things high prices would prohibit. As mentioned earlier, market protection to local monopoly companies leaves many nations in poverty; India is a good example, where the consumer pays more for less, thus, reducing their lot in life. For example, in India, local retailers are protected from international and local chain stores, limiting them to two hundred locations nationwide. As a result, the consumer is paying the premium for the benefit of local retailers. It is this type of state-controlled mercantilism that leads to a diminishment in consumer welfare.

Competition of commerce offer consumer choice. A good example is visiting an auto dealership or a grocery store, or better still, Amazon. Any person who lived in the Soviet Union during the Communist era knows all about lack of consumer choice, unreliable cars, and empty shelves in grocery stores. Multinational corporations (MNCs) that do business in poorer countries offer higher wages than local competitors, while cross-fertilizing skills and processes in the new country they operate in. Subsequently, this helps lift people out of poverty in these developing countries while improving the capital knowledge of the country. For example, foreign auto companies operating in Mexico such as Ford and Volkswagen pay almost three times more than local firms, including a host of benefit packages, thus helping many to lift themselves out of economic hardship.

It is fair to state that governments do not create jobs, unless one considers taxing people heavily to subsidize a welfare state as a long term societal strategy.

During the waning years of the Roman Empire, many people who had been given daily coins after serving in the army could be found in the Roman Colosseum watching gladiators fight, and other barbaric exhibitions, while they made little societal contributions. Does this sound familiar today with the West, living off the avails of entitlements and salivating at the pugilistic misadventures of MMA fights?

BACK TO THE TECHNO-CULTURE

We interrupt this regularly scheduled program for a special news bulletin!

"It's a bird! It's a plane!"

"No, Mommy, no! It's an eight-hundred-pound digital gorilla."

By now, if we have trolled through the comment boards after e-news articles or Twitter chains and have been exposed to digital verbiage, we see that they are mostly posted anonymously. The first few posts sound within the range of reason, but often they go downhill into a diatribe that spirals into the limited parameters of profanity the English language possesses. When people don't agree with each other, it usually ends up escalating into some type of name-calling rants in the digital world. In the case of adults, diametrically they pugilistically dual each other in the great digital Roman Coliseum, then they go to their children's local school board meeting to protest against bullying in the school yard. But hey, you know the beat goes on!

You see, these people who comment on Yahoo, MSN, blogs, classic newspapers gone digital, and consolidators like Digg.com, use their anonymity to metamorphose into eight-hundred-pound digital gorillas, pimple cream in one hand and a box of potato chips elegantly sprinkled by the side of their keyboards (as part of their artistic repertoire), since the stress of being a digital motor mouth might have them break out. Most often, what all this does is further reduce their chances of a meaningful social interaction.

Their only real concern is their mommies cutting them off their digital belching when they stop paying the ISP bills. But then again, a computer hack might track him down through his ISP address and lay down a good old-fashioned whipping. When this happens, of course they will manipulate anyone who listens now that they are on the receiving end of bullying. They may eventually get their parents to create a walkathon against bullying without realizing that many of the parents who participate in this seemingly good cause are bullies themselves. Yes, the same ones you hear screaming at their kids' minor league sports games perhaps they themselves came up short as kids, but are convinced their own kids will be the next Pele, Jordan, or Gretzky, coddled and all, while their ISP pipes serenade them 24/7.

Of course, it would be too simple to assume that youths are the only ones laying on the posting rants, because more mature middle-aged machismo-type males and blabbermouth females, who take time away from all the intellectual discovery of watching reality TV shows and all that Oprah has to offer, also participate in this digital orgy of democratic expression. Or better still, mild-mannered Starbucks patrons, equipped with their voguish technology, are tapping away on their Samsung Galaxy 6s or tablets on free Wi-Fi (remember that free is important, unless it involves giving away their own labour for free), as they expose the inner workings of the mind. Then again, they might be doing something more profound by posting conspiracy theories, usually built by convincing anyone who will listen, that 9/11 was a government job. Of course, this comes without having a rudimentary understanding of civil engineering, structural and stress analysis, metallurgic theory, or the meticulous preparation required to demolish a building.

This is why no trained and practiced engineer or credible investigator would give credence to most of these arcane conspiracy theories believed mostly by people who might be spending too much time in digital town halls, with self-ordained PhDs in emotional illogic and a self-proclaimed sixth sense, which gives them a false entitlement of elitist perception for their gullible cronies to digest.

The world seems to be turning many of the social media tools into some type of digital supermarket tabloid, where rhyme and reason and critical thinking are being tossed aside to make room for innuendo, groupthink, and diluted rhetoric, since OMG and various other sites provide hashish for the mind in a spiralling debacle of idleness. Yes, we are being gifted with this new age of enlightenment, but hopefully we will not turn it into digital apathy and enslavement that might prevent us from actually progressing.

The age of digital democratization is here, as we all have dreamy and tear-filled hopes of mindless expressive egalitarianism as the majority of thought bullies the minority. Because, after all, if enough people believe it, then it must be true! However, this could also be construed as collective misguidance. Just like when once upon a time people believed that the world was flat. When we peel it down to its crude nature, the "tenets of digital democracy" are a type of savagery that dilutes us into an inebriated form of groupthink that somehow makes us collectively righteous.

So, then, these same people who have come with the latest word on righteousness, "bullying," are now rallying the cry to define our latest quest for progression or regression, depending which side of the fence one sits on. For example, when we look at plain schoolyard bullying, of which, like many, I was often on the receiving end, at least it taught us how to deal with fear and uncertainty, all the while strengthening our spirits to learn how to cope with the nature of the human beast.

This is an important and unpleasant skill to learn during the rite of passage, but today, with weapons, the stakes are much higher. Of course, there are many other forms of bullying that we see on Facebook and other digital platforms. Then again, one could argue that the abusive nature of office politics and climbing up the corporate and governmental cliff is a form of bullying. But what is becoming clear is that the sociological architects who are designing our rallying cries are using social media as a vehicle to bully an unsuspecting public, while coercing people to think like them or risk being labelled a "phobia this" or "phobia that" without even understanding the meaning of the word as it is defined in the *Oxford Dictionary*. Of course, things degenerate more when the media-designed jingle of verbiage has come up with the use of the word "intolerant" as an emotive weapon to stigmatize people who have the audacity to present credible and intellectual critical thinking that opposes the suffocation, intolerant and weakly constructed tenets of political correctness.

But in the end, those accusing others of intolerance are often intolerant themselves when their model of societal norm is logically challenged with facts and empirical evidence. Eventually, the politically correct water down their intellectually challenged repertoire into a weak platform of societal engineered demagoguery that often degenerates into childish rants and venomous smearing, if you don't toe the line. So as opposed to debating someone's ideas, the politically correct smear a person's character, while hypocritically espousing the values of democratic thinking, and this is what makes them so dangerous.

And by manipulating all the multiple media outlets into fear, they can conduct a witch hunt against anyone who does not think like them, like some type of digitally enhanced renaissance of McCarthyism. So, in many respects, the politically correct and their clan of social architects *are* the new McCarthyism. Of course, we can take solace that even after all this, we are under the delusionary belief that individual freedoms can hold up against the intolerance of groupthink. And the intellectual immaturity of the politically correct lacks the ability to credibly attack one's ideas and as a result degrades themselves by attacking the person, with cheapened media clichés.

We are living in this world of liberal inspired political correctness, and it is being lapped up as *de facto* morality by the masses; so why is it that we are hearing so much digital diatribe that contradicts this? Since, after all, we all know that liberal thinking is morally superior and self-anointed! Is it perhaps the frustration of walking on eggshells creating a festering tension that is coming out as a latent manifest variable in social media? In digital land, both for brands and political opinions, the comment boards offer anonymity, and this seems to suggest that people are talking out of both sides of their mouths. The one side is in person, where they toe the line with words of politically correct obedience to their masters, that quite possibly mask their true feelings, and the other side is where their true feelings are espoused on the Internet.

So now that we have discussed a host of technologies going as far back as the Industrial Revolution and the rapid innovation of the century, while considering its effects on both consumers and commerce, it might be an opportune time to discuss the social media suspects, to try to make some sense out of all this.

ROASTING THE SOCIAL MEDIA, TECHNO-CULTURE, AND THE USUAL SUSPECTS

Techno-Culture Cool

The techno-culture has its share of "nouveau cool" with its impressive array of techno-culture speak, some of it quite titillating, some of it bordering on an abomination of the English language. Of course, to participate and become part of the new in-crowd, a vocabulary of about twenty-five words may be expressed—not all necessarily to be spelled out—coupled with a sense of shallowness as one publicly states one's beliefs in certain causes. In participating in this digital orgy of sorts, one hopes to be on the just side of history as we compare our attempts to cover up the savageness within, with the immunisation that technological civility can offer.

It is the new cool, where clothing fashion is complemented by technical gadgets, or is it the other way around, since we are coming around with the "Internet of things" and considering wearing gadgets that are digitally connected. In other words, we are on the verge of reconciling our bodies with artificial intelligence and becoming cyborgs of sorts. Even better, as opposed to discussing the origins of the universe or disco, large groups of individuals defend the credo of a cult-like devotion to a corporation like Apple, as the twentysomethings tap away at the local house of java as some form of public foreplay or a digital breeding call. Much time is available for this, since their futures have been sold down the river in many cases. The promised dreams of a robust service economy have not quite panned out yet, since these kids' futures are being outsourced abroad while they're sipping away at their cups of java. Still, they never quite understand that the scent of Western demise might lie within the relationship between advanced manufacturing and inventiveness. And while we are on this subject of the West, its future as a civilization might lie in its robust will to defend itself on all fronts against envy inspired hypocrites, both internal and external, as well as the naïvety of ideological self-flagellation. Because when all is said and done, if the West completely opened up its gates of immigration tomorrow morning, it would be a flood resembling Noah's Ark.

Now getting back to the social media, pictures are sent and uploaded to Instagram, Facebook, Snapchat, Vine, blogs, and the like, while insecure iterations of self-promoting narcissism are belched out on YouTube. And, yes, some of them are almost as good as MMA pre-fight videos.

It is no wonder then that aliens do not want to visit us, since they would have to check themselves in at the local psychiatric ward after being exposed to this latest version of what is now our digital world. But all is not bad; each day we invent new social media superheroes, since we use the various tools of the Internet to unknowingly create a comparative misery index of our lives against those of others, in order to help make sense of both our individual and collective existence.

Yes, we are living within the marvels of the third Industrial Revolution, and just like all revolutions, some of the by-product is bad, some is good, and much is grey. Ultimately, the way it frees and imprisons us might not matter much, since we might all be too dazed to know the difference. And perhaps now might be a good time to name some of the suspects.

Facebook

Facebook is a social-networking place where we can stay connected with friends and make new digital friends without necessarily ever having met them in person. It's a place where we record the daily chronicles of our lives as a testament not only for the world to see but perhaps as a vehicle to ease the pain of loneliness, while measuring our misery and glee index against others to ensure it stays within the normative parameters of our emotional distribution curves. Facebook is a place where we seem to "like" things that we might not really like while sharing the daily rituals of life in an oasis of digital pretension.

It is a place where we advertise and upload the ongoing events of our lives, yearning for the collective approval, like some lapdog wanting to impress its master. This is done by way of "likes", "shares", and "comments". Facebook is similar to receiving digital lollipops, much like a child desperately asking for approval from a parent, as the child yearns for perpetual attention.

It's a place where stardom seems within reach through a cocktail of an intertwined and narcissistic barrage of rapid quips that spirals into egotistical eroticism. This is complemented by provocative gestures in the race to the lower echelon of desperation, a place where ambition meets the tragedy of reality.

Simultaneously, a host of segmented ad campaigns pop up and clamour for our attention, to join their fan pages so we can advertise our pop cultural titillations and our moral causes to the world in collective righteousness. All this while not having the courage to leave the past and too fearful to consider the challenges of the future, somehow we hang on to our shallow acquaintances of days gone by, like some type of digital high-school reunion that just won't end, since we can't seem to get our eyes off the rear-view mirrors.

Victims of our own curiosity, we unknowingly become masochists as we collectively share the pain and romanticism of nostalgia without understanding that "God created the past so we could leave it there," in order to meet the mystique of the future. But perhaps Facebook is a testimony to the existence of our lives that will outlive our mortality, and in a sense, show that once upon a time a life gifted us with a type of optimism that we could live forever, if only in a digital format.

Twitter

"News on the hour or by the second!" Welcome to the world of Twitter, where the muzzled and other self-proclaimed serfs wailing in their culture of victimization or change can perform their text-based diatribe. For those who never made it to *America's Got Talent* or were born too late to perform on Ed Sullivan's show or perhaps want to perform a techno-cultural version of Walter Cronkite, Twitter is the next best thing.

Celebrities have their followers, or should I say "digital sheep," following their selected Hollywood cultists in the hope of being part of something that gives a connection and perhaps a deeper meaning to their lives. Reporters have now been reduced to 140 characters as they participate side-by-side in reporting the news, watching their careers fade into relative obscurity against the disruption of Twitter and the like.

True, Twitter is an incredible tool for organizing campaigns, a coup d'état, or disaster relief efforts, assuming that ISP providers are not down. However, often it is used as a form of stage for people to display the chips on their shoulders from not being heard, so they rant in the hope of saying something profound and earth-moving that will change the world and beyond. In many respects, their followers are people who are like fans at a gladiator match; they cheer for the glory and jeer at the tragedy, but are at best wannabe participants in the writing of history.

It seems stylish to organize a coup d'état to overthrow a dictator, as was the case in Egypt, only to be replaced by an Islamicist Party, and eventually the military, in order to keep the religious zealotry types in line and away from political power. Of course, to them democracy is a one-time vehicle to prop up a theological despot in power, based on their self-professed view of what the divine's message really is. In the summer of 2013, Twitter exploded on Turkey's Prime Minister Tayyip Erdogan's face, along with his gang of religiously infused despots posing as statesmen, when they were quite perturbed at the power of Twitter and how it helped create a rally of the oppressed. Perhaps Mr. Erdogan could purchase a girly calendar and get a grip on what century he's living in, and reconcile with empirical facts, his prevaricated denial of Turkish history.

Yes, Twitter has many other fine uses. For example, how about we overthrow our bosses and organize a massive street protests against the latest corporate villains (the same ones we pressure for higher share prices)? This sounds like a brilliant idea, until we come to the realization that being the boss is not what it's cracked up to be, since one has to put up one's own personal assets to make payroll, or if the firm is public, one has to deal with activist shareholders salivating at the mouth for the opportunity to reap the fruits of frivolous litigation on a director.

The name of the game these days is "let's find any boogeyman", except of course ourselves. After all, who needs a mirror to look into? This way we don't have to deal with the beast within. The list of bad guys is endless; we could all tweet into the dustbins of vengeance, corporations, politicians (that we collectively and misguidedly elect), bankers, car companies, charities that are a front for businesses. And the list is almost endless—certainly read-ers could draw up their own lists. Of course, we could have a cause to empower women by employing Twitter, but women, who are on equal footing for the most part here in the West, often employ the standard practice of beating on the Western man (their favourite whipping boy), since it is a no-lose proposal, while conveniently ig-noring the plight of the tragic and shameful treatment of women in countries like Saudi Arabia, Pakistan, Yemen, and the other regular suspects. They often ignore their sisters in countries like this, since they fear being branded racists by Orwellian demagogues. It shows that they do not have the courage to take their cause to the next level and wipe out gender-based oppression on a global scale, and it is this hypocrisy that needs to be challenged within.

But then again, if only Lady Gaga would retweet our latest insight into rumours of who wore what at the latest Hollywood gala, we could finally be discovered for our intellectual and philosophical prowess while having a legacy in history alongside Socrates.

But often, Twitter becomes a place for people to vent their anger as they perform their latest renditions of an old-school Hulk Hogan interview. Today, though, all one has to do is give a digital steroid fix to one's Twittermaniacs as they unwittingly join a cause or event that might just not pan out as they had hoped. For all that the "140 character universe" offers, it perhaps exasperates the loneliness of the digital-age since keystrokes and letters cannot replace the warmth of a real friend.

Twitter, of course, serves for much more, including sponsored tweets, overvalued shares, and retailers advising their followers on when their favourite products will be on sale, engaging consumers in dialogue, of course, bullying, and better still, *#getalife*! Yes, the fans are going wild cheering their latest digital cause, until the following morning they hashtag a new cause, because they forgot about the last cause.

THE DECLINE OF TELEVISION

Before the advent of the Internet and especially YouTube, television was the master of our attention span. Television was where families once gathered to watch great events and not-so-great events. The three-channel universe was the genesis of advertising agencies—the award-winning *Mad Men* series depicts this masterfully—as each week they formulated new jingles for consumer packaged goods companies.

It was a time when one sponsor would dominate the advertising of certain programs, especially in the 1950s. It is that nostalgic place where the *Mad Men* series finds itself as it celebrates the golden age of commercials and ad agencies. Television was where families watched the famous *Bonanza* series on Sunday nights. It was where *I Love Lucy* was introduced into our lives, and in 1964, it was those four lads from Liverpool that the world first was introduced to by Ed Sullivan.

Television has become the motion-picture history of our times since the late 1940s, capturing the indelible moments in of our lives and times while collecting them and giving them historical relevance.

Television was where a world saw the horror of a slain President, the assassination of Martin Luther King and then Bobby Kennedy as the dreams of idealism faded. It was where Walter Cronkite reported the carnage of Vietnam; it was where we saw the *Eagle* land on the moon. It was where a helicopter took a president away into the annals of history as a nation reflected on the tragedy; it was where we were first told about the death of Elvis Presley. It was through this lens that the world first saw the fall of the Berlin Wall and the end of the Cold War, only to realize that the world was a more stable place with two contenders as opposed to one.

Television was what brought the horror of 9/11 and the renaissance of religious zealotry in a way that is plainly embarrassing to modern civilization, while frankly holding back the progress of civilization to a higher level of purpose.

The lens of television saw the LAPD chase a certain football player doing his best rendition of Mario Andretti while taking us on a lovely tour of Los Angeles; it was where we heard about the loss of Michael Jackson.

Television has entertained and inspired us with its rich programming while at the same time letting us drop out of the world and dull our senses.

Television, with its rich array of programming, reads like the chronology of our lives, from *Ed Sullivan, Days of Our Lives, Mission: Impossible, The Adventures, Laugh In, All in the Family, Maude, Miami Vice, Cheers, CSI Miami,* and, of course, *Dancing With the Stars.* Certainly there was much more than this, but that would be a book on its own.

The news anchors, as was the case with Walter Cronkite and Lloyd Robertson, were more trusted than state leaders, and probably for good reason. And there was and is some lovely magazine-style reporting on *60 Minutes* and the like that promised to change the world as it tried to peel back the layers to find the truth, only to find out that the horror of the truth is too unbearable for most.

Television is a place where we have compared our morals to reconcile our lives against the misery index of the collective world at large; it is a place where we try to make sense of this mysterious, definitive, yet unexplained miracle called life. And much like the social media, television serves as a vehicle to ensure that we are not alone.

Up until 1994, the media of mass communication that dominated our world included, television, radio, and print. We all know by now that something was to appear that would disrupt this model, when the Internet came along in the mid-1990s. Thus, the line has become blurry as to what television is and what the difference is with computer-driven technologies such as smartphones and tablets, since to many, they are all screens, some push and some pull. The word "convergence" came into common parlance back in 1999 as it was hotly debated as to how the TV and the computer would converge. The answer is now revealing itself.

For the millennials, this has already happened, since they see little difference between getting their news and entertainment on iPhones, tablets, laptops, but rarely on TVs. To many, network news is so passé (unless one is into talking heads on CNN that go from crises to crises, spewing out second-rate propaganda). All these vehicles are just hardware that deliver content, which is what TV did in the first place. However, TV pushed information at you, while the Internet is more of a pull medium, where you can select information at a time of your convenience. Of course, these other platforms, meaning tablets and the like, are not as rich and grand as watching a large TV monitor, but then again, the millennials and others might not care. Consequently, the only thing holding back the demise of TV is really the Baby Boomers, who have not grown up with today's fascinating technologies, even though their generation invented most of the foundations. But it's true that many households are cutting their cable cords and living in the online world, where much of TV content is replicated.

Just as a small example, Netflix is producing its own programming, much like the networks, and one series that comes to mind is *House of Cards,* which received nine nominations at the Sixty-Fifth Primetime Emmy Awards, putting it in the same league as television programs. At the Netflix monthly fee of about eight dollars, cable executives—who are still pimping out and padding content—are probably reading Christensen's *Disruptive Innovation* until the wee hours of the morning, or at least they should be. This landmark moment marks the first time that television's top awards have recognized a program delivered online as equal in quality to the best that TV has to offer.

Cable companies realize that they are up against the convenience and the pull nature that social media and PVR offer, which allow us to record programs into a hard drive. Gone are the days where one would record shows on videocassettes or DVDs, and then pile them up like the Eiffel Tower in the living room, which again is taking advertising agencies for a loop.

Television stations still have their signals brokered through cable companies, and their days might be numbered by this type of pipeline pimping as it is becoming evident that television stations will pretty well deliver their content via the Internet directly for millennials, gen-Xers, and more tech-savvy Boomers to enjoy on tablets, smartphones, and laptops.

As the line between television and the online world becomes blurrier, cable and Internet delivery will likely go into what macroeconomists term "perfect competition," meaning the deliverables will become a commodity with no room for differentiation, and the determining factor of consumer behaviour will be price alone. In fact, we see this today as the share prices on cable companies are under pressure from unstable future earnings as a result of margin erosion, but we will let time deliberate on this. YouTube is perhaps the greatest game-changer to come along since television, and naturally, it now deserves proper mention.

YouTube

Founded in 2005 by Chad Hurley and Steve Chen and purchased by Google in 2006, it is one of the key drivers of social media in terms of shifting the ground we currently walk on. The idea is a simple one; it basically entails uploading a video online, but it is ingenious and has affected the world in so many ways: delivery of educational material, uploaded newsreels, propaganda campaigns, conspiracy theories, narcissistic behaviour, our own YouTube channels, how-to videos, and the list goes on. YouTube is where each person has the opportunity to do his or her own rendition of a professional wrestling interview, although none quite as good as the Iron Sheik. YouTube, much like the rest of social media, is a classic example of Metcalfe's law, this time on steroids.

Going back to education for a moment, one can really learn more complex subjects like calculus and its associated derivatives and rates of change. You may visit:

www.youtube.com/watch?v=jbIQW0gkgxo.

Or perhaps one would want to learn statistical inference and properties of normal distribution to better understand the central tendency theorem and mean reversion. Please visit:

http://www.youtube.com/watch?v=cgxPcdPbujI.

I trust that all digital debaters are quite conversant on the above, but the point is that university lectures are supplemented by YouTube videos, or actually if a person has the discipline, he or she could educate themselves on a host of subjects anywhere from the arts to the sciences. At the same time, this is an excellent tool for online degrees, since most accredited universities deliver online education, including the prestigious London School of Economics, a place where Sir Mick Jagger studied commerce. Thus, an individual can obtain an undergraduate degree today in commerce from LSE and many more—but more on online education later.

There were many musical bands that we never saw during our youth or never saw them on TV or in live concerts. Remember, not too long ago, if you missed the program, you missed it, unless you could record it on your video equipment. But today you can go on YouTube and watch Mick Jagger during his performance on *The Ed Sullivan Show* in 1965; please see http://www.youtube.com/watch?v=ROAKlnaMuRw.

Or perhaps see the Jackson 5 in 1970: http://www.youtube.com/watch?v=M-aSjHnbw18.

Or James Brown on the *Ed Sullivan Show:* http://www.youtube.com/watch?v=t08ejaQqWjY.

Or experience the genius of the Beatles during their 1965 Shea Stadium concert:

https://www.youtube.com/watch?v=EbcebPRoMLM.

YouTube changes the painful but addictive nature of nostalgia, since it really plays on our innate sense of wanting visuals, and it serves as a forum to compare the pop stars of yesteryear with today's. Looking back at all the icons of our youth, no matter what our age, and measuring it against today, it helps us understand the passage of time and lets us better measure our dreams against the reality we have created. Then again, this generation has not produced a Ray Charles, Jagger or Lennon, McCartney, and a Shirley Bassey, not even close.

YouTube always allows us to compare quarterback Broadway Joe Namath from 1968 with Aaron Rodgers of today or compare Iron Mike Tyson with Muhammad Ali, or better still, compare the legendary running back James Nathaniel "Jim" Brown from the 1950s and '60s with Adrian Lewis Peterson.

Okay, now that we are on a roll, how would Bobby Orr look in today's NHL, injury-free and outfitted with modern skates and training against some of the lead-foots that occupy NHL blue lines, then again, what would it be like to see Pele compared with Maradona or Rooney? Then again, how would Kennedy interpret our times?

Today we can watch back-to-back videos on YouTube and get into some titillating debates while munching away on nutritionally packed bags of nacho chips and wings, simultaneously having the middle-aged compare their heroes with today's while awaiting for their cholesterol results from their physician. Better still, we could always have a comparison on YouTube of civility at soccer games between Italian and English soccer fans as they spiral to the bottom of acceptable conduct and define a new term, "rowdyism," as they start painfully reminding us about our Neanderthal past. Then again, one could watch the best of street fights and barroom brawls, in which there are always some very intellectually inspiring participants involved who decided to take some time off from consulting NASA on the next Mars mission.

If it is entertainment you want, you will receive it amply, and unlike the spectators of Rome, you will not have to go back to the Roman Colosseum during the time of the empire.

For example, consider music, most-watched TV programs, if you like, or the classic top-forty hits of days gone by. For the most part, this has been replaced by YouTube's most-watched videos of the day. YouTube is easily streamed to the television now, and there is no real reason to watch cable TV, since everything is available, including full high-definition movies and music videos. YouTube is a large part of the reason people are cutting their cable services.

Much of what we see on YouTube is homemade, some of it borderline, some of it quite inventive, and the rest of it in between. Today, there is a whole army of YouTubers that want to be discovered and become famous, until they realize that being famous makes one even lonelier and often leads to despair; just ask Marilyn Monroe or Britney Spears. Nonetheless, many just want to rant and be heard as a form of healing all that ails them within their souls. Eventually, wisdom teaches the most treacherous of narcissists that anonymity has its privileges, and happiness is left open to interpretation.

But YouTube is much more than this; it is news, replays, channels, announcements, TV commercials, and it doesn't end there. We can watch product reviews or a significant other sending a message to the world on why her ex is so.… Broken hearts aside, YouTube delivers a visual experience that aligns with our primitive desire to see while allowing us to watch instructional videos ranging from advice on resolving technical issues, to do-it-yourself home repairs, to computer fixes, and cooking instructions. But wait, there are YouTube channels for various interests, political opinions, repeats of television events, gang fights, dog fights, bar fights, music bands, cops beating up suspects or suspects beating up cops, and, of course, first news videos of local and political events that contradict the official line of so-called authorities. Oh! Did I forget to mention arcane conspiracy theories?

But often, and sometimes sadly, people simply want to be heard via YouTube with their views, messages, and techno-culture confessions to find some type of warmth that can peel off the layers of being alone and sad in a world that is so connected electronically but not spiritually.

It's no wonder television cable is rope-a-doping—a term coined when Cassius Clay hung out in the corner ropes to avoid a beating—trying to figure out a way to compete with what you want, when you want. Hence, cable is firing back with PVRs and on-demand shows and then some in this world of disruptive change. In some respects, it seems that we are living in a time where this medium of television has passed us, well at least in the youth segment and the Netflix crowd. Perhaps YouTube is the techno-culture's *Ed Sullivan Show* that plays 24/7, and we just don't know it yet. But one thing is for sure: the hits just keep on coming!

The possibilities that YouTube offers are nearly infinite, and one day, perhaps, the events of our lives will be digitally documented and recorded against our tombstones to see if our values and ideals stand the test of time and comparative history. Maybe YouTube will deliver this ultimate gift to future generations, allowing them to come to terms with what was and is.

Smartphones

Was it Batman or Captain Kirk who seemed to have been the first cell phone user? For sure, the gadgetry envisioned from these shows greatly influenced industrial design, including the flip phone, which gained its design inspiration from *Star Trek*. First came car phones that were used by very few people in the 1970s and then started to come into early majority adoption in the late eighties. The handheld cell phone, which really started to become the norm in the 1990s, was a status symbol one could observe as the "it" people and wannabes were seen roller blading in Santa Monica with a phone in hand. Because after all, basking in the sun and the sea of cultural shallows quintessentially defines the tenets of Southern California life.

Today, smartphones create unfathomable efficiencies, addictions, and idleness all wrapped into a package that is essential, liberating, yet enslaving. But this much is for sure, smartphones, starting first with the BlackBerry and then iPhone and Galaxy and the like, have changed our world. After all, how can one be techno-cool without one? Instant messaging, texting, taking pictures, downloading music, sending e-mails, tweeting, and of course, selfies can be instantly uploaded to Instagram. Today's smartphones are becoming practical computers in many respects, where one can utilize them as a GPS, get live traffic maps, exchange pictures, document notes, obtain weather conditions on the move, surf the net, update Facebook pages, and use best flyer apps like Flipp to document lowest prices and force retailers to price match all specials. But it doesn't end there; other uses include—and I admit I am only touching the surface here—alarm clocks, appointment calendars, watching shows, and of course using them as calculators (since many people at the end of modern-day high school still do not know their multiplication tables as they are on their way to enriched lives of quantitative illiteracy, which in some respects is as bad as not being able to read).

As functional as smartphones are, they are perhaps a techno-culture fashion statement with their array of industrial designs, colours, and so forth. But for some, it is essential that their nails are manicured as part of their digital *haute couture* as they swirl their finger before they press the "send" button to send off a profound message into cyberspace, probably not to MIT on heat exchange theory for rocket thrust systems for the next NASA launch. Or perhaps they are reaching out to their digital superheroes that exist only in their minds as a form of a hallucinatory diversion, or perhaps judging by facial expressions, it could be a text fight with their significant other. The possibilities are endless!

How can we have a conversation about smartphones without bringing up smartphone etiquette, or lack thereof? Did we mention digital zombies who are glued to their handhelds as if the messiah were returning and they are waiting for that moment of hope that is about to come out of the screen? It doesn't end there. Take, for example, that etiquette in elevators has greatly changed since the 1960s and *Mad Men*. We no longer have to look at each other uncomfortably, since we stare into our phones as a way of telling people to get out of our faces, or perhaps we are trying to cry out that what we are texting is important. Of course, how we are glued to our smartphones is something that was never envisioned by most, and certainly not by Steve Ballmer of Microsoft. Ballmer's inability to see the mobile market was the prime reason he is no longer the CEO of Microsoft, as that company missed the train on the mobile software market. Today, smartphone software is powered by two big players, Google's Android and Apple's iOS, as they both wrestle for the championship belt.

The social interaction theatre has changed. As an example, even the ritual of arguments between a boyfriend and girlfriend is done differently—please remember, these arguments can still occasionally be won by the male at this stage, since they are not married yet—this will, of course, changes once the knot is tied and the male becomes intelligent and learns how to play dead. As we all know, relationships eventually lead to some type of conflict, whereas once upon a time, arguments were limited to in-person or telephone conversations or a "Dear Johnny" letter, but all this has changed.

If one is perceptive, they can easily see a woman in a state of argument with her boyfriend/spouse just by watching how she looks and presses the buttons on her phone. After all, who has time for lunch when one has all these different and titillating technology delivery systems to conduct a love life with?

For example, does she argue by phone, text, e-mail, Facebook message, or Skype? She can always get really upset and simply "unfriend" her other half on Facebook! Of course such abrasive action could lead to both emotional and monetary heartache. The richness of all the new technology allows the exhausting possibilities of launching digital darts to the heart until all things come full circle, and then they make up on Skype, or if things are really bad, they send a "we are through" text message to each other. Then all one has to do is try and remember the password to his or her Lavalife account, in order to join the digital lonely hearts club band and repackage an online profile, which lies somewhere between truth and fiction! Obviously, he or she should be mindful of the digital footprints left behind during the battle royal, since all this could appear on social media if one decides to create a stew of frothy digital vengeance. So, there's no need to break up in person with all the available technology. Just send a text and then flame on Facebook. After all, wasn't this the reason all this technology was invented for in the first place?

Gone perhaps are the "Dear Johnny" letters, or the classical, "I want to see you and tell you something important", as a way of dropping someone in person. Use of the more traditional verbiage such as, "It's not you, it's me" or the famous, "I need time alone to find myself," better known as the soft slide, has gone the way of Michael Jackson's moonwalk. These time-honoured traditions are too time-consuming in the techno-shallow-culture, when a simple text will do, stating that she relegated him on the last train out of town.

Thus, traditions of fighting on the phone and then getting back together for make-up sex seem to be distant memories. But then again, someone might invent an app for make-up sex!

Moving to motion pictures or television series, consider Hollywood films, which are about visual motion and sound, but more people now send and receive text messages on the fly in the real world, and talking has taken a back seat, comparatively speaking, as our communication is mostly digital. However, Hollywood writers almost completely ignore the function of the smartphone within a movie, since aiming cameras at people's digital messages will not fill theatres. TV shows such as *House of Cards* use text captions, whereas a series like *Breaking Bad* ignored texting and had sophisticated drug dealers speaking clearly about their intentions over the phone, as did *Sons of Anarchy*. Anyone with some knowledge of unscrupulous behaviour knows certain subjects cannot be discussed over the phone, so then realism in this aspect is missing from many new films. Ultimately, filmmaking will find a way to reconcile and visually admit smartphones as being the hub of people's lives.

There are a host of addictions that affect us mere mortals, from alcoholism to porn, food, heroin, marijuana, tobacco, idleness, and the like, but so far we are not sure that anything we have seen in our lifetime has obsessed the collective human psyche like the current smartphone technology. Certainly, no religion comes close to controlling the mind, even in its extreme forms, when compared with the hypnotic dominance our smartphones have over our minds. People walk down streets glued to their sets in the middle of oncoming traffic, while stressed out caffeine infused psychotics drive on our roads with one hand on the wheel and the other on the phone as they scream at other motorists from behind the safety of their autos. And, of course, when an e-mail or text message comes in, they are conditioned to look at immediately, as they do their best rendition of imitating Pavlov's Dog.

These types of digital addictions and followers border on cultish as the Galaxies, iPhones, and operating systems that help anchor social media in one neat, compact package come exploding out of the screen with unrivalled information, while numbing the mind.

How we interact with other humans behind our digital screens has, in some respects, stymied our ability to cope with the reality of our unfettered minds. As much as the efficiency of all this technology is a marvel, it comes with *caveat emptor* because, as one technology entices us with the promise of liberating our choices, it also seems to simultaneously hold our minds hostage in a very peculiar way.

MORE THREATS AND DISRUPTIVE CHANGES

Disruptive change is the history of mankind ranging from collective farming in Mesopotamia, the cradle of civilization, to the building of the pyramids, the structures of Rome and Greece, and, of course, the two industrial revolutions that have dizzied our minds as we have evolved as humans to meet the manifest destiny of our infinite curiosity and unbridled imaginations. It is perhaps these two qualities in our makeup that deliver us to glory and agony.

The changes that we see today were almost unimaginable not too long ago, and some of it we saw in the industrial design possibilities of gadgets that first appeared on *Star Trek*, and perhaps the best way to create an ending to the evolution of all this "technology speak" would be to look at some of the changes that now define the world we live in today.

Encyclopedia Britannica

Once upon a time, *Encyclopedia Britannica* was the standard foundation of reference learning, as parents collected the complete volumes that were sold door to door or were available even in grocery stores as incentives to purchase groceries, part of a shopping loyalty program. This was how I obtained my series. The *Encyclopedia Britannica* was a general summary collection of mankind's knowledge, something like the libraries of Alexandria, and served as a vehicle to learn and interact with our parents. In some ways, discussing this newfound knowledge is how parents and children learned from each other. Of course, the medium of printed-book collecting was limited and static when we compare this with the dynamic, wide-in-breadth, and inclusive contributory nature of *Wikipedia*.

Wikipedia in many respects has become the collective documented knowledge of humanity, at least in summary format, and it evolves dynamically in real time, unlike print and the classic encyclopedia. Already, if not much later, the word "encyclopedia" might be relegated into the classic and rarely used reservoir of the English language as it becomes a faded memory, replaced by a more robust *Wikipedia*.

Blogs

A blog is another incredible tool, which really is a perpetual diary of knowledge or opinions a blogger shares with the world on an easy-to-use website platform, since the blogger does not require a computer programming background to manage a blog. Some of the better-known blog programs include WordPress, Tumblr, Blogger, and Technorati. Blogging is a robust cloud platform allowing people to create insights on a host of topics, some of which include social issues, technology, cars, marketing, financing, education, tutorial support, homemaking and then some. Some well-known bloggers have a large set of followers something like a digital religion, and some are just spewing words into cyberspace; nonetheless, it is an incredible vehicle of dynamic exchange and knowledge to share.

Online Education

Education has always been thought of as a way out of poverty, and the traditional setting ensured that drilled-down knowledge was imparted by grade-school teachers, and in fact, this is still quite useful in math and a host of different subjects. After all, when learning the sciences and engineering, discipline is a must. With all the technological vehicles we have nowadays, from YouTube to school sites and student-driven blogs, the delivery of education is rapidly evolving. One can study online to achieve a full university-level degree program, and in fact, this is exactly what the London School of Economics, Liverpool University, as well as Heriot-Watt and many more offer, realizing that all the knowledge of math, business studies, literature, science, and so on can be taught online by a host of digital delivery methods. This approach works, as long as the university has a mechanism to have students write proctored exams that ensure the integrity of the degree, yet this system might not be good for everybody. One should consider that even within the brick-and-mortar schools, plagiarism and blatant cheating is rampant, and when I taught at college, I had to become quite aware of the creative techniques students employed, who felt that cheating was quite acceptable. So a word to the wise: when hiring graduate students, look up the university's reputation for exam fraud and plagiarism, since I can assure you that these types are being passed off as graduates to the world of commerce and elsewhere.

In making the case for online learning, many professors post their lectures online, which can easily be followed by students, while the type of knowledge available online is something like the libraries of Alexandria on steroids. In the classical normal on-campus learning environment, many times students come to class tired or lose their attention spans, and in the case of night classes, intellectual stamina can be waning after a hard day's work. However, when one is relaxed at home, one is in an optimum frame of mind to focus better, assuming one has discipline. Let's say that the student can go through a host of accounting questions and compare them with perfect answers, supported by drawn-out diagrams and documentation from the professor as to how the answer was reached. The one major reason most students might have an advantage studying at the college-level brick-and-mortar school setting might be that at a younger age, they might not yet have developed the discipline to sit down without a pre-set time. However, everything one needs in textbooks is now available in searchable *.pdf*s online, which makes life easier and makes going through indexes of key words a breeze. In contrast, I am sure we all still try to remember where a passage was in a certain book and spend considerable amount of time flipping through pages.

Thus, is there really a reason for a student to physically attend a prestigious university to study psychology? Alternatively, the subject can be studied online at any university with support vehicles such as YouTube, blogs, Facebook, and video conferencing and still get the left-wing bias that academia acutely suffers from. Remember that many of these professors can still spew out from their academia tower, their left-wing Keynesian mandates against the hypocrisy of their well-padded bourgeois salaries, complemented of course by four-months-a-year vacation entitlements.

Personal opinions aside, this much is for sure, technology is changing education forever, and in many disciplines, most younger students have a better grasp of social media marketing than their professors do, especially those who were brought up in the ad world of *Mad Men*, in the three-channel universe from the sixties. So, then, the question becomes, in the future, who is teaching who? On a personal note, when I taught business management studies, including statistics, marketing, and corporate finance at the designation level, I used to wonder sometimes why I was getting paid for something that was clearly explained in books. Oh well!

We now live in a service economy, and things have not quite panned out as social engineers, most economists, and other crystal-ball readers had hoped for, since perhaps few of these crystal-ball readers have ever run a firm. We are possibly now finally seeing the new technology delivering what was always promised to us namely, "perfect information", but ironically, the problem is that all this imperfect information that was economically inefficient back then is what kept many people employed while fostering secretive supply chains.

The Utopia of the Service Economy—Well, Sort Of!

When we peel the service economy down to the core, it is, in many aspects, nothing more than skimming off the fundamental economy. Subsequently, when all is said and done, service industries do not produce things or create products that need to be manufactured, which results in the highly skilled peripheral careers like robot technicians, CNC designers, artificial intelligence, and industrial engineers. This constitutes much of the core capital required to ensure that our inventions in the West are refined through clean manufacturing techniques that hyper automation can offer. Manufacturing and engineering are concomitant with a nation's inventiveness and capital stock, while being the foundation of a robust economy. To support this position, please look at all the inventions referred to in the first and second industrial revolution sections of this book, and you may verify the correlation for yourself. Excellent examples include China, Brazil, Japan, and, of course, Germany, which, unlike most of the rest of Europe, spends less time debating and more time creating. What is also important is that manufacturing allows engineers to walk into the plant, speak to the technicians, and see how their design works through a plant's process systems. This allows them to go back to their CAD-CAM (computer automated design and manufacturing) design studio and improve the product continuously. This is especially important during a teething stage of a new product or part.

What many people don't realize is that the manufacturing of the future will look nothing like it did in the past, whereas robotics, 3D printers, CNC derivatives, and other "smart machines" will do nearly all the work and highly skilled technicians will maintain and program them. Much of this was already discussed in the *History of Invention* section of this book.

The Detroit of the future will ask for a much higher level of skill sets, and low-skilled workers will not be able to hide under the canopy of unions to keep their entitlements, since the consumer agenda is to attain more for less money and will act in its own self-interest, as brilliantly articulated and timelessly evidenced by Adam Smith in *The Wealth of Nations*. Thus, the consumers' agenda of self-maximization is also in it for itself, and when it comes to their own self-interest, they are not in the benevolence business. Of course, this comes at an expense when going shopping and supporting goods that are "Made in China," since they are unwittingly writing the epitaph of Western manufacturing and the diminishment of Western inventiveness. After all, it was Western inventiveness that really brought the rest of the world out of the dark ages, and in many respects, it still does.

But of course, governments will create jobs and save the day by taxing those villainous people who create enterprise and employment as they spend themselves into insurmountable deficits and bribe voters with their own money, or even worse, capital borrowed under their name. This will naturally end one day and will come to a reckoning when the capital markets snub government bonds based on fiat currency. As a side note, the interference of the Fed with easy money, is causing distorted valuations in asset prices, low interest addiction as well as interfering with the business cycle and not allowing the economy to rinse out its inefficiencies both on a macro and micro economic scale. The end result will be, that this false economy, when it does hit the wall, based on debt and speculation, will have some severe economic and social consequences. I call it *kick the can down the road economic planning*, but this would be a subject for another book. But the things that will create meaningful jobs are advanced technology and the manipulation of technologies that create competitive advantage.

Without rigorous training in advanced technologies such as artificial intelligence, we will be deprived of a robust middle class. The old middle class still looks to yesterday's entitlements like a back-alley drunkard nostalgically looking at his last empty bottle. But then again, delving further into this subject is another matter altogether, so now, with an attempt to stay the course, it might be a good time to get back to other disruptive changes.

Google

In 1998, Google was created by Larry Page and Sergey Brin, and it was about to change and accelerate the world into the information age. It is Google that has come to define the backbone of the techno-culture or information age, as it was the missing link to drive our knowledge-based world into warp speed, while providing infinite access to knowledge like no other technological vehicle to date. As it states on its website, "Google's mission is to organize the world's information and make it universally accessible and useful," and that's exactly what it has done.

If Microsoft, the personal computer, and Apple were the vehicles that made software easy to use and brought desktops to the world, Google is the vehicle that has organized human knowledge at our fingertips and has more than likely made the largest contribution to democratization since the Greeks came up with democracy.

If Henry Ford created the assembly line and gave birth to industrial engineering, if the Wright brothers gave the world the first sustainable flight, if Leonardo da Vinci defined eclectic genius, if Beethoven defined the classics, if the Beatles through *Sgt. Pepper* legitimized pop music as a form of art, and if transportation is what eventually gave birth to great cities, it can be said that Google has this same place, in both absolute and relative terms, as one of humanity's great inventions and sociocultural contributions. Google has created a shift that has allowed all the miraculous associated technologies to flourish while enlightening minds with rapid-fire knowledge at everyone's fingertips, and this is their gift to the story of mankind.

Not too long ago, one had to go to the library to research facts, but today we just google it as libraries try to remain relevant. The story of Google does not end there; its Android operating system is the fuel for the information age, supported by the fact that it commands about eighty-five percent of the world's market share in mobile phones (see: http://www.businessinsider.com/android-ios-market-share-data-and-apples-iphone-6-2014-8).

So, then, the mobile market is dominated by Google, as well as all the techno addicts who can't get their faces out of them. One of its great coup d'état was buying and further developing Android and then sharing it for free with Samsung. This has ensured that Android is the new language of the mobile environment while catching Windows

8 flat-footed and instilling rear-view fear into Apple. Thus, when one wants the weather with no time to watch scantily dressed weather girls—which is TV weather reporting's last great hope—one can pick up the Samsung and get the weather on the road, since it tracks one's location. Oh! Did I forget about the fact that getting a free mobile operating system comes with a catch? Google gets to show its display ads on the mobile for giving the software operating system free to the customer and to Samsung.

Google affects nearly every facet of our lives, going well beyond simple searches. Cloud computing uploads no longer require people to have their files on a USB stick, since they can upload their files to Google Drive, which unfortunately is not suitable for companies needing levels of employee permission. Diametrically, Microsoft Office365 cloud is much more sophisticated for companywide virtual cloud setting applications, which mimics a client server with many of its security features.

The story gets juicer still with Google, since Gmail, maps—including satellite views and traffic maps—news, and Google Play, where films and music can be downloaded, are only part of the story. The term "I googled it" has been brought into the English language as common speak, just as once upon a time the term "Xerox it" was for "photocopy it." "Google" is one of the most common words used in the English language—or is "selfie" the most common? Even high-school and university exams are at peril, since instructors have to ensure that students are not googling answers or texting questions to each other in the middle of the exam.

Want to put an end to a debate about an objective topic like who invented calculus? The answer is Sir Isaac Newton, all of which would come up on a Google search. Does a Google answer put an end to a debate? Not necessarily.

Simple things of folklore have been left in the dustbins of cultural history, such as the board games Scramble, Snakes & Ladders, and, of course

Monopoly, which all taught us lessons. We can no longer live in obscurity as individuals, since more than likely Google will find you, unless you are an expert at sweeping yourself clean on social media, but then again, you would be accused of living like a hermit in this day and age.

Interested in buying a house? Google will give you both satellite and street-view images to better understand what is in the neighbourhood, just in case your lovely real-estate agent forgot to mention that there was a rehab clinic for convicted axe murderers at the end of your future street.

Google's clean page can deliver the business news but lacks the richness of Yahoo's finance section that still is probably the best free site in the world on stocks and equities, in terms of quantitative and qualitative analysis. Still, as a news hub, it is not as rich as OMG on celebrities' lives and gossip, but at the same time, it is very pronounced with paid display ads while creating an industry of Google SEO (Search Engine Optimization) specialists.

Can't spell? That's no problem; Google knows how to complete your search and corrects your spelling or gives you credible alternatives. In fact, the legitimacy of new words in the English language can first be checked on Google, while at the same time, it is by far a much better spell-checker than Microsoft Word, which is relatively flat-footed.

Or perhaps you ordered your last vehicle without a GPS, that's no problem at all, since you can use Google's turn-by-turn instructions, along with their map. So much for General Motors and OnStar. Even if you are in heavy traffic, you can go to Google Maps and turn on the traffic option to get a live update on traffic conditions. Want to value your brands? Just do a Google search and see where it shows up; otherwise, you could hire SEOs with no knowledge of your business to bring up your rankings.

The story of Google is too deep to go into here, but we know our lives are inextricably linked with it. For example, if Google went down for thirty days, what effect would it have on our lives? What would be the ramifications on our schools, businesses, our way of life, lost efficiencies, and conveniences we take for granted? What if your IT team couldn't use Google to solve a tech problem, while a computer virus attacked and nobody could google the digital remedy?

Possibly the effect of Google going down would be so critical that it could cause economic erosion on a global scale and cost firms so much money that it could lead to an unscheduled stock-market correction or possibly a deep recession, as today's commerce heavily depends on information and concomitantly the speed to operate. The effects would be more pronounced in education, since the loss of Google would make most students functionally illiterate until they got their tech fix.

When all is said and done, the final litmus test for a business's worth is this: if a company no longer exists in the marketplace, are its brands and services endearing enough to create a consumer void that can't easily be filled? Would the consumer or channel really miss its services? In the case of Google, the world without it today is almost unimaginable.

LinkedIn
LinkedIn allows individuals to post their résumés online while sharing business contacts in one nice electronic hub for the whole world to see. Résumés were traditionally presented only when someone needed a new position or a job, but today people put out their *curriculum vitae* in front of the world's HR digital theatre, namely LinkedIn. Once upon a time, résumés were constructed by stretching the truth for only a few eyes to see, such as head-hunters, and HR departments, and the upside was that there was privacy and the exaggeration of accomplishments were less exposed.

Today, though, one can post some of the best tall tales and selective information on LinkedIn's platform for the whole world to see, but the problem is that few really realize these are permanent digital footprints. Unwittingly, the selective reasoning that makes up many résumés on LinkedIn comprises what can best be described as "digital perjury," which could blow back in one's face like lipstick on a married man's shirt collar. Many people have multiple variations of their résumé, and this begs the question, does the one presented at an interview match the LinkedIn profile? This of course could put someone into a foggy situation where most potential employers will do a cross-check to verify how much of what was said was—borrowing a term from the seventies—is "jive talkin'"!

LinkedIn is obviously much more than that; it is a place where business connections can be accumulated, join business groups, find the correct buyers' contact information to sell products by doing advanced searches, poach employees from the competition, post résumés, and send private messages, read and comment on articles, post comments as well as view companies' LinkedIn pages. It can even be said that LinkedIn has replaced the classic business Rolodex and contributes to the diminishment of traditional business cards, as do e-mail and v-cards in general.

LinkedIn, in many respects is the Facebook of business professionals, and it is a game-changer. In the nineties people created business portals, much of it is now redundant and made irrelevant by LinkedIn. Just a few years ago, people joined multiple business sites to make contacts, and much of this has been made redundant by LinkedIn.

LinkedIn is the one of the ultimate disruptive forces that has put many personnel agencies out of business. Ironically, the same way job sites such as Workopolis put an end to help-wanted print ads as we knew them in newspapers, we now see job sites on the receiving end of this disruptive change, compliments of LinkedIn's help-wanted section.

Unlike the East, in the West, it was not common to really see people's pictures on their résumés, and in fact, putting your picture on your résumé was once considered a no-no! This has changed because even if your résumé has no picture, most people on LinkedIn have their sometimes-air-brushed pictures alongside their digital *curriculum vitae*. Just like Facebook, we celebrate job anniversaries, or better still, when we find a new job; this is announced for the digital sphere to see, and in some instances, it seems to be the same people finding new jobs every eight months or so.

How we present ourselves professionally in the Internet age has changed due to LinkedIn, as we watch each other's careers and make connections, make comments, join groups, read articles, and send private messages. It seems safe to say that LinkedIn is part of social media. But this much is for sure: LinkedIn is one of the great disruptive changes of our times and allows one to create a Rolodex of contacts that was unimaginable not so long ago.

So there we have it! A quick ride through the techno-culture and how we got here, as we consider the phenomena of today's technology compared with the breakthroughs of first flight and electricity. So, then, one might ask which inventions were greater, both in absolute and relative terms. What impacted the human story more acutely, the car or the Internet? For that matter, did the telephone have a larger impact than e-mail? Did the jet plane change the world more than the computer? Did the first train change the world more than the smartphone? Was electricity humanity's last great innovative accomplishment? Did the moon landing change the psyche of mankind more than any other event to this date?

The answer to these questions just might lie in how we perceive and interpret the human journey.

Editorial & Comment Section

PERSPECTIVES AND TIME

Once upon a time, the weatherman gave us our weather, and today we can just pick it up on our smartphones equipped with GPS and get the weather temperature variances as we drive from the suburbs to the city. And to wait for the middle of the evening news to get your weather seems arcane, unless of course the weatherman is replaced by a sensuously dressed weather lady—probably a better bet for any male still with a pulse.

Even the rite of passage of all fine young men of gawking at girly magazines has gone by since *Penthouse, Playboy,* and *Hustler* are found in thinning magazine sections that cannot compete with all the burlesque offered on the Internet. Or better still, how about some of those scantily dressed young ladies in various stages of desperation on Facebook and Instagram posting their best renditions of the whore of Babylon?

This much is for sure: the world around us has changed substantially since 1995, when the word "Netscape" came into common speak, and we were all on dial-up. Microsoft, even though it still dominates desktop applications in business, has not been able to extrapolate this to the social media and especially smartphones, but its new hopes lie in cloud applications. In 1995, Coca-Cola was the highest-valued brand in the world, followed by a host of consumer packaged goods brands such as Tide laundry detergent, a host of auto companies, and of course IBM. Today, the number-one ranked brand is Apple, Coca-Cola is second, and as a side note, once upon a time, Coca-Cola was more recognized around the world than the American flag, but to-day's techno-culture brands are far more recognized than Coca-Cola (Interbrand's Top 100 Ranked Brands: http://www.interbrand.com/en/best-global-brands/2013/top-100-list-view.aspx).

This list includes Facebook, Google, Samsung, eBay, Amazon.com, and Adobe. Suspiciously, Yahoo was off the list, as was Twitter, and in Twitter's case it might have something to do with its inability to make a profit. Nevertheless, these are the new kids on the block playing king of the hill.

Change is sometimes humanity's travesty and sometimes its saviour, but it is still sprinkled within the history of the human story. The third Industrial Revolution has arrived, and the promise of technology is the marvel that in many respects quintessentially rewards mankind's ability for its relentless dreaming, curiosity, and unwavering commitment to progress. Knowledge inoculates us from humanity's shared history of savagery and foolishness within our times and before. However, it is this pursuit of technology and science that best engenders our collective minds to look five hundred years down the road so as to put our irrelevant conflicts of today into perspective. Seeing the world this far out is perhaps the ultimate expression of the human experience, or at least the hallmark of advanced thinking that gives rise to collective unselfishness.

Yes, the genie is out of the bottle, and regardless of how we romanticize about the past, it will not come back because it had its place on stage, as do all great plays of the theatre. The technology we are seeing today is only the beginning, and yes, some of it is bad, much of it good, and some is still within our intellectual deliberation, until, of course, history stores it in orderly perspective. But in the meantime, with a world lacking real heroes and leaders, we can always turn to digital superheroes as a form of comfort until real leadership finally arrives again, may it be digitally or in physical actuality.

The Leaderless World

In terms of world government, it is true that there are many leadership positions in the world, but sadly they are for the most part all vacant, as talking heads pose as leaders. Yes, sounds rolls off their lips, but no real words are spoken. Today, many we refer to as leaders are only in leadership positions, while lacking the boldness and intellectual reservoir to make visionary or tough decisions, and see the future as Winston Churchill or John F. Kennedy once did. These current leaders' only goals are political, which is to win the next election, and the scorched earth they leave for future generations to grapple with—for example, unsustainable government debt and societal entitlements—is not their true concern. On the other side of the equation, few in the electorate make wise decisions, so one must ask, how qualified are they to vote in the first place. Yes, this line of thinking might sound elitist, but the election results give rise to this thought. I then propose that we are in a world with no real leadership and a confused electorate that votes but rarely thinks, with the result being that we end up with the government we deserve. This is the conundrum that we live in but cannot seem to escape from, since the horse's nose can't stop staring at the other horse's tail, just like a carousel the music plays, but the mirage won't stop. But hey…that's the latest in democracy, so just stare at the symptoms and forget the cause as the band plays on!

Frozen in Time

Just to put into perspective the pace we have moved at, consider, for example, that if someone with good educational credentials and worldly experience was frozen in time, let's say just twenty years ago, and then woke up to the year 2014, he or she would more than likely be considered functionally illiterate and quite possibly unemployable.

Considering the changes in our modern vocabulary, or in many cases lack thereof, trying to comprehend modern techno-culture speak would be challenging. Here are a few terms that did not exist in our wider culture twenty years ago:

"Did you google it?"

"Text me?"

"I saw it on YouTube or Netflix."

"I read Digg."

"I put up the pictures on Instagram."

"I missed my math class but picked it up on YouTube."

"Check out my new Facebook profile."

"Sorry, I don't watch CNN for breaking news."

"I have Twitter on my Samsung for that.

"Send me a link."

"E-mail me."

It would be plausible to argue that this person, after dropping out of the world and coming back twenty years later, would be dysfunctional, somewhat not conversant, and have difficulty fitting into today's world. It is this comparative perspective that most people under twenty-five do not have, but they are hopefully reading this, and might begin to understand. Sadly, even today there is a whole crowd over forty-five out there that is already dysfunctional in much of today's technology.

KINGS AND QUEENS

The human plight of the haves and have-nots is as old as recorded civilization itself, dating back to Mesopotamia. But if we look at how royalty and the well-heeled lived just 125 years ago, it would by most accounts be a life of deprivation compared with today's middle class and underclass. Much of this progress is due to the free-market system. For example, today's homes have indoor plumbing, air conditioning, and we have a much more comfortable ride to work than even Queen Victoria enjoyed. Basic cars have more features than a 1910 Rolls-Royce, and gaslights and candles have been replaced by electricity. Of course, water is clean in much of the world, computers and the information age have equipped the population with more information at its fingertips than perhaps President Kennedy had during the Cuban Missile Crisis, and, of course, medical breakthroughs have afforded much of the world better healthcare than the most affluent had 125 years ago or even twenty-five years ago. True, there is a gap between classes, but that is the quintessential nature of humanity.

As middle class jobs are being outsourced to countries like India and the Philippines by the likes of Microsoft, and manufacturing is being outsourced to China, of course it is firms like those that are being given the tag of villain. Little mention is being given to the fact that America has one of the highest corporate tax rates in the developed world, followed by a host of laws and red tape that punish employers. The story weaves and gets juicer when we deliberate further and consider that consumers are not without their faults in the outsourcing dilemma, since they go to the retail shelf and online with their own self-interest first, namely to self-maximize by purchasing more for less with little regard for the macroeconomic consequences of their actions.

Just walk into an American shopping mall and see the second-rate goods that point to a consumer with little appreciation for qualitative differentiation. See if you can find Italian or German suits and shoes that are much more superior to the mass-market offerings. So then, to bring about this outcome of more for less, firms must outsource or perish as sustainable market participants while their shareholders put pressure on them to outperform the market, and these shareholders are in many cases the same consumers that are helping hollow out the manufacturing infrastructure of the West. Who, then, is the catalyst of all this outsourcing? Firms or self-serving consumers? Is the consumer's action in any way causing the dilemma of being bitten back by loss of jobs? Or are lower expectations eroding this gifted dream we call "the West?" The plot thickens when we stop pointing fingers and realize we are all participants in this ad hoc symphony of economic self-flagellation.

Many of these jobs the West cannot afford to keep with the current labour costs and suffocating tax structures, while most employees in developed countries do not want repetitive, low-paying jobs, which, as argued earlier, are going to become automated. These jobs will be taken over soon by employing advanced automated manufacturing systems, and the people who can set them up and keep them humming will more than likely be the forming a new middle class.

Regardless of dreams of a classless utopia—like the one in Cuba or the former Soviet Union, where doctors earned the same as custodians—that mask the destructive tendencies of resentment and idleness, the fact of the matter is that, unfortunately, not everyone can be Beethoven, Dr. Nash, Bill Gates, Cassius Clay, Count Basie, Einstein, or the Beatles. Of course, wealth distribution, coupled by cries of choking the wealthy are titillating election time promises, but even if we taxed the top five percent at the ninety percent tax bracket, it would not even make a dent into our current or accumulated deficit. Much of it has occurred in the name of financing in the way of higher taxes to support social programs that have resulted in multi-generational welfare addiction as a way of life. These are empirically failed strategies that just don't work, and much of its failed ideology emanating from President Johnson's *Great Society* vision in 1965.

Technology, progress, and its natural bedfellow, free-markets, have delivered a quality of life that was unfathomable only a hundred years ago, and has greatly helped increase consumer welfare while bringing the types of comfort and products that we often take for granted.

But we know this much: we are in an age of an acute paradigm shift, and what we do with it is possibly mankind's manifest destiny.

This being said, it seems we are searching for a morality or a sense of advanced values that will define our own sense of supreme virtues, but sadly, this often ends up being a form of elitism on its own.

THE DEMOCRATIZATION OF WHAT?

Now, we have this great so-called level playing field that is being cheered as some type of equalizer for the proletariat, to bring it out of its eternal state of victimization. When we start trolling news articles, we quickly see that grown people hiding under pseudonyms are able to use the comment section of an online article to exert their alter egos or any sense of rage they were not able to dispose of at their places of work or perhaps in their school days.

This is the world we live in, where the underlying savagery of the collective human psyche relentlessly appears on the social media. Yes, this is the world where links are posted on Facebook, Twitter, blogs, and the like, asking people to read articles that may or may not be based on truth.

If only the CIA had this type of communicative grey area propaganda in the 1950s, it could have overthrown a hundred Guatemala's—this is where the CIA actually took over a radio station in Guatemala and then organized a mob at the parliament—simply by sending out propaganda hashtags on Twitter. Or better still, doctoring graphic images using Photoshop and then letting people emotionally debate fact from fiction, rather than the arduous task of dropping leaflets, which are not without environmental footprints.

Then, of course, today's CIA should perhaps create a Facebook page and ask people to "like" the newly installed dictator or the religious psychotics who are currently posing as freedom fighters. They too should be afforded a fan page on Facebook to celebrate their repugnant morality, until of course they metamorphose into the latest "made by America" Frankenstein and bite back at their masters like some out-of-control pit bull. Or until someone figures out that the old boss is much better than the new boss; at least the neighbourhood had stability, which brings us back to the philosophy of "if it isn't broke, don't fix it."

It is in this magical place called the social media, and the Internet in general, which seems to be the last great hope for egalitarian justice for the masses, as a vehicle to share all sorts of information in the never-ending quest to change the world, instead of realizing that we might have to change ourselves first. Indeed, social media and all its various components—some good, some bad, and some that history will still deliberate on—is somehow going to create this utopian oasis of distributive justice.

Yes, this is the place where twentysomethings in the West are going to vent out their values for the rest of the world to hear and adopt, to help the masses, both in the West and beyond to come out of their collective comatose state and simultaneously change the world. Yes, they want to expose that terrible boogieman called free-markets that has, as evidenced earlier in this book, delivered nearly every technological advancement that this world and its inhabitants enjoy and often take for granted. Or perhaps, middle age people should join the G-20 protestors and get some aerobic exercise in the afternoon, instead of attending all those boring dinner parties, while they can work on their rusty pitching skills, by showing the young on how to properly throw Molotov cocktails. The police benefit as well, as they can work off all that high calorie junk food they eat during their shift. This way everyone wins, including the employment created for window replacement technicians in the aftermath. This seems like a better *jobs creation program* than what governments create.

One must also consider the fact that the average lower-middle class, down to the working and welfare class has more creature comforts and more access to information than Queen Victoria did just a hundred years ago. For example, consider the ocean of knowledge that is easily accessible at a library that contains more intelligence than the plutocracy and governments of yesterday had. The deliverance of all this technology that we have discussed, including radio, television, access to emergency services, the Internet, smartphones, cloud software, the refrigerator, modern stove, mixers, dishwashers, cameras, Facebook, Instagram, Apple, Twitter, and Microsoft, have increased the quality of life for many, on a global scale. Today, in the West we have access to clean water, and in most cases, health care, rapid transport, indoor plumbing, autos, telephone, as well as air conditioning.

Unfortunately, all this advancement is not the case in many parts of the developing world. Progress is being made, and most live better than their parents did fifty years ago, and certainly a hundred years ago. I personally have visited some of the poorest places in the world, including Ethiopia (no, I did not stay at hotel like most Westerners do), and regardless of their abject poverty, Ethiopians are very cultured and proud people that somehow find joy in life that might be missing in ours. Further, their respect for life brings them above the level of using poverty as a convenient vehicle to justify violence. One's culture and way of life plays a major role, and this is something people in the West could learn from, to help dispel the myth that poverty justifies and equates with violent crime. It certainly doesn't help, but does not give *carte blanche* either. However, as much as we have good intentions to help these developing countries, it sadly amounts to our poor giving money to their ruling class to continue subjecting their poor against the background of indoctrinated corruption that prevails within the veins of the society.

So then, going back to justifying violence and anarchy, consider how the people of New Orleans conducted themselves during the Katrina hurricane, for example, hooliganism, police looting stores, murders and the raping of women, and contrast this of how the Japanese conducted themselves during their tsunami and subsequent nuclear disaster.

My father grew up in abject poverty and hardship, and came to the West with thirty-five dollars in his pocket in 1962, but he made no excuses, was accountable, and did not resort to crime.

Even if one measures power and equality through access to information, the average Internet user has better exposure to information than the three networks had during the Vietnam War, both in relative and absolute terms. On *Wikipedia* and the CIA's World Factbook, one can get a quick glimpse of a nation's GDP, demographics, number of airstrips, military capabilities, and where they are located, by employing Google Satellite. President Kennedy did not know where every commercial airliner was on its flight path in real time, but today these details can be found on flight trackers, and one can even track ships online. All these technological inventions have improved the quality of life for many.

DEBT AND BENEVOLENCE - STRANGE BEDFELLOWS

Progress can be measured by a host of different criteria including the input of social programs that have for the most part failed us, and bears much responsibility for leaving the world with sixty-one trillion dollars of debt and if we add in worldwide provincial, regional and state debts, the number easily exceeds a hundred trillion dollars. This is not only unsustainable, but will come back to haunt us. Sadly, it is this sense of benevolence, all with good intention, of course, that eventually creates its by-product of entitlement and multi-generational welfare dependency, as opposed to self-reliance. Roosevelt's *New Deal* in the Great Depression perhaps was the acute point in American history of first introducing social safety nets. But what really tipped it over the edge in an effort to eradicate poverty and offer education for the poor, was President Lyndon Johnson's 1965 *Great Society* doctrine. For the most part, this societal engineering has been a colossal failure both socially and economically, while it has kept generations in poverty, since welfare assistance has evolved into entitlements and has become a way of life.

For example, consider the public K-12 education system in the United States, which is at best mediocre, whereas they feel it is okay to pass students who should be failing. The story is developing along the same lines in Canada, since we now have this liberal notion that we should not fail any students, since it might psychologically scar them. Of course, politicians are strong proponents of the public education system in its current state, yet send their own children to private schools.

Okay then, I suppose in the real world, if your products and services are not purchased, you fail, and if this book that I spent four years writing does not sell, I do not get to pass "Go" and financially collect. In fact, Bill Gates made this type of point with a class of high school students, to help bring students out of their academic cocoon.

In Canada the current National debt is six hundred billion dollars, and this translates into about fifty-four thousand dollars per household, and if we include provincial debt, that number at least doubles into over a hundred thousand dollars per household, for a grand total of over one trillion in debt. In the United States the federal accumulated debt is over eighteen trillion dollars, which means about a hundred and fifty thousand dollars per household and if you added in the states' debt, we might double this number to three hundred thousand per household, with a grand total of $30,000,000,000,000. This is hardly the sign of good and sustainable governance.

If one believes that personal choices, both economic and social, are the fundamental building blocks of freedom, which then nourishes democratic thinking, why is it then that we are so docile about bloated governments that demand nearly fifty percent of our salaries in taxes? Does this mean that as individuals we do not have the acumen to spend our own money, or do enlightened governments have a right to collectively spend it on our behalf? It all depends on one's sense of what freedom really means.

Our social programs should be designed to give people a helping hand until they can be self-reliant again, not four generations of welfare dependency being passed off as societal compassion. Then I ask, imagine a world where government reverted to the role they are meant to occupy, meaning efficiency, accountability, offer the rules of commerce, provide infrastructure, maintain the rule of law, and, of course, not to get into trillions of dollars in debt. Then imagine this world of no chronic government debt and fifty percent of your taxes were reduced!

This would result in an economy with sustainable growth, where more people would have more money to spend and to give to so many worthwhile charities. Encouraging governments to become bigger by using social programs as a manipulative tool to gain favour of a largesse existence will only serve to encourage their voracious appetite for taxation, and in the end, this unsustainable spending will oppress a society.

Greece is only the beginning; if we continue, eventually we are more than likely looking at government default of debt in the developed world, including the United States, which would shake the economic foundations of global stability. Let's consider that the United States at near zero percent interest needs to issue new bonds just to pay interest on its current bonds when they come due, and if in any given year, more U.S. Treasury Bonds could come due and possibly exceed their entire tax revenue, which is just over three trillion dollars a year, this is just plain sad and reckless.

Quite possibly the big reason the Feds can't measurably move interest rates up is that the cost of financing government debt in the way of bonds would be so high, it would collapse *the house of cards* and all this false economy, including its social programs. Bringing interest rates back to five percent alone would mean that at least thirty-three percent of your tax money goes towards paying interest on the accumulated government debt from the current twenty percent. This type of careless spending would adversely affect the truly needy.

Moving across the ocean to Europe; Italy would need only a small shove like one hundred to two hundred basis points in interest rates to send it over the edge into debt default—and the rest of Europe is not far behind. Then with higher interest rates, pensioners who have saved money will be rewarded for their efforts, as opposed to getting into risky equity investments.

The United States has one of the highest corporate tax rates in the developed world at about thirty-five percent, which is quite oppressive. Further increases in this tax rate would contract the economy, cause more off-shoring and increase unemployment. Punishing a nation's employers might not serve as the most convenient boogieman to point at, but...

Ah! I have the solution, just tax the wealthiest! After all, stealing from the wealthy has worked so well in Venezuela recently, and Ethiopia in the 1970s, where the business class and the nations' intelligentsia were either killed, imprisoned or had to leave the country, leading to indescribable living conditions and a barren market place. Now that we have focused our attention to the business class, we should not forget our favorite whipping boys, namely the very wealthy, and in the case of the United States, if the government confiscated the wealth of the fifty richest people, which would be about seven hundred billion dollars, it would not even pay five percent of the National debt. Ah well! So much for the people's revolution.

Bloated, inefficient and debt ridden governments are not going to provide the solutions to our problems, quite the contrary, problems will mount with their unsustainable debt, poor deliverables and inefficient governance. And certainly, it is not government that creates jobs, it is commerce that provides jobs, since almost any jobs government does provide have only been taken away from the private sector, by magically taking a dollar and turning it into fifty cents.

This is the frank and alarming story that I present to you. But as a beginning, there is a first baby step we could take on the road to healing. Next time there is a federal election, just after the candidates come around with promises like Santa Clause; ask them to consider the following: before any new promises are made to the electorate, it might be prudent for them to provide the cash flow charts as to how they will retire the accumulated debt over the next ten years, simultaneously reduce taxes by fifty to sixty percent, while discussing the quantitative sustainability of our public pensions over the next ten to thirty years. Then present them a utopia where taxes and government are minimal, deficits do not exist, and we express freedom by making our own economic choices by keeping most of what is ours, namely, our earnings. Hence; being in a position as a society to help the truly needy as opposed to an emotional ideology that chases the tail, but does not know which head to match it to.

But here is the bottom line, socialism as an ideology and its off-spring of addictive entitlements, when peeled to the core, is turning out to be the demonstrative denial of the failures of communism, while being largely responsible for leaving behind an untenable mountain of debt that might turn out to be the most enigmatic story of our times.

A Recent Trip to The Movies
We always need a villain to blame, perhaps to absolve us from finding the mirror to look at ourselves. This type of mentality really comes to light in a recent motion picture titled *Elysium*. The synopsis of the movie is that the Earth and civilization have run amuck with poverty, crime, lawlessness, lack of adequate infrastructure, health care, and so on, to the point that human life on Earth is quite unbearable. Something like Detroit, or parts of the third world. It is the year 2154, and there are two classes: the very wealthy who have abandoned the Earth in favour of a pristine, utopian, man-made space station called Elysium, and the rest, who live on the overpopulated, destroyed Earth. I guess by 2154 it becomes apparent that Obama and his adversaries did not save the middle class, and the Detroit auto industry and all that jazz, or didn't deliver on "hope and change." So, then, the movie fast-forwards into giving us a glimpse into mankind's future plight. Undeniably, the people who live on this space station have a luxurious lifestyle, with the types of advances that surpass *Star Trek*, including high-tech medical systems that rival the resurrection. They also have a strict immigration policy of keeping the destructive types out.

Of course, the character named Max, who is the new leader of the proletariat on Earth, finds a way to invade the space station to democratize things for the overpopulated people on the Earth, and then, lo and behold, he crashes the defense systems of the Elysium Space Station, and a hero is born for the underclass. Naturally, the moviegoer leaves the theatre rooting for the underclass, blinded by self-righteousness, without really thinking that the destructive ways learned on Earth will be extrapolated to this utopian space station, to mimic the mess they created on Earth, without recognizing for a moment that perhaps the lack of work ethic of those left behind might have had something to do with the societal apocalypse. However, in the name of democratization, egalitarianism, and all that funky equitable distributive speak, the roughneck types win, probably armed with statistics about how five percent of the population control eighty percent of the wealth, but they conveniently forget that the poorer classes make very little contribution to the tax base, as is the case with much of the lower middle class. However, what is not considered in the film is how these types perhaps ruined the Earth in the first place! Is it the fault of greedy bankers or willingly greedy accomplices like us? Ah! The nature of the beast!

It is this beautiful Earth we all live on for now, until the human story evolves and we can find a new planet or space station to destroy, not intentionally, of course, since madness and good intentions are strange bedfellows, nevertheless, they are accomplices. So then, perhaps this Earth has three types of people. The first types are the builders and creators of human ingenuity, who understand purpose and understate all that they have given the world; we see many examples in this book.

Then there are the destroyers and destructives that spend their lives in a toxic brew of envy as a badge of honour, while masking their idleness and their true destructive intent. Like some scene out of an old tearful play, they do a superlative rendition of a mix between modern Luddites and Robin Hood, with a bit of intellectual hooliganism to boot. Of course, they love the idea of redistributing wealth—as long as it is not theirs. These are usually the types that are in entitlement positions or are associated with self-ordained social engineers that speak in sounds, but no words of substance come out, while they do not understand that envy is not a philosophy or a form of accomplishment, and it has been absent from humanity's reservoir of achievements. This type of thinking is a diminutive human trait that is toxic and throws away accountability as well as accomplishment, with its repertoire of excuses. But hey...the train keeps rolling so why let facts get in the way of emotion?

Finally, there is the third camp of people making up this world who are in a state of "oooh and ahhhh" as they try to make sense of all the wonders around them and find something to soothe themselves from the travesty of life, while they ponder what camp to cheer for. They are often glued to their various digital addictions, pretending that all this knowledge will somehow give them clarity of thought that is reconcilable with their sometimes-shifting and foundationally precarious value systems. These are the ones that the government mostly woos at election time with their latest message of, *"Pappa's got a brand new bag"*.

But no matter how we try to democratize the human adventure, when we peel back our layers of sophistication, we still operate like wolf packs, with the alphas leading the way. Thus, like it or not, our natural *modus operandi* is a hierarchical society, and it is because of this that we have reverence for leaders—who are for the most part absent on the world stage today—that bring us out of our seats to applaud them, sort of as a way station until we find out if there is a God after we die.

With the exception of death, the enablement of knowledge and, more importantly, the application of know-how seems to be the ultimate equalizer, assuming one does not waste it in idle and meaningless debates. So, then, will the digital world and all its associated social media phenomena deliver the Holy Grail and take us to the promised land of enlightenment? In the interim, we do have social media to consider and all that it promises as a participative equalizer that in some aspects plays out like a theatrical tragedy.

Newspaper Boys Do Deliver

Somehow we have ended up here, but coming to the present has taken us on a fascinating journey, from swinging London in 1966 while finally mustering the courage to answer the question of what was wrong with Batman and finally acknowledging the fact that the judicial and social safety-net system failed the Joker, Riddler, and cast of alleged crooked cronies through no fault of their own. We took a look at the future through the world's fair of Expo 67. Possibly, only a newspaper boy can answer the great questions of our times by listing the greatest trash-talkers of all time, while coming to terms with the need for anti-heroes, and deeply considering the dichotomy between the virtuous and the vilified, subsequently proving that there is an inextricable link of twisted admiration. Together we have seen how Team Canada in the 1972 Hockey Summit Series saved Canada's soul and ensured that our gift to the world was not snatched before our very eyes against the backdrop of the Cold War.

Our journey has revisited that magic moment when we accomplished Camelot's dream and finally landed a man on the moon on that magical night that forever changed our collective psyche. As we are approaching the end of print media as we know it, and the subsequent last days of newspaper delivery boys, the epic tale that has eluded historians and sociologists has finally been told as we summoned the courage to tell the story of the rise and fall of disco! We then moved to the techno-culture, if only for a moment before it dawned on us that perhaps we should explain how we got here through a voyage that took us back to the two prior Industrial Revolutions, in order to make comparative sense of our present. We considered many of the inventions from those eras, including the steam engine, the Model T Ford, electricity, and flight, and then some, all of which changed the course of history forever. And finally, we immersed ourselves in the breathtaking technology of today and understood that it did not come from nowhere, and perhaps we had to stand on the shoulders of giants that have since passed to bring ourselves to today's magical moment, which we should never lose sight of.

But sadly, not all the enigmatic inquiries of the human story were answered in this written journey; for example, is there life after disco? Or did not have the courage to ask the difficult questions; why did the coyote keep ordering all this equipment from Acme to catch the roadrunner? Why didn't the coyote, if he was such a genius, just buy a bucket of KFC chicken and save himself the anguish and the money? And, of course, we have not answered the question of the future of rap music's reservoir of gratuitous lyrics, since there are only so many words in the English vocabulary that rhyme with Yo before rappers lose the ability to write more lyrics infused with plebeian speak. Or why they dress in lowly *haute couture* that at best looks like it came from a clown convention that went amok. But perhaps rap music is an outlet for a generation to express its anger and frustration that not even its mentors understand.

There are parts of recent history that were never quite considered, such as when the Berlin Wall fell, or why the concept of freedom did not catch on like wildfire in so much of the rest of the world and has been sadly replaced by apathy and hashtags.

We never deliberated on 9/11 and how it has changed the world and led to senseless and endless wars without the courage to define the enemy, as we fight him on one front and help him on another, leaving friend and foe in a state of perpetual confusion.

We never considered that the world that during the polarized Cold War era was more stable than it is now. In the aftermath of the fall of the Soviet empire, the remaining superpower squandered its moment to lead by example and enlighten, while emerging China does not have the morality or a socioeconomic political system worth emulating. All empires need to be worth mimicking in order to be successful, and this was certainly the case with the British Empire, since people simply wanted to look up to it in so many aspects, and in many respects, it is still true today. And sadly, some parts of the world embrace a backward way of life, fuelled by religious zealotry and theological fascism that shamefully does not belong in this century, yet somehow we import it into the West and explain it away in the name of tolerance.

Thus, we are left without a beacon of hope in a rudderless conundrum of vacant world leadership, and it is this world that we currently live in. The shame is that we are polarized by a multitude of shallow philosophies and agendas that have no real chance of coming together into something meaningful, while we evade collective betterment and vision for the plight of the human journey two hundred years from now.

For it is ignoring this responsibility that hinders our development of an enlightened vision.

THE FUTURE OF TOMORROW

We are now in the grasp of the third Industrial Revolution, which will make cities smart and energy renewable, much different than the fossil fuels we see today. As the electric car or fuel cells become the new choice for transportation energy, we will see world systems, including power plants, connected by the Internet. Jeremy Rifkin discusses some of this in length; please see http://www.thethirdindustrialrevolution.com, where he proposes the five pillars of the third Industrial Revolution.

Little things like timed traffic lights, will soon be gone, since these traffic lights will be controlled by the smart technology of modern traffic flow that Google traffic and the like provide. The gasoline engine's time will soon come to an end, and we will reminisce to our grandchildren about how we once had gas stations. When this moment comes, we will be gifted with perspective when we realize that it was an economically inefficient and antiquated way to distribute energy, as world-set high oil prices and greedy governments taxing of energy defied the tenets of both ecological and economic freedom. Some gas stations will be protected by museums as commercial artifacts, though, as stark reminders on how we destroyed our ecology and sent our young to fight in what will one day be referred to as the "oil wars" that we are currently embroiled in, and yes, this is the same oil we buy to help support terrorism.

The factory of the future will be minus the greasy overalls, as easy-to-implement industrial robots will run the plant with twenty technically trained people in the office and two people on the plant floor. Printing in 3D will create customization and lower barriers to entry for short run production, but the technology still has shortcomings and lacks economies of scale. Nanotechnology will become a feasible reality, and this just might be the technology that will help surgeons in the future, as robots are starting to now. The scanning technology that offers prognosis and diagnosis of illnesses of the human body that was introduced to our imaginations in 1966 by Dr. Leonard McCoy in the original *Star Trek* series will soon become reality. All this is around the corner as the MRI and CAT scans in healthcare systems are the relatively rudimentary stepping stones that point to the future of how a smart system will measure our health and create a medical road map of what we will face.

The Internet of things might include gadgets and systems that are strapped on or surgically inserted into our bodies to help us make perfect decisions, like some type of cyborg. And hopefully this will help us make better collective decisions during elections. We see this with how much of our days revolve around our smartphones—and there are now wristwatches on the market that have some of the same features as our smartphones.

Software technology will advance us into artificial intelligence, where computers will emulate human decision-making patterns. Eventually, artificial intelligence might see itself as more stable than humans and could possibly take us out; in fact, movies have already been made about this subject matter. But there's no need to worry; it will be nothing more than a contest between control freaks, one stable and the other not.

One day, and not that far off, we will be colonizing planets and building large space stations, with each one having a new philosophy that likeminded people can live on in relative peace, as opposed to the animosity towards each other and unsustainable confrontational existence we have on Earth. That way we can debate from different space stations and planets, each with its own separate system of economic and political way of life, and immigration may be allowed to these planets and space stations based on one's value system.

The new millennium promises some means of uncertainty, but for the bold, it is a time of opportunity. We have been inundated with all the great predictions of vogue, but perhaps the time has come to put it all in perspective.

In the twentieth century, from our imaginations to reality, we discarded the horse, flew gracefully with the birds, harnessed the power of the atom, and on that storied July night in 1969 greeted the stars. It is a time to give credit to the shoulders of giants we stand on; we bow with humility for those who innovated, inspired, and tampered with our imagination. It is a time not to underestimate our ability or resolve in this most gifted and exciting time to be alive.

As we head into the new age of advanced technologies, and hopefully advances in philosophies, we will learn to embrace the boldness of this new inventiveness, and these new disruptive technologies will deliver their promises somewhere on the near horizon. Because someplace in our imagination, a mother cradles the next Henry Ford, in someone's garage the next Bill Gates, Steve Jobs and Elon Musk dreams, somewhere there stands on a mountain another set of brothers named Wright who this time are reaching for the stars and will accept nothing less.

Because, with a new set of unfathomable realities lies our ability to stretch our psyches to a new set of breakthroughs and achievements that will set the new norms—this is the road we have always travelled. It is in this spirit that we move forward with a new set of visions that increase our intellectual elasticity in order to meet the challenges that lie ahead, while we define our new summit of knowledge.

THE FINAL EDITION

But still, nostalgia comes calling as I fall back to the day when I waited for the *Globe and Mail* and *Toronto Telegram* newspaper trucks to deliver my bundles so I could start my newspaper route and have a step up on the world. Perhaps I miss the romantic sounds of pages being turned and the head start of knowledge that the newspaper gave me. Newspapers allowed me to survey the world with a tender mind and realize how we understood it in the idealism of our youth, yet, without understanding the fatalistic nature of life and all that awaited us—some good, some bad, and some unexplainable, but all weaved into a dream.

Newspapers today, as a last gasp, are experimenting with paywalls with limited or mixed success, as most were never global papers, and charging for their subscriptions to compete against the free information provided digitally is challenging, since a new generation gets its info on Vice, Digg, Twitter, Yahoo, MSN, Drudge, and the like. But sadly, much of what is expressed today in the digital media seems like a digital supermarket tabloid in various stages of desperation. Once upon a time, though, writers that were larger than life had expertise in their chosen areas, they entertained us as they tried to help us make sense out of everything around us.

Even though we all secretly love the lady called print newspaper, we all know that she cannot keep up with the fluid and robust nature of up-to-the-minute news that digital media can provide. Digital media can give us many pictures and videos of the events that touch the visual area of our psyches to support the text that tries to reason with our logical sides. Digital media offers a multitude of reader feedback on articles in the way of comment section on the fly that in some ways mimics Twitter. Unlike classic letters to the editor, the comments section offers anonymity. Hence, a reader's true manifest variables are expressed in the digital world as we see some very sharp bows and arrows being exchanged, often spiralling into a digital barroom brawl.

323

Yet, one longs for those dreamy days of obtaining knowledge through the sound of a paper crinkling, as each page told a story. And we were knowingly being romanced by the stories and the ritual of turning pages, while the proof of being learned was the dark ink on the tips of our fingers as we pondered the miracle of our lives as individuals against the community we lived in. Yes, this lady is much older now, but once upon a time, she walked with such grace and spoke with such eloquence because, when all is said and done, the classical print newspaper told the story of our times and lives.

Time is the greatest gift we have; time marches on, steady and relentless, to its own beat, and to those that do not capture the moment and find purpose it leaves us with faded memories that shed a tear at the core of our their souls. It leaves us trying to come to terms with what was possible versus what we have done, while we try to reconcile the fact that we now have more in the past and less in the future, and time eventually delivers the sobering hand of reality.

Yes, we are more connected to each other than ever, yet so lonely.

But somewhere in the back of all my memories, I still daydream in a hectic fourteen-hour workday about all that I wish we could produce—and one last hockey game in Thorncliffe Park with my childhood friends. I dream of those cold Canadian winter mornings with books in hand, off to school. I imagine once more sitting in the grey seats at Maple Leaf Gardens and watching Bobby Orr go end-to-end with his magical presence and incomparable skills. Somewhere, I dream back to the moments where all was possible and the awe we all felt with the crackling sound of Neil Armstrong's words as he flirted with mankind's destiny.

Somewhere, as we create one thing, we dream of that special time in childhood when minds were limitless and full of ideas, if we only had enough courage to pursue them.

Somewhere, this child lives in us all, that soft spot in our psyches where we compare our dreams to what we have become.

Somewhere in midlife we weigh the romantic nostalgia of the past against the inevitable fatalism of the future and live in a present that tries to come to terms with both, as we flirt with normalcy.

We are hurled into an uncertain yet exciting era, and it should never be squandered. So, then, it is this space that we occupy, it is this time we live in, it is this dream that we all have in this unexplainable temporariness called life that we pass through. As we look into the past, we might romanticize about the crinkling sounds of papers filling our minds as they once did, instead of the modernism of digital media.

But I still remember a time when we leafed through the newspaper, folding through the pages of the events and memories that defined our lives, some that are glorious and some that are painful; either way, they are both needed to give meaning to the other.

Yes, we are inebriated by the nostalgia and selective extractions of the past that give us joy and tragedy, weaved into a cloth we knowingly drape ourselves in against the curiosity and unknowingness of the future. Memories are beautiful but often garbed in pain, with one foot grasping nostalgic romanticism, the other looking at the future with both fear and curiosity. Perhaps this is the story of human progress. But in our grasp, we have been bestowed with the gift of life; its only real sadness is when it's spent in idleness.

Hope, it is said, is the future we wish to participate in, so we live each day as we enter our own personal theatre to watch the tragic yet glorious play of what was promised, compared with what we have become.

But sometimes I still curiously peek at the street corner and still see that beautiful lady called the newspaper, with her unmistakable flowing hair and grace, who is all dressed up but has nowhere to go. Yes, she is older now, static perhaps, and her eyes are tired, but once upon a time, she was so dynamic that she filled our minds with all that was possible as she gifted us the news of the world. For so long, and with such reliability, she told us the story of our lives that, when assembled together, gave us the chronicle of our times, neatly folded in a news-paper. So, then, we give her one last gaze in a heartfelt farewell as she gracefully exits the stage.

The moments in our lives are all journalized into a summit of knowl-edge and experiences we neatly tuck away into our psyches, gift-wrapped but rarely opened, but perhaps one day you will find the reason and the moment to deliver your own newspaper.

Notes

Front Page News

Why Newspapers Matter

People Section

Swinging Sixties

1. *Look at life. Swinging London of sixties*: https://www.youtube.com/watch?v=Dzzn3_UthQo

2. *Expo 67*: https://en.wikipedia.org/wiki/Expo_67

3. Parke Puterbaugh, *The British Invasion: From the Beatles to the Stones, The Sixties Belonged to Britain*, Rolling Stone Magazine (July 14, 1988)

Arts & Entertainment Section

Batman and 1960s Hip!

1. *Batman* (TV series): https://en.wikipedia.org/wiki/Batman_(TV_series)

News Section

Out of This World

1. J. M. Roberts, *The New Penguin History of The World*, pg. 466

2. *Soviet atomic bomb project*: https://en.wikipedia.org/wiki/Soviet_atomic_bomb_project

3. Boris Johnson, *The Churchill Factor: How One Man Made History*, pg. 284-289

Sports Section

Frozen Ice

The Magic of September 1972

1. Patrick White, *'72 SUMMIT SERIES The story of the Summit Series, as it's never been told before,* The Globe & Mail (Sept 15th, 2012) Focus Section pg. f1-f9

2. *1972 Canada-Soviet Hockey Series (Summit Series):* http://www.thecanadianencyclopedia.ca/en/article/1972-canada-soviet-hockey-series/

3. *Summit Series*: https://en.wikipedia.org/wiki/Summit_Series

The Main Event

4. Gary Will's *Toronto wrestling history*: http://www.garywill.com/toronto/index.htm

Lifestyle Section

The Rise and Fall of Disco

1. *Culture in the 1950s*: http://www.shmoop.com/1950s/culture.html

2. Rock 'n Roll Hall of Fame, *Chuck Berry timeline*: https://www.rockhall.com/inductees/chuck-berry/timeline/

3. *Swinging London*: https://en.wikipedia.org/wiki/Swinging_London

4. *Motown*: https://en.wikipedia.org/wiki/Motown

5. *Motown Junkies*: http://motownjunkies.co.uk/index/

6. David Edwards and Mike Callahan, *The Motown Story*, http://www.bsnpubs.com/motown/gordystory.html

7. Gilbert Cruz, *A Brief History of Motown*, Time Magazine (Jan. 12, 2009)

8. Salvador Barajas, *Top 10 Instrumental Songs from the '60s*: http://listverse.com/2011/01/31/top-10-instrumental-songs-from-the-60s/

9. *Beat Music*: https://en.wikipedia.org/wiki/Beat_music

10. *Studio 54*: https://en.wikipedia.org/wiki/Studio_54

11. Christopher Andersen, *Mick, The Wild Life and Mad Genius of Jagger*, pg.184-185

12. *History of disco dance*: http://www.buzzle.com/articles/history-of-disco-dance.html

13. Diana Mankowski, *That's The Way They Liked It: Disco Fashion*, http://www.ultimatehistoryproject.com/disco-fashion.html

14. *Donna Summer*: https://en.wikipedia.org/wiki/Donna_Summer

15. *Disco:* https://en.wikipedia.org/wiki/Disco

16. Lisa Robinson, *Boogie Nights*, Vanity Fair (February 2010)

17. *Bee Gees*: https://en.wikipedia.org/wiki/Bee_Gees

18. *Saturday Night Fever*: https://en.wikipedia.org/wiki/Saturday_Night_Fever

19. *The Story of Saturday Night Fever*: https://www.youtube.com/watch?v=AZ6jxglUmbw

20. *Memorable Quotes for Saturday Night Fever*: http://www.imdb.com/title/tt0076666/quotes

21. *100 Greatest Disco Songs*: http://digitaldreamdoor.com/pages/best_disco-songs.html

22. Disco Savvy, *A chronicle of disco music from 1972 to the present*: www.discosavvy.com

Homes Section

Oh! Those Real-Estate Agents

1. Susan Pigg Business Reporter, *Competition Bureau loses its MLS-access case against TREB*, The Toronto Star (Apr 15 2013)

2. Charles P. Kindleberger and Robert Aliber, *Manias Panics and Crashes, A History of Financial Crises*, pg. 62-116

Business & Technology Section

1. Randall W. Forsyth, *Liquid Courage: The deals are all about consolidation, not innovation,* Barron's Magazine (Feb 18th, 2013) pg. 9-10

2. Clayton M. Christensen, *The Innovator's Dilemma*, pg. 3-24 and pg. 207-210

3. Edinburgh Business School Marketing, *Environmental Analysis: Tools to Identify Attractive Markets*, Module 4 pg. 2

4. Steven P. Schnaars, *Marketing Strategy A Customer-driven Approach*, pg. 64-91

The Techno-Culture, the Twenty-Five-Word Universe, and the Sea of Shallows

5. *Technoculture*: https://en.wikipedia.org/wiki/Technoculture

A Brief History of the Internet

Technology and Disruptive Change

The Industrial Revolution

The Second Industrial Revolution

1. *Second Industrial Revolution*: https://en.wikipedia.org/wiki/Second_Industrial_Revolution

2. Professor Joel Mokyr Robert H. Strotz, *The Second Industrial Revolution, 1870-1914,* (August 1998) http://faculty.wcas.northwestern.edu/~jmokyr/castronovo.pdf

3. Ryan Engelman, *19th Century, 20th Century, The Second Industrial Revolution, 1870-1914:* http://ushistoryscene.com/article/second-industrial-revolution/

4. *9 Life-Changing Inventions the Experts Said Would Never Work*: http://ecosalon.com/9_life_changing_inventions_the_experts_said_would_never_work/

5. *Car:* https://en.wikipedia.org/wiki/Car

6. *Ford Model T*: https://en.wikipedia.org/wiki/Ford_Model_T#Mass_production

7. *Electricity:* https://en.wikipedia.org/wiki/Electricity

8. *Electric Power*: https://en.wikipedia.org/wiki/Electric_power

9. *History of electric power transmission*: https://en.wikipedia.org/wiki/History_of_electric_power_transmission

10. Rosalie E. Leposky, *A Brief History of Electricity* (2003): http://www.ampersandcom.com/ampersandcommunications/ABriefHistoryofElectricity.htm

11. *History of the telephone*: https://en.wikipedia.org/wiki/History_of_the_telephone

12. *History: Alexander Graham Bell (1847 - 1922):* http://www.bbc.co.uk/history/historic_figures/bell_alexander_graham.shtml

13. *History of broadcasting*: https://en.wikipedia.org/wiki/History_of_broadcasting

14. *History of radio*: https://en.wikipedia.org/wiki/History_of_radio

15. *Invention of radio*: https://en.wikipedia.org/wiki/Invention_of_radio

16. *History of IBM*: https://en.wikipedia.org/wiki/History_of_IBM

17. *History of Jet Engine*: https://en.wikipedia.org/wiki/History_of_the_jet_engine

18. *Jet Engine*: https://en.wikipedia.org/wiki/Jet_engine

19. *de Havilland Comet*: https://en.wikipedia.org/wiki/De_Havilland_Comet

20. *History of Aviation - First Flights:* http://www.avjobs.com/history/

21. *History of aviation*: https://en.wikipedia.org/wiki/History_of_aviation

22. *Wright brothers*: https://en.wikipedia.org/wiki/Wright_brothers

23. *History of CNC Machining: How the CNC Concept Was Born*: http://www.cmsna.com/blog/2013/01/history-of-cnc-machining-how-the-cnc-concept-was-born/

24. *CNC Machine Overview and Computer Numerical Control History*: http://www.cnccookbook.com/CCCNCMachine.htm

25. *Industrial Robot*: https://en.wikipedia.org/wiki/Industrial_robot

26. *History of Television*: https://en.wikipedia.org/wiki/History_of_television

27. *Television*: https://en.wikipedia.org/wiki/Television

28. *Early Television Stations*: http://www.earlytelevision.org/don_lee_everest.html

29. *Culture in The 1950s, Television Enters the National Living Room*: http://www.shmoop.com/1950s/culture.html

30. Mitchell Stephens, *History of Television, Grolier Encyclopedia*: https://www.nyu.edu/classes/stephens/History%20of%20Television%20page.htm

31. Time Magazine Archive, *Early years of TV*: http://content.time.com/time/archive/collections/0,21428,c_television_history,00.shtml

32. Greg Christison, *John Logie Baird's genius brings us the world*, Daily Express (May 12, 2013): http://www.express.co.uk/news/uk/398873/John-Logie-Baird-s-genius-brings-us-the-world

33. Bob Malone, *George Devol: A Life Devoted to Invention, and Robots* (September 26, 2011): http://spectrum.ieee.org/automaton/robotics/industrial-robots/george-devol-a-life-devoted-to-invention-and-robots

34. *George Charles Devol, Jr.*: https://en.wikipedia.org/wiki/George_Devol

35. *Larry Tesler, (Xerox PARC, Apple, Amazon, and Yahoo!)* : https://en.wikipedia.org/wiki/Larry_Tesler

36. *MAC History*: http://www.mac-history.net/computer-history/2012-03-22/apple-and-xerox-parc

37. Arun Rao and Piero Scaruffi, *A History of Silicon Valley, The Largest Creation of Wealth in History A Moral Tale, (2012):* http://www.scaruffi.com/politics/sv.html

38. Piero Scaruffi, *Lab Inventors: Xerox PARC and the Innovation Machine (1969-83):* http://www.scaruffi.com/svhistory/sv/chap84.html

39. *Xerox Alto*: https://en.wikipedia.org/wiki/Xerox_Alto

40. *PARC (company)*: https://en.wikipedia.org/wiki/PARC_(company)

41. Adam Smith, *The Wealth of Nations*, 1994 Random House, pg. 15 & 485

42. Rex Murphy, *The modern university risks becoming a cocoon of self-indulgence and anti-intellectualism*, National Post (March 27, 2015)

43. Innovation pessimism, *Has the ideas machine broken down?* The Economist, (Jan, 12, 2013): http://www.economist.com/news/briefing/21569381-idea-innovation-and-new-technology-have-stopped-driving-growth-getting-increasing

44. Manufacturing, *The factory of the future*, The Economist (Oct. 30, 2013): http://www.economist.com/blogs/schumpeter/2013/10/manufacturing

A Farewell to the Twentieth Century

1. Richard Nixon, *1999, Victory Without War*, pg. 57-58, 100, 106-108, 228, 259, 269-270, and 308

Then and Now

Back to the Office of days gone by

1. *IBM Selectric typewriter*: https://en.wikipedia.org/wiki/IBM_Selectric_typewriter

2. *Car Phone:* https://en.wikipedia.org/wiki/Car_phone

3. *On Hold: The telephone generation gap*: Globe & Mail, (Aug 30th 2013) Section b11

The Rise and Fall of Television

Back to the Techno-Culture

1. *Digital Revolution:* https://en.wikipedia.org/wiki/Digital_Revolution

2. Jeremy Rifkin, *The Third Industrial Revolution; How Lateral Power is Transforming Energy, the Economy, and the World (2011)*: http://www.thethirdindustrialrevolution.com/

3. Comparative Advantage, *The boomerang effect,* The Economist (April 21, 2012): http://www.economist.com/node/21552898

More Threats and Disruptive Changes

Editorial & Comment Section

Perspectives & Time

Kings and Queens

1. Lawrence James, *The Rise & Fall of the British Empire*, pg. 170, 207, 457, 508-9

The Democratization of What?

Debt and Benevolence - Strange Bedfellows

1. Peter D. Schiff, *The Real Crash, America's Coming Bankruptcy*, pg. 259-275

The Future of Tomorrow

1. Manufacturing, *The third industrial revolution*, The Economist (April 19, 2012): http://www.economist.com/node/21553017

2. *Dr. Ray Kurzweil -- The Impact of Accelerating Information Tech on War and Peace:*https://www.youtube.com/watch?v=DAkoSGaueX0

3. Dylan Love, *By 2045 'The Top Species Will No Longer Be Humans,' And That Could Be A Problem,* Business Insider (July 5, 2014)

4. *Artificial Intelligence (Ai)*: https://en.wikipedia.org/wiki/Artificial_intelligence

51074776R00193

Made in the USA
Charleston, SC
14 January 2016